Ninja Foodi Cookbook

for Beginners and Advanced Users

365 Days Easy, Affordable, and Delicious Ninja Foodi Recipes to Pressure Cook, Steam & Crisp, Air Fry, Bake/Roast, Sear/Sauté, and More.

Natasha Barber

Copyright © 2021 by Natasha Barber All rights reserved.

The content contained within this book may not be reproduced, duplicated, or transmitted without direct written permission from the author or the publisher. Under no circumstances will any blame or legal responsibility be held against the publisher, or author, for any damages, reparation, or monetary loss due to the information contained within this book, either directly or indirectly.

Legal Notice: This book is copyright protected. It is only for personal use. You cannot amend, distribute, sell, use, quote or paraphrase any part, or the content within this book, without the consent of the author or publisher.

Disclaimer Notice: Please note the information contained within this document is for educational and entertainment purposes only. All effort has been executed to present accurate, up to date, reliable, complete information. No warranties of any kind are declared or implied. Readers acknowledge that the author is not engaged in the rendering of legal, financial, medical, or professional advice. The content within this book has been derived from various sources. Please consult a licensed professional before attempting any techniques outlined in this book. By reading this document, the reader agrees that under no circumstances is the author responsible for any losses, direct or indirect, that are incurred as a result of the use of the information contained within this document, including, but not limited to, errors, omissions, or inaccuracies.

Table of Contents

Table of Contents 3
Introduction 7
   What is a Ninja Foodi 7
   How to use Ninja foodi pressure cooker? 7
   How to clean Ninja foodi pressure cooker? 8

Measurement Conversions 9
   BASIC KITCHEN CONVERSIONS & EQUIVALENTS 9

Snacks, Appetizers & Sides 10
- Dried Beet Chips 10
- Artichokes With Melted Butter 10
- Crispy Cheesy Zucchini Bites 10
- Faux Daikon Noodles 10
- Asian Chicken Nuggets 10
- Zesty Brussels Sprouts With Raisins 11
- Rise And Shine Breakfast Casserole 11
- Garlic And Mushroom Crunchies 11
- Cheesy Chicken Dip 11
- Sweet Potato Skins 11
- Crispy Brussels Sprouts With Aioli Sauce 12
- The Original Zucchini Gratin 12
- Spiralized Carrot 12
- Horseradish Roasted Carrots 12
- Cheesy Stuffed Onions 13
- Sweet Potato Fries 13
- Loaded Smashed Potatoes With Bacon 13
- Crispy Fries 13
- Dill Butter 14
- White Bean Hummus 14
- Teriyaki Chicken Wings 14
- The Original Braised Kale And Carrot Salad 14
- Spaghetti Squash And Chicken Parmesan 15
- Quick Turkey Cutlets 15
- Turkey Scotch Eggs 15
- Cheesy Smashed Sweet Potatoes 15
- Delicious Bacon- Wrapped Drumsticks 15
- Chili Chicken Dip 16
- Chicken Wings 16
- Stuffed Chicken Mushrooms 16
- The Kool Poblano Cheese Frittata 16
- Cauliflower And Egg Dish 17
- Cheeseburger Boats 17
- Hungarian Cornmeal Squares 17
- Strawberry Snack Bars 17
- Spinach Hummus 18
- Turkey And Wild Rice Salad With Walnuts 18
- Chicken Pork Nuggets 18
- Crispy Spiced Cauliflower Bites 19
- Beef Chicken Meatloaf 19

Breakfast 20
- Kale-egg Frittata 20
- Tropical Fruit Steel Cut Oats 20
- Bacon And Cheese Custards 20
- Easy Cheesy Egg Bake 20
- Chorizo Omelet 21
- Apple And Cranberry Oatmeal With Vanilla 21
- Cheesy Egg Bake With Ham 21
- Poached Breakfast Eggs 21
- Swiss Bacon Frittata 22
- Butternut Breakfast Squash 22
- Ham & Broccoli Frittata 22
- Savory Custards With Ham And Cheese 22
- Deviled Eggs(1) 23
- Strawberry Muffins 23
- Cranberry And Toasted Almond Grits 23
- Curried Chickpea And Roasted Tomato Shakshuka .. 23
- Very Berry Puffs 24
- Cranberry Lemon Quinoa 24
- Breakfast Egg Pizza 24
- Pumpkin Breakfast Bread 24
- Hanging Bacon 25
- Easy Homemade Yogurt 25
- Pancetta Hash With Baked Eggs 25
- Butternut Squash Apple Soup With Cinnamon 25
- Cinnamon Sugar Donuts 25
- Apricot Oatmeal 26
- Sweet Potato Hash And Eggs 26
- Maple Giant Pancake 26
- Spinach Casserole 27
- Prosciutto Egg Bake 27
- Cheesy Tex-mex Breakfast Egg Bake Casserole 27
- Walnut Orange Coffee Cake 27
- Bacon And Gruyère Cheese Quiche 28
- Butter Cookies 28
- Pecan Steel-cut Oats 28
- Cinnamon Bun Oatmeal 28
- Chili Cheese Quiche 29
- Stuffed Baked Potatoes 29
- Mediterranean Quiche 29
- Bbq Chicken Sandwiches 30
- Applesauce Pumpkin Muffins 30
- Cheddar Shrimp And Grits 30
- Southern Grits Casserole 30
- Homemade Vanilla Yogurt 31
- Cinnamon Oatmeal With Cream Cheese 31
- Japanese Pancake 31
- Chocolate Chip And Banana Bread Bundt Cake 32
- Ninja Foodi Hard-boiled Eggs 32
- Strawberry Oat Breakfast Bars 32
- Paprika Hard-boiled Eggs 32

Vegan & Vegetable 33

- Green Squash Gruyere 33
- Quinoa Stuffed Peppers With Pesto 33
- Sesame Radish 33
- Mushroom Goulash 33
- Eggplant Casserole 34
- Broccoli & Pesto Penne 34
- Artichoke With Mayo 34
- Mushroom Brown Rice Pilaf 34
- Southern Pineapple Casserole 35
- Rustic Veggie Tart 35
- Worthy Caramelized Onion 35
- Cauliflower Chunks With Lemon Sauce 35
- Cheesy Spicy Pasta 36
- Cheesy Green Beans With Nuts 36
- Caramelized Sweet Potatoes 36
- Veggie Loaded Pasta 36
- Potato Filled Bread Rolls 37
- Aloo Gobi With Cilantro 37
- Ritzy Vegetable Mix 37
- Roasted Vegetable Salad 37
- Stuffed Manicotti 38
- Slowly Cooked Lemon Artichokes 38
- The Veggie Lover's Onion And Tofu Platter 38
- Cheesy Chilies 38
- Green Cream Soup 39
- Okra Bhindi Masala 39
- Spanish Rice 39
- Tomato And Poblano Stuffed Squash 39
- Mushroom And Swiss Cheese Tarts 39
- Creamy Polenta & Mushrooms 40
- Mesmerizing Spinach Quiche 40
- Italian Spinach & Tomato Soup 40
- Risotto And Roasted Bell Peppers 41
- Hawaiian Tofu 41
- Hearty Veggie Soup 41
- Chives And Radishes Platter 41
- Complete Cauliflower Zoodles 41
- Cauliflower Cakes 42
- Zucchini Cream Soup 42
- Veggie And Quinoa Stuffed Peppers 42
- Zucchini And Artichoke Platter 42
- Green Lasagna Soup 43
- Minestrone With Pancetta 43
- Italian Sausage With Garlic Mash 43
- Pineapple Appetizer Ribs 43

Soups & Stews 44

- Creamy Italian Sausage, Potato, And Kale Soup 44
- Creamy Pumpkin And Squash Bisque With Apple 44
- Delicious Hungarian Goulash Soup 44
- Pho Tom 45
- Garlicy Roasted Cauliflower And Potato Soup 45
- Vegetable And Lamb Stew 45
- Coconut Shrimp And Pea Bisque 46
- English Pub Split Pea Soup 46
- Spanish Chorizo And Lentil Soup 46
- Italian Sausage Soup 46
- Haddock And Biscuit Chowder 47
- Beef And Pork Chili 47
- Butternut Squash And Orzo Soup 47
- Chicken And Black Bean Enchilada Soup 48
- Lasagna Soup 48
- Chicken Potpie Soup 48
- Roasted Red Pepper And Caramelized Onion Soup With Grilled Cheese 49
- Curry Acorn Squash Soup 49
- Italian Sausage, Potato, And Kale Soup 49
- Whole Farro And Leek Soup 50
- Coconut And Shrimp Bisque 50
- Tomatillo Chicken Thigh Stew 50
- Roasted Tomato And Seafood Stew 51
- Tex-mex Chicken Tortilla Soup 51
- Spicy Pork Stew With Black Benas And Tomatoes 51
- Loaded Potato Soup 52
- Chicken Enchilada Soup 52
- Lentil Spinach Soup With Lemon 53
- Goulash (hungarian Beef Soup) 53
- Vegetable Wild Rice Soup 53

Fish & Seafood 54

- Mackerel En Papillote With Vegetables 54
- The Great Poached Salmon 54
- Curried Salmon & Sweet Potatoes 54
- Dijon Flavored Lemon Whitefish 54
- Lemony Shrimp 55
- Apricot Salmon With Potatoes 55
- Haddock With Sanfaina 55
- Seafood Paella 56
- Salmon With Dill Sauce 56
- Steamed Shrimp With Asparagus 56
- Tuscan Cod 56
- Nawesome Cherry Tomato Mackerel 57
- Sweet & Spicy Shrimp 57
- Basil Lemon Shrimp & Asparagus 57
- Lemon Cod Goujons And Rosemary Chips 58
- The Ginger Flavored Tilapia 58
- Crab Alfredo 58
- Garlicky Shrimp With Broccoli 58
- Cod Over Couscous 59
- Great Seafood Stew 59
- Shrimp Fried Rice 59
- Creamy Crab Soup 60
- Classic Crab Imperial 60
- Very Low Carb Clam Chowder 60
- Citrus Mahi Mahi 60
- Tuscan Cod With Red Potatoes 61
- Cod Cornflakes Nuggets 61
- Curry-flavored Shrimp 61
- Parmesan Tilapia 61
- Buttery Scallops 62
- Shrimp And Sausage Paella 62
- Baked Cod Casserole 62
- Pineapple Rice With Coconut-crusted Shrimp 62
- Spiced Red Snapper 63
- Spanish Steamed Clams 63
- Pepper Smothered Cod 63
- Coconut Cilantro Shrimp 64
- Salmon Chowder 64

Ranch Warm Fillets 64	White Wine Mussels With Saffron Threads 66
Shrimp Scampi With Tomatoes 64	Heartfelt Sesame Fish 66
Salmon Paprika 64	Buttery Lemon Cod Over Couscous 66
Panko Crusted Cod 65	Delightful Salmon Fillets 67
Spicy Shrimp Pasta With Vodka Sauce 65	Garlic Sauce And Mussels 67
Speedy Clams Pomodoro 65	Seafood Minestrone 67
Shrimp Spaghetti With Parmesan 65	Fish Finger Sandwich 67
Salmon Florentine 66	Buttery Salmon With Green Beans And Rice 68
Favorite Salmon Stew 66	

Beef, Pork & Lamb 69

Rosemary Pork Roast 69	Philippine Pork Chops 77
Mississippi Pot Roast With Potatoes 69	Beef Short Rib & Ale Stew 77
Rich Beef Rendang 69	Ham, Bean & Butternut Soup 77
Italian Rigatoni, Sausage, And Meatball Potpie 69	The Calabacita Squash Meal 78
One Pot Ham & Rice 70	Maple Glazed Pork Chops 78
Pork, Green Beans, And Corn 70	Short Ribs With Mushroom And Asparagus Sauce 78
Crispy Pork Chops 70	Sausage & Roasted Red Pepper Linguine 78
Bacon Strips 70	Spicy "faux" Pork Belly 79
Paprika Pork And Brussels Sprouts 71	Chipotle Burgers 79
Pineapple Rack Ribs 71	Premium Mexican Beef Dish 79
Greek Lamb Gyros 71	Baby Back Ribs With Barbeque Sauce 80
Beef Stew With Beer 71	Balsamic Pot Roast Of Beef 80
Beef Lasagna 72	Beef And Turnip Chili 80
Cuban Flank Steak 72	Italian Pot Roast 80
Pork And Peanut Lettuce Wraps 72	Sesame Beef Ribs 81
Lime And Ginger Low Carb Pork 72	Asian-glazed Pork Shoulder 81
The Chipotle Copycat Dish 73	Cranberry Pork Bbq Dish 81
Lamb Chops And Potato Mash 73	Chicken And Crispy Dumplings 81
Tomato-basil Bread Pizza 73	Beer Braised Bacon & Cabbage 82
Cauliflower And Chickpea Green Salad 73	Orange Chicken And Broccoli 82
Calzones With Sausage And Mozzarella 74	Pesto Pork Chops & Asparagus 82
Beef Prime Roast 74	Baked Ziti With Rich Meat Sauce 83
Farro, Fennel And Arugula Salad 74	Chinese Bbq Ribs 83
Maple Apples & Pork Chops 75	Quinoa, Nut, And Chickpea Stuffed Butternut Squash ... 83
Spanish White Quinoa 75	All-tim Favorite Beef Chili 84
Simple Beef & Shallot Curry 75	Parmesan Broccoli Florets 84
Generous Shepherd's Pie 75	Beef Congee 84
Cajun Red Beans And Rice 76	Mushroom And Cheddar Poutine 84
Crispy Korean-style Ribs 76	Lone Star Chili 85
Zinfandel Braised Beef 76	Super Cheesy Pepperoni Calzones 85

Poultry 86

Awesome Ligurian Chicken 86	Turkey Rellenos 91
Barbeque Chicken Drumettes 86	Poached Chicken With Coconut Lime Cream Sauce 91
Greek Style Turkey Meatballs 86	Honey Garlic Chicken 91
Cabbage And Chicken Meatballs 87	Garlic-herb Roasted Chicken 92
Fluffy Whole Chicken Dish 87	Your's Truly Lime Chicken Chili 92
Shredded Chicken & Black Beans 87	Mexican Style Green Chili Chicken 92
Taiwanese Chicken Delight 87	The Borderline Crack Chicken 93
Spicy Chicken Tortilla Soup 87	Chicken With Bbq Sauce 93
Cheesy Chicken & Zucchini Rolls 88	Chicken And Broccoli Stir-fry 93
Italian Chicken Muffins 88	Saucy Chicken Breasts 93
Chicken With Black Beans 88	Crispy Chicken With Carrots And Potatoes 94
Chicken With Bacon And Beans 88	Hawaiian Pinna Colada Chicken Meal 94
Chicken With Rice And Peas 89	Turkey & Pasta With Lemon Pesto 94
Ginger Orange Chicken Tenders 89	Stir-fried Chicken And Broccoli Rice Bowl 94
Crunchy Chicken Schnitzels 89	Lime And Cilantro Chicken Meal 95
Apricot Bbq Duck Legs 90	Lemon Chicken 95
Chicken Gumbo 90	Salsa Verde Chicken With Salsa Verde 95
Garlic And Butter Chicken Dish 90	Authentic Belizean Stewed Chicken 95
Korean Barbecued Satay 90	Coq Au Vin 96
Chicken & Black Bean Chowder 90	Chicken Posole 96
Cheesy Chicken And Broccoli Casserole 91	Turkey Cutlets 96

Chicken Pasta With Pesto Sauce 97	Chicken Burgers With Avocado 98
Chicken With Cilantro Rice 97	Sesame Chicken Wings(2) 98
Sticky Drumsticks 97	Spinach And Chicken Curry 98
Lemon Turkey Risotto 97	Bacon & Cranberry Stuffed Turkey Breast 99

Desserts 100

Blackberry Crisp 100	Carrot Cake 105
Egg And Ham Pockets 100	Mexican Chocolate Walnut Cake 105
Sweet And Salty Bars 100	Almond Milk 105
Classic Cheesecake 100	Mocha Cake 105
Coconut Lime Snack Cake 101	Blueberry Lemon Pound Cake 106
Chocolate Mousse 101	Chocolaty Fudge 106
Butterscotch Almond Brownies 101	Chocolate Brownie Cake 106
Rhubarb, Raspberry, And Peach Cobbler 102	Fried Snickerdoodle Poppers 107
Pineapple Cake 102	Raspberry Lemon Cheesecake 107
Steamed Lemon Pudding 102	Irish Cream Flan 107
Pecan And Cherry Stuffed Apples 102	Bacon Blondies 107
Moon Milk 103	Peach Cobbler 108
Dark Chocolate Brownies 103	Créme Brulee 108
Banana Rum Pudding 103	Apricots With Honey Sauce 108
Hearty Crème Brulee 103	Chocolate Cake 108
Fried Oreos 104	Cherry Almond Bar Cookies 109
Coffee Cake 104	Hearty Apricot Cobbler 109
Molten Lava Cake 104	

RECIPE INDEX 110

Introduction

For so many people, there are a few unspoken rules when it comes to cooking. It needs to be quick, it needs to be tasty, and it needs to be good for you. However, in the constant hustle and bustle of life, too often we sacrifice at least one of these areas to get the job done and move on to the next thing. Multi-cookers claim to do it all, and slow cookers have long been touted for their versatility and convenience. After all, they do the work for you: just toss ingredients into the pot and come back to a perfectly cooked meal. Pressure cookers take it a step further, making your food incredibly tender, exceptionally fast.

But what about texture? Tender food is great, but no one wants to eat stews and soups every night. We all crave the crispy and crunchy. What are chicken wings without a crispy exterior? Who wants to eat potpie without a flaky

crust?

Enter the Ninja Foodi Pressure Cooker, the pressure cooker that crisps—a revolutionary appliance changing the multi-cooker game. That means, with the Foodi Pressure Cooker, you can make roast chicken that is juicy and tender within and beautiful bronzed and crisp outside.

This Ninja Foodi cookbook will introduce you to the functions and benefits of this revolutionary appliance. Whether you are new to the Foodi or you are a Foodi fanatic, I will break down cooking with the Ninja Foodi Pressure Cooker, giving you tips and tricks, and helping you unleash its full potential—flavor, texture, and speed. And, of course, I'll introduce you to a wide variety of recipes so you can use it every day. The 500 recipes in the Ninja Foodi cookbook offer air-frying, pressure-cooking, and sauté recipes from breakfast through dinner.

What is a Ninja Foodi

A pressure cooker can cook almost anything but its biggest flaw is it cannot make foods crispy. The Ninja Foodi solves this problem by combining the regular pressure cooker with an air fryer. You can use the new feature to air fry foods and dehydrate. As expected though, this does lead to a higher cost than a pressure cooker.

How to use Ninja foodi pressure cooker?

It is perfect for the individual who wants the freshest, most delicious cooking experience. The Foodi eliminates the need to stir food, freeing up one of your hands to do other things while it cooks. And with its automated lid sealing system, you can be confident that food will not boil over. This Pressure Cooker is an easy-to-use, modern pressure cooker perfect for people who want to spend less time in the kitchen.

1. ·Set the cooking time on the pressure cooker using the digital timer on the control panel.
2. ·Make sure you don't cook your food in an aluminum pan.
3. ·Avoid using plastic spoons, bowls, plates, and cooking utensils.
4. ·Stick to wearing clean, neatly pressed clothes.
5. ·Once the cooking time is complete, the food is automatically removed from the cooker.
6. ·Allow the food to cool down in the cooker before

Ninja Foodi Cookbook

removing it.
7. ·For easy removal, place the food in a strainer and run cold water through it.
8. ·Dry the food with a clean cloth before serving.

How to clean Ninja foodi pressure cooker?

The popularity of the Ninja Foodi FD401 Programmable Pressure Cooker and Air Fryer has skyrocketed in recent years because it cooks meals quickly without using too much oil. It can be challenging to clean this appliance, but the following tips should help you get your Ninja looking new.

- ·First, disconnect the power from your pressure cooker.
- ·To clean the pressure cooker & air fryer, you need lemon, soapy water, a brush, and a sponge.
- ·Mix 4-5 pieces of lemon juice with water inside the cooker.
- ·Then, close the lead and boil the water.
- ·After boiling the water, open the lid.
- ·Now, on the lid, you can see grease, oil, which has boiled due to the warmth of the hot water.
- ·Then wipe the lead with a paper towel to remove the oil & grease.

- ·If you see food particles stuck after wiping, you can use a soft brush to remove the food particles.
- ·Then keep washing well with soapy water.
- ·After washing, wipe with a clean towel.
- ·Then leave to dry, but should not be allowed to dry in the sunlight.
- ·Use for cooking again after drying.

Measurement Conversions

BASIC KITCHEN CONVERSIONS & EQUIVALENTS

DRY MEASUREMENTS CONVERSION CHART
3 TEASPOONS = 1 TABLESPOON = 1/16 CUP
6 TEASPOONS = 2 TABLESPOONS = 1/8 CUP
12 TEASPOONS = 4 TABLESPOONS = 1/4 CUP
24 TEASPOONS = 8 TABLESPOONS = 1/2 CUP
36 TEASPOONS = 12 TABLESPOONS = 3/4 CUP
48 TEASPOONS = 16 TABLESPOONS = 1 CUP

METRIC TO US COOKING CONVERSIONS
OVEN TEMPERATURES
120 °C = 250 °F
160 °C = 320 °F
180° C = 360 °F
205 °C = 400 °F
220 °C = 425 °F

LIQUID MEASUREMENTS CONVERSION CHART
8 FLUID OUNCES = 1 CUP = 1/2 PINT = 1/4 QUART
16 FLUID OUNCES = 2 CUPS = 1 PINT = 1/2 QUART
32 FLUID OUNCES = 4 CUPS = 2 PINTS = 1 QUART = 1/4 GALLON
128 FLUID OUNCES = 16 CUPS = 8 PINTS = 4 QUARTS = 1 GALLON

BAKING IN GRAMS
1 CUP FLOUR = 140 GRAMS
1 CUP SUGAR = 150 GRAMS
1 CUP POWDERED SUGAR = 160 GRAMS
1 CUP HEAVY CREAM = 235 GRAMS

VOLUME
1 MILLILITER = 1/5 TEASPOON
5 ML = 1 TEASPOON
15 ML = 1 TABLESPOON
240 ML = 1 CUP OR 8 FLUID OUNCES
1 LITER = 34 FL. OUNCES

WEIGHT
1 GRAM = .035 OUNCES
100 GRAMS = 3.5 OUNCES
500 GRAMS = 1.1 POUNDS
1 KILOGRAM = 35 OUNCES

US TO METRIC COOKING CONVERSIONS
1/5 TSP = 1 ML
1 TSP = 5 ML
1 TBSP = 15 ML
1 FL OUNCE = 30 ML
1 CUP = 237 ML
1 PINT (2 CUPS) = 473 ML
1 QUART (4 CUPS) = .95 LITER
1 GALLON (16 CUPS) = 3.8 LITERS
1 OZ = 28 GRAMS
1 POUND = 454 GRAMS

BUTTER
1 CUP BUTTER = 2 STICKS = 8 OUNCES = 230 GRAMS = 8 TABLESPOONS

WHAT DOES 1 CUP EQUAL
1 CUP = 8 FLUID OUNCES
1 CUP = 16 TABLESPOONS
1 CUP = 48 TEASPOONS
1 CUP = 1/2 PINT
1 CUP = 1/4 QUART
1 CUP = 1/16 GALLON
1 CUP = 240 ML

BAKING PAN CONVERSIONS
1 CUP ALL-PURPOSE FLOUR = 4.5 OZ
1 CUP ROLLED OATS = 3 OZ 1 LARGE EGG = 1.7 OZ
1 CUP BUTTER = 8 OZ 1 CUP MILK = 8 OZ
1 CUP HEAVY CREAM = 8.4 OZ
1 CUP GRANULATED SUGAR = 7.1 OZ
1 CUP PACKED BROWN SUGAR = 7.75 OZ
1 CUP VEGETABLE OIL = 7.7 OZ
1 CUP UNSIFTED POWDERED SUGAR = 4.4 OZ

BAKING PAN CONVERSIONS
9-INCH ROUND CAKE PAN = 12 CUPS
10-INCH TUBE PAN =16 CUPS
11-INCH BUNDT PAN = 12 CUPS
9-INCH SPRINGFORM PAN = 10 CUPS
9 X 5 INCH LOAF PAN = 8 CUPS
9-INCH SQUARE PAN = 8 CUPS

Snacks, Appetizers & Sides

Dried Beet Chips

Servings: 1
Cooking Time: 8 Hours
Ingredients:
- ½ beet, peeled and cut into ⅛-inch slices

Directions:
1. Arrange the beet slices flat in a single layer in the Cook & Crisp Basket. Place in the pot and close the Crisping Lid.
2. Press Dehydrate, set the temperature to 135°F(55°C), and set the time to 8 hours. Select Start/Stop to begin.
3. When dehydrating is complete, remove the basket from the pot and transfer the beet chips to an airtight container.

Artichokes With Melted Butter

Servings: 6
Cooking Time: 12 Minutes
Ingredients:
- 3 globe artichokes, stems and top leaves trimmed, if desired
- 2 teaspoons kosher salt
- 1 lemon, halved
- 4 tablespoons butter, melted

Directions:
1. Add ½ cup water, the artichokes, and the salt to the Foodi's inner pot. Squeeze the lemon halves over the artichokes and then add them to the pot as well. Lock on the Pressure Lid, making sure the valve is set to Seal, and set to Pressure on High for 12 minutes. When the timer reaches 0, quick-release the pressure and carefully open the lid.
2. Serve the artichokes with melted butter.

Crispy Cheesy Zucchini Bites

Servings: 6
Cooking Time: 10 Minutes
Ingredients:
- 2 zucchini, cut in 3/4-inch thick slices
- Nonstick cooking spray
- ½ cup panko bread crumbs
- 1 tbsp. parmesan cheese
- 1 tbsp. lite mayonnaise
- ½ tsp garlic powder
- ½ tsp onion powder
- ¼ tsp seasoned salt
- ¼ tsp pepper

Directions:
1. Pour enough water to cover the bottom of the cooking pot about 1 inch. Set to sauté on high heat and bring to a boil.
2. Add zucchini, reduce heat to low and simmer 3-5 minutes or just until tender. Drain and pat dry with paper towels.
3. Lightly spray the fryer basket with cooking spray and place it in the cooking pot.
4. In a small bowl, stir together bread crumbs, cheese, garlic powder, onion powder, salt, and pepper.
5. Spread one side of each zucchini slice with mayonnaise and place in a single layer in the basket. Sprinkle crumb mixture over top of each slice.
6. Add tender-crisp lid and set to air fry on 450°F (230°C). Bake 3-5 minutes, or until golden brown. Serve immediately.

Nutrition:
- InfoCalories 48, Total Fat 1g, Total Carbs 7g, Protein 1g, Sodium 196mg.

Faux Daikon Noodles

Servings: 6
Cooking Time: 15 Minutes
Ingredients:
- 2 tablespoons coconut oil
- 1 pound boneless and skinless chicken thigh
- 1 cup celery, diced
- 1 cup carrots, diced
- ¾ cup green onion, chopped
- 6 cups chicken stock
- ½ teaspoon dried basil
- 1 teaspoon salt
- 1/6 teaspoon fresh ground pepper
- 2 cups daikon noodles, spiralized

Directions:
1. Set the Ninja Foodi to Saute mode and add coconut oil, allow the oil to warm up
2. Add chicken thigh and Saute for about 10 minutes
3. Take the chicken out and shred it up
4. Add carrots, onions to the pot and cook for 2 minutes
5. Add the rest of the and lock up the lid
6. Cook for 15 minutes on HIGh pressure
7. Do a quick release carefully. Enjoy your "Faux" noodles!

Asian Chicken Nuggets

Servings: X
Cooking Time: 20 Minutes
Ingredients:
- 1 lb. chicken breasts, boneless, skinless & cut in 1-inch pieces
- 1 tsp salt
- ½ tsp pepper
- 2 eggs
- 1 cup Panko bread crumbs
- ¼ cup lite soy sauce
- ¼ cup honey
- 4 cloves garlic, diced fine
- 2 tbsp. hoisin sauce
- 1 tablespoon freshly grated ginger
- 1 tablespoon Sriracha
- 2 green onions, sliced thin
- 2 tsp sesame seeds

Directions:
1. Place the rack in the cooking pot and top with a sheet of parchment paper.
2. Sprinkle the chicken with salt and pepper.
3. In a shallow dish, beat the eggs.
4. Place the bread crumbs in a separate shallow dish. Working in batches, dip the chicken first in the eggs then bread crumbs, pressing to coat the chicken well.
5. Place the chicken on the parchment paper in a single layer. Add the tender-crisp lid and select air fry on 400 °F (205°C). Bake the chicken 10-15 minutes until golden brown and cooked through, turning over halfway through cooking time. Transfer to serving plate and keep warm.
6. Set the cooker to sauté on med-high heat. Add the soy sauce, honey, garlic, hoisin, ginger, and Sriracha, stir to combine. Cook, stirring frequently, until sauce thickens, about 2 minutes.
7. Add chicken and toss to coat. Serve immediately garnished with green onions and sesame seeds.

Nutrition:
- InfoCalories 304, Total Fat 7g, Total Carbs 27g, Protein 32g, Sodium 1149mg.

Zesty Brussels Sprouts With Raisins

Servings: 4
Cooking Time: 45 Min
Ingredients:
- 14 oz. Brussels sprouts, steamed /420g
- 2 oz. toasted pine nuts /60g
- 2 oz. raisins /60g
- 1 tbsp olive oil/15ml
- Juice and zest of 1 orange

Directions:
1. Soak the raisins in the orange juice and let sit for about 20 minutes. Drizzle the Brussels sprouts with the olive oil, and place them in the basket of the Ninja Foodi.
2. Close the crisping lid and cook for 15 minutes on Air Crisp mode at 370 °F or 185°C. Remove to a bowl and top with pine nuts, raisins, and orange zest.

Rise And Shine Breakfast Casserole

Servings: 6
Cooking Time: 10 Minutes
Ingredients:
- 4 whole eggs
- 1 tablespoons milk
- 1 cup ham, cooked and chopped
- ½ cup cheddar cheese, shredded
- ¼ teaspoon salt
- ¼ teaspoon ground black pepper

Directions:
1. Take a baking pan bowl, and grease it well with butter. Take a medium bowl and whisk in eggs, milk, salt, pepper and add ham, cheese, and stir. Pour mixture into baking pan and lower the pan into your Ninja Foodi
2. Set your Ninja Foodi Air Crisp mode and Air Crisp for 325 degrees F (160°C) for 7 minutes
3. Remove pan from eggs and enjoy!

Garlic And Mushroom Crunchies

Servings: 4
Cooking Time: 8 Hours
Ingredients:
- ¼ cup vegetable stock
- 2 tablespoons extra virgin olive oil
- 1 tablespoon Dijon mustard
- 1 teaspoon dried thyme
- 1 teaspoon of sea salt
- ½ teaspoon dried rosemary
- ¼ teaspoon fresh ground black pepper
- 2 pounds cremini mushrooms, cleaned
- 6 garlic cloves, minced
- ¼ cup fresh parsley, chopped

Directions:
1. Take a small bowl and whisk in vegetable stock, mustard, olive oil, salt, thyme, pepper and rosemary. Add mushrooms, garlic and stock mix to your Ninja Foodi
2. Close lid and cook on SLOW COOK Mode for 8 hours
3. Open the lid and stir in parsley. Serve and enjoy!

Cheesy Chicken Dip

Servings: 6
Cooking Time: 2 Hours
Ingredients:
- 1 lb. cheddar cheese, cubed
- 2 cups chicken, cooked & shredded
- 4 oz. cream cheese, cubed
- 1 cup tomatoes, diced
- 1 cup black beans, drained & rinsed
- ½ cup black olives, pitted & sliced
- 1 jalapeno, seeded & diced
- 2 tbsp. taco seasoning

Directions:
1. Place all ingredients in the cooking pot and stir to mix.
2. Add the lid and set to slow cooking on low heat. Set timer for 2 hours. Let dip cook, stirring occasionally until hot and bubbly and the cheese has melted.
3. Stir well then transfer to a serving dish and serve warm.

Nutrition:
- InfoCalories 507, Total Fat 35g, Total Carbs 12g, Protein 35g, Sodium 1022mg.

Sweet Potato Skins

Servings: 4
Cooking Time: 20 Minutes
Ingredients:
- 2 sweet potatoes, baked & halved lengthwise
- 1 tsp olive oil
- 2 cloves garlic, diced fine
- 1 tbsp. fresh lime juice
- 2 cups baby spinach
- ½ cup chicken, cooked & shredded
- 1 tsp oregano
- 1 tsp cumin
- 2 tsp chili powder
- ½ cup mozzarella cheese, grated
- ¼ cup cilantro, chopped

Directions:
1. Scoop out the center of the potatoes, leaving some on the side to help keep the shape.
2. Set the cooker to sauté on med-high heat and add the oil.
3. Once the oil is hot, add garlic, lime juice, and spinach. Cook 2-3 minutes until spinach is wilted.
4. In a large bowl, mash the sweet potato centers until almost smooth.
5. Stir in chicken, oregano, cumin, and chili powder. Stir in spinach until combined.
6. Place the rack in the cooking pot and top with parchment paper.
7. Spoon the potato mixture into the skins and top with cheese. Place on the rack.
8. Add the tender-crisp lid and set to bake on 400°F (205°C). Bake 15-20 minutes until cheese is melted and lightly browned. Let cool slightly then cut each skin in 4 pieces and serve garnished with cilantro.

Nutrition:
- InfoCalories 132,Total Fat 2g,Total Carbs 20g,Protein 9g,Sodium 155mg.

Crispy Brussels Sprouts With Aioli Sauce

Servings: 4
Cooking Time: 10 Minutes

Ingredients:
- 1 tablespoon butter
- ½ cup (125 mL) chopped scallions
- ¾ pound (340 g) Brussels sprouts
- Aioli Sauce:
- ¼ cup (63 mL) mayonnaise
- 1 tablespoon fresh lemon juice
- ½ teaspoon Dijon mustard
- 1 garlic clove, minced

Directions:
1. Press the Sauté button and melt the butter.
2. Add the scallions and sauté for about 5 minutes until softened. Stir in the Brussels sprouts and cook for an additional 1 minute.
3. Assemble pressure lid, making sure the pressure release valve is in the Seal position. Select Pressure and set to high. Set time to 4 minutes. Press Start to begin.
4. Meanwhile, stir together all the ingredients for the aioli sauce in a small bowl.
5. When the timer beeps, perform a quick pressure release. Carefully remove the lid.
6. Remove the Brussels sprouts from the cooker and serve alongside the aioli sauce.

The Original Zucchini Gratin

Servings: 4
Cooking Time: 15 Minutes

Ingredients:
- 2 zucchinis
- 1 tablespoon fresh parsley, chopped
- 2 tablespoons bread crumbs
- 4 tablespoons parmesan cheese, grated
- 1 tablespoon vegetable oil
- Salt and pepper to taste

Directions:
1. Pre-heat your Ninja Foodi to 300 degrees F for 3 minutes
2. Slice zucchini lengthwise to get about 8 equal sizes pieces
3. Arrange pieces in your Crisping Basket
4. Top each with parsley, bread crumbs, cheese, oil, salt, and pepper
5. Return basket Ninja Foodi basket and cook for 15 minutes at 360 degrees F
6. Once done, serve with sauce. Enjoy!

Spiralized Carrot

Servings: 4
Cooking Time: 13 Minutes

Ingredients:
- 1 cup of water
- 4 big carrots
- 1 teaspoon liquid stevia
- 1 tablespoon turmeric
- 1 tablespoon butter
- ½ teaspoon ground ginger

Directions:
1. Wash and peel the carrots. Use a spiralizer to make the curls or spirals.
2. Put the carrot spirals in the Ninja Foodi's insert.
3. Combine the liquid stevia, water, turmeric, and ground ginger together in a mixing bowl.
4. Stir the mixture well. Set the Ninja Foodi's insert to" Sauté" mode.
5. Add the butter to the carrot mixture and sauté it for 3 minutes.
6. Stir the vegetables frequently. Add the stevia mixture and Close the Ninja Foodi's lid.
7. Cook the dish on" Sauté" mode for 10 minutes.
8. Once the carrot spirals are cooked, remove them from the Ninja Foodi's insert, strain them from the stevia liquid.
9. Serve.

Nutrition:
- InfoCalories: 62; Fat: 3.1g; Carbohydrates: 8.3g; Protein: 0.8g

Horseradish Roasted Carrots

Servings:4
Cooking Time: 10 Minutes

Ingredients:
- 1 pound carrots, peeled and cut into 1-inch pieces
- ½ cup vegetable stock
- 2 tablespoons grated horseradish
- ¾ cup mayonnaise
- ½ teaspoon kosher salt
- ½ teaspoon freshly ground black pepper
- Minced parsley, for garnish

Directions:
1. Place the carrots and stock in the pot. Assemble pressure lid, making sure the pressure release valve is in the SEAL position.
2. Select PRESSURE and set to HI. Set time to 2 minutes. Select START/STOP to begin.
3. When pressure cooking is complete, quick release the pressure by turning the pressure release valve to the VENT

position. Carefully remove lid when unit has finished releasing pressure.
4. In a small bowl, combine the horseradish, mayonnaise, salt, and pepper. Add mixture to the cooked carrots and stir carefully. Close crisping lid.
5. Select BROIL and set time to 6 minutes. Select START/STOP to begin.
6. After 3 minutes, open lid to check doneness. If further browning desired, close lid and continue cooking.
7. When cooking is complete, garnish with parsley and serve immediately.

Nutrition:
- InfoCalories: 323,Total Fat: 30g,Sodium: 632mg,Carbohydrates: 13g,Protein: 1g.

Cheesy Stuffed Onions

Servings: 6
Cooking Time: 1 Hour
Ingredients:
- 3 onions, peeled & cut in half horizontally
- 1 tbsp. olive oil
- ¼ cup cream cheese, reduced fat, soft
- 2 tbsp. sour cream, fat free
- 1 clove garlic, diced fine
- 1 tsp fresh rosemary, diced fine
- 1/8 tsp salt
- 1/8 tsp pepper
- 2 tbsp. panko bread crumbs
- 1 tbsp. butter, melted
- 1 tsp bacon bits

Directions:
1. Place onions, cut side up, in the cooking pot. Drizzle with oil.
2. Add the tender-crisp lid and select air fry on 400°F (205°C). Cook onions for 40 minutes. Transfer to wire rack and let cool enough to handle.
3. Carefully remove the center of the onion so you have a shell.
4. In a small bowl, combine cream cheese, sour cream, garlic, rosemary, salt, and pepper. Spread over and into the onions.
5. In a separate small bowl, combine bread crumbs, butter, and bacon.
6. Place the rack in the cooking pot and top with a sheet of parchment paper. Place the onions back in the pot and sprinkle the tops with bacon mixture.
7. Add the tender-crisp lid and set to bake on 400°F (205°C). Bake onions another 10-15 minutes or until golden brown. Serve.

Nutrition:
- InfoCalories 93,Total Fat 6g,Total Carbs 8g,Protein 2g,Sodium 127mg.

Sweet Potato Fries

Servings: 4
Cooking Time: 20 Minutes
Ingredients:
- Nonstick cooking spray
- ½ tsp cumin
- ½ tsp chili powder
- ½ tsp pepper
- ½ tsp salt
- ¼ tsp cayenne pepper
- 2 sweet potatoes, peeled & julienned
- 1 tbsp. extra-virgin olive oil

Directions:
1. Lightly spray fryer basket with cooking spray.
2. In a small bowl, combine cumin, chili powder, pepper, salt, and cayenne pepper.
3. Place potatoes in a large bowl and sprinkle spice mix and oil over them. Toss well to coat.
4. Place the fries, in small batches, in the basket and place in the cooking pot.
5. Add the tender-crisp lid and select air fryer on 425°F (160°C). Cook fries 15-20 minutes, until crispy on the outside and tender inside, turning halfway through cooking time. Serve immediately.

Nutrition:
- InfoCalories 86,Total Fat 3g,Total Carbs 13g,Protein 1g,Sodium 327mg.

Loaded Smashed Potatoes With Bacon

Servings: 4
Cooking Time: 30 Minutes
Ingredients:
- 12 ounces (340 g) baby Yukon Gold potatoes
- 1 tsp. extra-virgin olive oil
- ¼ cup shredded Cheddar cheese
- ¼ cup sour cream
- 2 slices bacon, cooked and crumbled
- 1 tbsp. chopped fresh chives
- Sea salt

Directions:
1. Put the Crisp Basket in the pot. Close the Crisping Lid. Select Air Crisp, set the temperature to 350°F (175°C), and set the time to 5 minutes. Press Start/Stop to begin to preheat the unit.
2. While preheating, toss the potatoes with the oil until evenly coated.
3. After the pot and basket are preheated, open the lid and place the potatoes into the basket. Close the lid, select Air Crisp, set the temperature to 350°F (175°C), and set the time to 30 minutes. Press Start/Stop to begin.
4. 15 minutes later, open the lid, lift the basket and shake the potatoes. Lower the basket back into the pot and close the lid to resume cooking.
5. After another 15 minutes, check the potatoes for your desired crispiness.
6. Take the potatoes out from the basket. Lightly crush the potatoes to split them with a large spoon. Top with the cheese, sour cream, bacon, and chives, and season with salt.

Crispy Fries

Servings:2
Cooking Time: 40 Minutes
Ingredients:
- 3 large russet potatoes
- 2 teaspoons kosher salt, plus more as needed
- Cooking spray

Directions:

1. Place the potatoes in the Foodi's crisping basket and set the basket into the Foodi's inner pot. Fill the pot with water to reach the maximum fill line. Then remove the potatoes, one at a time, to peel them before returning them to the water. Once the potatoes are peeled, put one on a cutting board and cut it into ½-inch fries . Return the cut potato to the water and repeat with the remaining 2 potatoes .

2. Reserve ½ cup of the water from the inner pot and drain the potatoes. Return the reserved ½ cup water to the potatoes in the Foodi's inner pot and add the salt. Lock on the Pressure Lid, making sure the valve is set to Seal, and set to Pressure on High for 0 minutes. When the timer reaches 0, quick-release the pressure and carefully remove the lid. Transfer the potatoes to a kitchen towel–lined baking sheet and blot them dry with another kitchen towel.

3. Spray the potatoes heavily with cooking spray, tossing gently to evenly coat them. Add them to the crisping basket, insert the basket into the Foodi inner pot, drop the Crisping Lid, and set the Foodi to Air Crisp at 275°F(190°C) for 10 minutes, or until the fries are limp and pale.

4. Lift the lid and spray the fries with more oil. Drop the Crisping Lid again and set the Foodi to Air Crisp at 400°F(205°C) for 30 minutes, or until the fries are browned and crisp. Lift the lid and sprinkle with more salt if you like, then serve hot.

Dill Butter

Servings: 7
Cooking Time: 5 Minutes
Ingredients:
- 1 cup butter
- 1 teaspoon minced garlic
- 1 teaspoon dried oregano
- 1 teaspoon dried cilantro
- 1 tablespoon dried dill
- 1 teaspoon salt
- ½ teaspoon black pepper

Directions:
1. Set "Sauté" mode and place butter inside the Ninja Foodi's insert.
2. Add minced garlic, dried oregano, dried cilantro, butter, dried dill, salt, and black pepper.
3. Stir the mixture well and sauté it for 4-5 minutes or until the butter is melted.
4. Then switch off the cooker and stir the butter well.
5. Transfer the butter mixture into the butter mould and freeze it.

Nutrition:
- InfoCalories: 235; Fat: 26.3g; Carbohydrates: 0.6g; Protein: 0.4g

White Bean Hummus

Servings: 8
Cooking Time: 8 Hours
Ingredients:
- 2 cups small white beans, soaked overnight
- 2 tbsp. pine nuts
- 1 tsp lemon zest, grated
- 1 tbsp. fresh lemon juice
- ¼ tsp garlic powder
- ¼ tsp salt

Directions:
1. Place beans with just enough water to cover them in the cooking pot. Add the lid and set to slow cooker function on low heat. Cook 8 hours, or until beans are tender.
2. Drain the beans, reserving some of the cooking liquid. Place beans in a food processor.
3. Wipe the cooking pot and set to sauté on low heat. Add the pine nuts and cook, stirring frequently, until lightly browned.
4. Add the lemon zest and juice, garlic powder, and salt to the beans. Pulse until almost smooth. If hummus is too thick, add reserved cooking liquid, a tablespoon at a time, until desired consistency.
5. Transfer hummus to a serving bowl and sprinkle with pine nuts. Serve.

Nutrition:
- InfoCalories 169,Total Fat 1g,Total Carbs 31g,Protein 12g,Sodium 81mg.

Teriyaki Chicken Wings

Servings: 6
Cooking Time: 30 Min
Ingredients:
- 2 lb. chicken wings /900g
- 1 cup teriyaki sauce /250ml
- 1 tbsp honey /15ml
- 2 tbsp cornstarch 30g
- 2 tbsp cold water /30ml
- 1 tsp finely ground black pepper /5g
- 1 tsp sesame seeds /5g

Directions:
1. In the pot, combine honey, teriyaki sauce and black pepper until the honey dissolves completely; toss in chicken to coat. Seal the pressure lid, choose Pressure, set to High, and set the timer to 10 minutes. Press Start.
2. When ready, release the pressure quickly. Transfer chicken wings to a platter. Mix cold water with the cornstarch.
3. Press Sear/Sauté and stir in cornstarch slurry into the sauce and cook for 3 to 5 minutes until thickened. Top the chicken with thickened sauce. Add a garnish of sesame seeds, and serve.

The Original Braised Kale And Carrot Salad

Servings: 4
Cooking Time: 30 Minutes
Ingredients:
- 10 ounces kale, roughly chopped
- 1 tablespoon ghee
- 1 medium onion, sliced
- 3 medium carrots, cut into half inch pieces
- 5 garlic clove, peeled and chopped
- ½ cup chicken broth
- Fresh ground pepper
- Vinegar as needed
- ½ teaspoon red pepper flakes

Directions:
1. Set your pot to Saute mode and add ghee, allow the ghee to melt

2. Add chopped onion and carrots and Saute for a while
3. Add garlic and Saute for a while. Pile the kale on top
4. Pour chicken broth and season with pepper
5. Lock up the lid and cook on HIGH pressure for 8 minutes
6. Release the pressure naturally over 10 minutes. Open and give it a nice stir
7. Add vinegar and sprinkle a bit more pepper flakes. Enjoy!

Spaghetti Squash And Chicken Parmesan

Servings: 4
Cooking Time: 20 Minutes
Ingredients:
- 1 spaghetti squash
- 1 cup marinara sauce (Keto Friendly)
- 1 pound chicken, cooked and cubed
- 16 ounces mozzarella

Directions:
1. Split up the squash in halves and remove the seeds
2. Add 1 cup of water to the Ninja Foodi and place a trivet on top
3. Add the squash halves on the trivet. Lock up the lid and cook for 20 minutes at HIGH pressure
4. Do a quick release. Remove the squashes and shred them using a fork into spaghetti portions
5. Pour sauce over the squash and give it a nice mix
6. Top them up with the cubed up chicken and top with mozzarella
7. Broil for 1-2 minutes and broil until the cheese has melted

Quick Turkey Cutlets

Servings: 4
Cooking Time: 22 Minutes
Ingredients:
- 1 teaspoon Greek seasoning
- 1 pound turkey cutlets
- 2 tablespoons olive oil
- 1 teaspoon turmeric powder
- ½ cup almond flour

Directions:
1. Add Greek seasoning, turmeric powder, almond flour to a bowl
2. Dredge turkey cutlets in it and keep it on the side for 30 minutes
3. Set your Foodi to Saute mode and add oil and cutlets, Saute for 2 minutes
4. Lock lid and cook on LOW-MEDIUM pressure for 20 minutes
5. Quick release pressure. Serve and enjoy!

Turkey Scotch Eggs

Servings: 6
Cooking Time: 20 Min
Ingredients:
- 10 oz. ground turkey /300g
- 4 eggs, soft boiled, peeled
- 2 garlic cloves, minced
- 2 eggs, lightly beaten
- 1 white onion; chopped
- ½ cup flour /65g
- ½ cup breadcrumbs /65g
- 1 tsp dried mixed herbs /5g
- Salt and pepper to taste
- Cooking spray

Directions:
1. Mix together the onion, garlic, salt, and pepper. Shape into 4 balls. Wrap the turkey mixture around each egg, and ensure the eggs are well covered.
2. Dust each egg ball in flour, then dip in the beaten eggs and finally roll in the crumbs, until coated. Spray with cooking spray.
3. Lay the eggs into your Ninja Foodi's basket. Set the temperature to 390 °F or 200°C, close the crisping lid and cook for 15 minutes. After 8 minutes, turn the eggs. Slice in half and serve warm.

Cheesy Smashed Sweet Potatoes

Servings: 4
Cooking Time: 70 Min
Ingredients:
- 2 slices bacon, cooked and crumbled
- 12 ounces baby sweet potatoes /360g
- ¼ cup shredded Monterey Jack cheese /32.5g
- ¼ cup sour cream /62.5ml
- 1 tbsp chopped scallions /15g
- 1 tsp melted butter /5ml
- Salt to taste

Directions:
1. Put the Crisping Basket in the pot and close the crisping lid. Choose Air Crisp, set the temperature to 350°F or 175°C, and the time to 5 minutes. Press Start/Stop to begin preheating.
2. Meanwhile, toss the sweet potatoes with the melted butter until evenly coated. Once the pot and basket have preheated, open the lid and add the sweet potatoes to the basket. Close the lid, Choose Air Crisp, set the temperature to 350°F or 175°C, and set the time to 30 minutes; press Start.
3. After 15 minutes, open the lid, pull out the basket and shake the sweet potatoes. Return the basket to the pot and close the lid to continue cooking. When ended, check the sweet potatoes for your desired crispiness, which should also be fork tender.
4. Take out the sweet potatoes from the basket and use a large spoon to crush the soft potatoes just to split lightly. Top with the cheese, sour cream, bacon, and scallions, and season with salt.

Delicious Bacon-Wrapped Drumsticks

Servings: 6
Cooking Time: 8 Hours
Ingredients:
- 12 chicken drumsticks
- 12 slices thin cut bacon

Directions:
1. Wrap each chicken drumsticks in bacon. Place drumsticks in your Ninja Foodi
2. Place lid and cook SLOW COOK mode for 8 hours. Serve and enjoy!

Chili Chicken Dip

Servings: 8
Cooking Time: 20 Minutes
Ingredients:
- 1 tbsp. olive oil
- 1 sweet onion, chopped fine
- 2 cloves garlic, chopped fine
- 2 jalapeño peppers, seeded & chopped
- 1 Poblano pepper, seeded & chopped
- 1 cup Greek yogurt
- 8 oz. cream cheese, fat free, soft
- ½ cup cheddar cheese, reduced fat, grated
- 4 oz. green chilies, diced
- 1 tsp salt
- 2 cups chicken breasts, cooked & shredded
- 1 tbsp. chili powder
- 2 tsp cumin
- ½ tsp pepper
- 1 tsp oregano
- Nonstick cooking spray
- ¼ cup cilantro, chopped

Directions:
1. Set the cooker to sauté on medium heat. Add oil and let it get hot.
2. Add the onion, garlic, jalapeno, and poblano peppers. Cook, stirring frequently, until vegetables are tender, about 3-5 minutes. Transfer to a bowl and let cool completely.
3. In a medium bowl, beat together yogurt, and cream cheese until smooth.
4. Turn the mixer to low and add onion mixture along with remaining ingredients, except cilantro. Beat until all ingredients are combined.
5. Spray a casserole dish with cooking spray. Spread dip evenly in the dish.
6. Place the rack in the cooking pot and put the dish on it. Add the tender-crisp lid and select bake on 400°F (205°C). Bake 15 minutes until bubbly. Sprinkle with cilantro and serve.

Nutrition:
- InfoCalories 189,Total Fat 7g,Total Carbs 15g,Protein 19g,Sodium 1004mg.

Chicken Wings

Servings: 2
Cooking Time: 40 Minutes
Ingredients:
- 1½ cups hot sauce
- 6 whole chicken wings, split into drumettes and flats
- ½ teaspoon kosher salt
- Celery sticks, for garnish (optional)
- Carrot sticks, for garnish (optional)
- Blue cheese dressing, for garnish (optional)
- Ranch dressing, for garnish (optional)

Directions:
1. Place ½ cup of the hot sauce and 1 cup water in the Foodi's inner pot and stir to combine. Place the wings in the crisping basket and set the basket into the inner pot. Lock on the Pressure Lid, making sure the valve is set to Seal, and set to Pressure on High for 2 minutes. When the timer reaches 0, quick-release the pressure and carefully remove the lid.
2. Sprinkle the wings with the salt. Drop the Crisping Lid and set the Foodi to Air Crisp at 390°F (200°C) for 40 minutes, or until crisp and blistered.
3. Lift the lid and remove the basket with the wings. Add the remaining 1 cup hot sauce to the pot, and toss the wings with the sauce in the pot. Transfer the wings to a platter and serve with your favorite accoutrements.

Stuffed Chicken Mushrooms

Servings: 4
Cooking Time: 15 Minutes
Ingredients:
- 12 large fresh mushrooms, stems removed
- Stuffing
- 1 cup chicken meat, cubed
- ½ pound, imitation crabmeat, flaked
- 2 cups butter
- Garlic powder to taste
- 2 garlic cloves, peeled and minced

Directions:
1. Take a non-stick skillet and place it over medium heat, add butter and let it heat up
2. Stir in chicken and Saute for 5 minutes. Add for stuffing and cook for 5 minutes
3. Remove heat and let the chicken cool down. Divide filling into mushroom caps
4. Place stuffed mushroom caps in your Crisping basket and transfer basket to Foodi
5. Lock Crisping Lid and Air Crisp for 10 minutes at 375 degrees F. Serve and enjoy!

The Kool Poblano Cheese Frittata

Servings: 4
Cooking Time: 25 Minutes
Ingredients:
- 4 whole eggs
- 1 cup half and half
- 10 ounces canned green chilies
- ½ -1 teaspoon salt
- ½ teaspoon ground cumin
- 1 cup Mexican blend shredded cheese
- ¼ cup cilantro, chopped

Directions:
1. Take a bowl and beat eggs and a half and half
2. Add diced green chilis, salt, cumin and ½ cup of shredded cheese
3. Pour the mixture into 6 inches greased metal pan and cover with foil
4. Add 2 cups of water to the Ninja Foodi. Place trivet in the pot and place the pan in the trivet
5. Lock up the lid and cook on HIGH pressure for 20 minutes
6. Release the pressure naturally over 10 minutes
7. Scatter half cup of the cheese on top of your quiche and broil for a while until the cheese has melted. Enjoy!

Cauliflower And Egg Dish

Servings: 4
Cooking Time: 4 Minutes
Ingredients:
- 21 ounces cauliflower, separated into florets
- 1 cup red onion, chopped
- 1 cup celery, chopped
- ½ cup of water
- Salt and pepper to taste
- 2 tablespoons balsamic vinegar
- 1 teaspoon stevia
- 4 boiled eggs, chopped
- 1 cup Keto Friendly mayonnaise

Directions:
1. Add water to Ninja Foodi
2. Add steamer basket and add cauliflower, lock lid and cook on High Pressure for 5 minutes
3. Quick release pressure. Transfer cauliflower to bowl and add eggs, celery, onion and toss
4. Take another bowl and mix in mayo, salt, pepper, vinegar, stevia and whisk well
5. Add a salad, toss well. Divide into salad bowls and serve. Enjoy!

Cheeseburger Boats

Servings: 9
Cooking Time: 20 Minutes
Ingredients:
- 3 bell peppers
- 1 lb. lean ground beef
- 1 onion, chopped fine
- ½ tsp salt
- ½ tsp pepper
- 2/3 cup ketchup, divided
- 1 tbsp. mustard
- 5 slices cheddar cheese, reduced fat

Directions:
1. Place the rack in the cooking pot and top with a sheet of parchment paper.
2. Cut peppers in 6 vertical pieces, using the indention lines as a guide. Remove ribs and seeds.
3. In a large bowl, combine beef, onion, salt, pepper, 1/3 cup ketchup, and mustard. Spoon mixture into peppers.
4. Place peppers on parchment paper, these will need to be cooked in batches. Add the tender-crisp lid and select bake on 375°F (190°C). Bake 20 minutes, or until meat is no longer pink.
5. Drizzle with some of the remaining ketchup and top with ¼ slice of cheese. Cook about 5 minutes more or until cheese has melted. Serve immediately.

Nutrition:
- InfoCalories 175,Total Fat 7g,Total Carbs 10g,Protein 18g,Sodium 479mg.

Hungarian Cornmeal Squares

Servings: 4
Cooking Time: 55 Minutes
Ingredients:
- 1¼ cup (63 mL) water, divided
- 1 cup (250 mL) yellow cornmeal
- 1 cup (250 mL) yogurt
- 1 egg, beaten
- ½ cups sour cream
- 1 teaspoon baking soda
- 2 tablespoons safflower oil
- ¼ teaspoon salt
- 4 tablespoons plum jam

Directions:
1. Pour 1 cup of water in the cooking pot. Set a reversible rack in the pot. Spritz a baking pan with cooking spray.
2. Combine the cornmeal, yogurt, egg, sour cream, baking soda, ¼ cup of water, safflower oil, and salt in a large bowl. Stir to mix well.
3. Pour the mixture into the prepared baking pan. Spread the plum jam over. Cover with aluminum foil. Lower the pan onto the reversible rack.
4. Assemble pressure lid, making sure the pressure release valve is in the Seal position. Select Pressure and set to high. Set time to 55 minutes. Press Start to begin. Once cooking is complete, perform a quick pressure release, carefully open the lid.
5. Transfer the corn meal chunk onto a cooling rack and allow to cool for 10 minutes. Slice into squares and serve.

Strawberry Snack Bars

Servings: 16
Cooking Time: 30 Minutes
Ingredients:
- Butter flavored cooking spray
- 1 cup butter, soft
- 2 oz. stevia
- 1 tbsp. sour cream, reduced fat
- 1 egg
- 1 cup flour
- 1 cup whole wheat flour
- 1 cup strawberry jam, sugar free
- 1 tbsp. brown sugar
- 2 tbsp. walnuts, chopped

Directions:
1. Spray an 8-inch square pan with cooking spray.
2. In a medium bowl, beat butter and Stevia until creamy.
3. Beat in sour cream and egg until combined.
4. Stir in both flours, ½ cup at a time, until mixture forms a soft dough.
5. Press half the dough in the bottom of the prepared pan. Spread the jam over the top. Then spread the other half of the dough gently over the top. Sprinkle the brown sugar and nuts over the top.
6. Place the rack in the cooking pot and place the pan on it. Add the tender-crisp lid and set to bake on 375°F (190°C). Bake 25-30 minutes until bubbly and golden brown.
7. Transfer to wire rack to cool before cutting.

Nutrition:
- InfoCalories 195,Total Fat 13g,Total Carbs 22g,Protein 3g,Sodium 97mg.

Spinach Hummus

Servings: 12
Cooking Time: 1 Hr 10 Min
Ingredients:
- 2 cups spinach; chopped /260g
- ½ cup tahini /65g
- 2 cups dried chickpeas /260g
- 8 cups water /2000ml
- 5 garlic cloves, crushed
- 5 tbsp grapeseed oil /75ml
- 2 tsp salt; divided /10g
- 5 tbsp lemon juice /75ml

Directions:
1. In the pressure cooker, mix 2 tbsp oil, water, 1 tsp or 5g salt, and chickpeas. Seal the pressure lid, choose Pressure, set to High, and set the timer to 35 minutes. Press Start. When ready, release the pressure quickly. In a small bowl, reserve ½ cup of the cooking liquid and drain chickpeas.
2. Mix half the reserved cooking liquid and chickpeas in a food processor and puree until no large chickpeas remain; add remaining cooking liquid, spinach, lemon juice, remaining tsp salt, garlic, and tahini.
3. Process hummus for 8 minutes until smooth. Stir in the remaining 3 tbsp or 45ml of olive oil before serving.

Turkey And Wild Rice Salad With Walnuts

Servings: 4
Cooking Time: 50 Minutes
Ingredients:
- 4 cups water
- 1 cup wild rice
- 2¼ tsps. kosher salt (or 1⅛ tsps. fine salt), divided
- 1 pound (455 g) turkey tenderloins
- 3 tsps. walnut oil or olive oil, divided
- 3 tbsps. apple cider vinegar
- ⅛ tsp. freshly ground black pepper
- ¼ tsp. celery seeds
- Pinch sugar
- ½ cup walnut pieces, toasted
- 2 or 3 celery stalks, thinly sliced (about 1 cup)
- 1 medium Gala, Fuji, or Braeburn apple, cored and cut into ½-inch pieces

Directions:
1. In the Foodi inner pot, add the water. Stir in 1 teaspoon of kosher salt and the wild rice.
2. Lock the Pressure Lid into place, set the valve to Seal. Select Pressure, adjust the cook time to 18 minutes. Press Start.
3. Meanwhile, sprinkle 1 teaspoon of kosher salt onto the turkey tenderloins and set aside.
4. After the rice is cooked, naturally release the pressure for 10 minutes, then quick release any remaining pressure. Open and remove the Pressure Lid carefully. The rice grains should be mostly split open. If not, select Sear/Sauté. Press Start. Simmer the rice for several minutes until at least half the grains have split. Drain and allow to cool slightly. Place to a large bowl to cool completely.
5. Close the Crisping Lid and preheat by selecting Bake/Roast, adjusting the temperature to 375°F (190°C) and the time to 4 minutes. Press Start.
6. Meanwhile, place the turkey into the Crisp Basket and use 2 teaspoons of walnut oil to brush.
7. Once the pot is preheated, place the basket in it.
8. Close the Crisping Lid and select Bake/Roast, adjust the temperature to 375°F (190°C) and the cook time to 12 minutes. Press Start.
9. At the same time, in a jar with a tight-fitting lid, add the remaining 1 teaspoon of walnut oil and the vinegar. Add the remaining ¼ teaspoon of kosher salt, the pepper, the celery seed, and the sugar. Cover the jar and shake until the ingredients are well combined.
10. After the turkey is cooked, take it out from the basket and allow to cool for several minutes. Cut it into chunks and place the turkey over the rice along with the celery, walnut pieces, and apple. Over the salad pour with about half the dressing and toss gently to coat, adding more dressing as desired.

Chicken Pork Nuggets

Servings: 6
Cooking Time: 20 Minutes
Ingredients:
- 2 cups ground chicken
- ½ cup dill, chopped
- 1 egg
- 2 tablespoons pork rinds
- 1 tablespoon heavy cream
- ½ cup almond flour
- 3 tablespoons butter
- 1 tablespoon canola oil
- 1 teaspoon black pepper

Directions:
1. Beat the egg in a suitable mixing bowl.
2. Add the chopped dill and ground chicken. Blend the mixture until it is smooth.
3. Sprinkle the dish with black pepper and cream.
4. Blend the nugget mixture again. Form the nuggets from the meat mixture and dip them in the almond flour and pork rinds.
5. Sprinkle the Ninja Foodi's insert with the canola oil and butter.
6. Set the Ninja Foodi's insert to "Pressure" mode. Once the butter mixture starts to melt, add the nuggets.
7. Close the Ninja Foodi's lid and cook the dish for 20 minutes.
8. Once done, check if the nuggets are cooked and remove them from the Ninja Foodi's insert.
9. Drain on a paper towel and serve.

Nutrition:
- InfoCalories: 217; Fat: 15.4g; Carbohydrates: 3.1g; Protein: 17.4 g

Crispy Spiced Cauliflower Bites

Servings: 12
Cooking Time: 15 Minutes
Ingredients:
- Nonstick cooking spray
- 1 egg
- 1 tbsp. water
- 1 cup whole wheat panko bread crumbs
- 1 tbsp. garlic powder
- ½ tsp onion powder
- 1 tbsp. fresh parsley, chopped
- 6 cups cauliflower florets
- ¼ cup light mayonnaise
- 2 tbsp. sweet chili sauce
- 2 tbsp. hot sauce

Directions:
1. Lightly spray the fryer basket with cooking spray and place in the cooking pot.
2. In a small bowl, whisk together egg and water.
3. In a separate small bowl, stir together bread crumbs, garlic powder, onion powder, and parsley.
4. Dip each floret first in egg then in bread crumbs. Place in fryer basket, in batches.
5. Add the tender-crisp lid and set to air fry on 400°F (205°C). Bake cauliflower 15 minutes or until golden brown and crispy.
6. In a small bowl, whisk together mayonnaise, chili sauce, and hot sauce. When all the cauliflower is done, drizzle sauce over the top and serve.

Nutrition:
- InfoCalories 77,Total Fat 3g,Total Carbs 11g,Protein 3g,Sodium 177mg.

Beef Chicken Meatloaf

Servings: 9
Cooking Time: 40 Minutes
Ingredients:
- 2 cups ground beef
- 1 cup ground chicken
- 2 eggs
- 1 tablespoon salt
- 1 teaspoon black pepper
- ½ teaspoon paprika
- 1 tablespoon butter
- 1 teaspoon cilantro, chopped
- 1 tablespoon basil
- ¼ cup fresh dill, chopped

Directions:
1. Combine the ground chicken and ground beef together in a mixing bowl.
2. Add egg, salt, black pepper, paprika, butter, and cilantro.
3. Add the basil and dill and add it to the ground meat mixture and stir using your hands.
4. Place the meat mixture on aluminium foil, shape into a loaf and wrap it.
5. Place it in the Ninja Foodi's insert. Close the Ninja Foodi's lid and cook the dish in the" Sauté" mode for 40 minutes.
6. Once done, remove the meatloaf from the Ninja Foodi's insert and let it rest.
7. Remove from the foil, slice it, and serve.

Nutrition:
- InfoCalories: 173; Fat: 11.5g; Carbohydrates: 0.81g; Protein: 16g

Breakfast

Kale-egg Frittata

Servings: 6
Cooking Time: 20 Min
Ingredients:
- 1 ½ cups kale; chopped /195g
- 6 large eggs
- ¼ cup grated Parmesan cheese /32.5g
- 1 cup water /250ml
- 2 tbsp heavy cream /30ml
- ½ tsp freshly grated nutmeg /2.5g
- cooking spray
- Salt and black pepper to taste

Directions:
1. In a bowl, beat eggs, nutmeg, pepper, salt, and cream until smooth; stir in Parmesan cheese and kale. Apply a cooking spray to a cake pan. Wrap aluminum foil around outside of the pan to cover completely.
2. Place egg mixture into the prepared pan. Add water into the pot of your Foodi. Set your Foodi's reversible rack over the water. Gently lay the pan onto the reversible rack.
3. Seal the pressure lid, choose Pressure, set to High, and set the timer to 10 minutes. Press Start. When ready, release the pressure quickly.

Tropical Fruit Steel Cut Oats

Servings: 4
Cooking Time: 19 Minutes
Ingredients:
- 1 cup steel cut oats
- ¾ cup frozen chopped peaches
- ¾ cup frozen mango chunks
- 1 cup (240 ml) unsweetened almond milk
- 2 cups (480 ml) coconut water or water
- 1 (2-inch) vanilla bean, scraped (seeds and pod)
- ¼ cup chopped unsalted macadamia nuts
- Ground cinnamon

Directions:
1. Mix the oats, coconut water, almond milk, mango chunks, peaches, and vanilla bean seeds and pod in the Ninja pressure cooker. Stir well.
2. Close the pressure lid. Set the steamer valve to sealing.
3. Select Pressure and the time to 5 minutes.
4. Once cooking is complete, allow the pressure to release naturally for 10 minutes, then quick release any remaining pressure. Press Stop.
5. When the pin drops, unlock and remove the lid.
6. Throw away the vanilla bean pod and stir well.
7. Spoon the oats into 4 bowls. Sprinkle cinnamon and 1 tablespoon of the macadamia nuts on top of each serving.

Bacon And Cheese Custards

Servings: 4
Cooking Time: 7 Minutes
Ingredients:
- 2 bacon slices, halved widthwise
- 4 large eggs
- ¼ cup heavy (whipping) cream
- 1 ounce (28 g) cream cheese, at room temperature
- ¼ tsp. kosher salt (or ⅛ tsp. fine salt)
- Freshly ground black or white pepper
- ¼ cup grated Gruyère or other Swiss-style cheese
- ¼ cup Caramelized Onions

Directions:
1. On your Ninja Pressure Cooker, select Sear/Sauté and press Start. Preheat for 5 minutes.
2. Add the bacon, and cook for 3 to 4 minutes, or until browned, turning occasionally. Transfer the bacon to a paper towel-lined plate to drain with a slotted spoon, leaving the fat in the pot. Using a basting or pastry brush to coat the bacon fat onto the inside of four custard cups or 1-cup ramekins. Set the cups aside. Wipe out the inner pot and replace it in the base.
3. In a small bowl crack the eggs. Then add the heavy cream, cream cheese, salt, and several grinds of pepper. Beat the mixture with a handheld electric mixer, until it is homogeneous with no clumps of cream cheese remaining.
4. Add the grated cheese and mix again to incorporate the cheese.
5. In the bottom of each custard cup, place a piece of bacon. Divide the onions evenly among the cups and pour the egg mixture over, dividing it as evenly as possible. Use in the bottom of each custard cup to cover each cup.
6. In the inner pot, add 1 cup of water. Place the ramekins on the Reversible Rack, then put in the pot.
7. Lock the Pressure Lid into place, set the steamer valve to Seal. Select Pressure and set the cook time to 7 minutes. Press Start.
8. When the cooking is complete, quick release the pressure. Open and remove the Pressure Lid carefully.
9. Carefully remove the custard cups from the pressure cooker with tongs. Allow to cool for 1 to 2 minutes before serving.

Easy Cheesy Egg Bake

Servings: 4
Cooking Time: 27 Minutes
Ingredients:
- 4 eggs
- 1 cup milk
- 1 teaspoon sea salt
- 1 teaspoon freshly ground black pepper
- 1 cup shredded Cheddar cheese
- 1 red bell pepper, seeded and chopped
- 8 ounces ham, chopped
- 1 cup water

Directions:
1. In a medium mixing bowl, whisk together the eggs, milk, salt, and black pepper. Stir in the Cheddar cheese.

2. Place the bell pepper and ham in the Multi-Purpose Pan or an 8-inch baking pan. Pour the egg mixture over the pepper and ham. Cover the pan with aluminum foil and place on the Reversible Rack.
3. Pour the water into the pot. Place the rack with the pan in the pot in the lower position.
4. Assemble the Pressure Lid, making sure the pressure release valve is in the Seal position. Select Pressure and set to High. Set the time to 20 minutes. Select Start/Stop to begin.
5. When pressure cooking is complete, quick release the pressure by moving the pressure release valve to the Vent position. Carefully remove the lid when the unit has finished releasing pressure.
6. When cooking is complete, remove the pan from the pot and place it on a cooling rack. Let cool for 5 minutes, then serve.

Chorizo Omelet

Servings: 4
Cooking Time: 30-35 Minutes
Ingredients:
- 3 eggs, whisked
- 3 ounces chorizo, chopped
- 1-ounces Feta cheese, crumbled
- 5 tablespoons almond milk
- ¾ teaspoon chilli flakes
- ¼ teaspoon salt
- 1 green pepper, chopped

Directions:
1. Add listed ingredients to a suitable and mix well.
2. Take an omelette pan and pour the mixture on it.
3. Pre-heat your Ninja Food on "BAKE" mode at a temperature of 320 °F (160°C).
4. Transfer pan with omelette mix to your Ninja Foodi and cook for 30 minutes, or until the surface is golden and the egg has set properly.
5. Serve and enjoy.

Nutrition:
- InfoCalories: 426; Fat: 38g; Carbohydrates: 7g; Protein: 21g

Apple And Cranberry Oatmeal With Vanilla

Servings: 4
Cooking Time: 27 Minutes
Ingredients:
- 2 cups gluten-free steel-cut oats
- ½ cup dried cranberries, plus more for garnish
- 2 apples, peeled, cored, and diced
- 3¾ cups water
- ¼ cup apple cider vinegar
- 1 tbsp. ground cinnamon
- ½ tsp. ground nutmeg
- ½ tsp. vanilla extract
- ⅛ tsp. sea salt
- Maple syrup, for topping

Directions:
1. In the pot, add the oats, water, vinegar, cinnamon, nutmeg, vanilla, cranberries, apples, and salt. Assemble the Pressure Lid, set the steamer valve to Seal. Select Pressure. Set the time to 11 minutes. Select Start/Stop.
2. After pressure cooking is done, release the pressure for 10 minutes naturally, then move the pressure release valve to the Vent position to quick release any remaining pressure. Remove the lid when the pressure has finished releasing.
3. Stir well of the oatmeal, top with maple syrup and more dried cranberries, and serve.

Cheesy Egg Bake With Ham

Servings: 4
Cooking Time: 27 Minutes
Ingredients:
- 1 cup milk
- 4 eggs
- 1 tsp. freshly ground black pepper
- 1 tsp. sea salt
- 1 cup shredded Cheddar cheese
- 8 ounces (227 g) ham, chopped
- 1 red bell pepper, seeded and chopped
- 1 cup water

Directions:
1. Add the milk, eggs, black pepper and salt in a medium mixing bowl, whisk them together. Add the Cheddar cheese and stir well.
2. In the Multi-Purpose Pan or an 8-inch baking pan, add the ham and bell pepper. Then pour the egg mixture over the ham and pepper. Use aluminum foil to cover the pan and place on the Reversible Rack.
3. In the pot, add the water. Place the rack with the pan in the pot.
4. Assemble the Pressure Lid, set the steamer valve to Seal. Select Pressure. Set the time to 20 minutes. Select Start/Stop to begin.
5. After pressure cooking is finish, move the pressure release valve to the Vent position to quick release the pressure. Remove the lid when the unit has finished releasing pressure carefully.
6. After cooking is finish, remove the pan from the pot and transfer it onto a cooling rack. Allow to cool for 5 minutes, and serve.

Poached Breakfast Eggs

Servings: 4
Cooking Time: 10 Minutes
Ingredients:
- 4 large eggs
- Nonstick cooking spray

Directions:
1. Lightly spray 4 cups of silicone egg bite mold with nonstick cooking spray. Crack each egg into a sprayed cup.
2. Pour 1 cup of water into the Ninja pressure cooker. Put the egg bite mold on the wire rack and lower it into the pot carefully.
3. Close the pressure lid. Set the steamer valve to seal.
4. Select Pressure and the time to 5 minutes.
5. Once cooking is complete, press Stop and quick release the pressure.
6. When the pin drops, unlock and remove the lid.
7. Run a spoon or a small rubber spatula around each egg and carefully remove it from the mold. The white should be cooked, but the yolk is runny.
8. Serve immediately.

Swiss Bacon Frittata

Servings: 6
Cooking Time: 23 Minutes
Ingredients:
- 1 small onion, chopped
- 1/2 lb. of raw bacon, chopped
- 1 lb. of frozen spinach
- 10 eggs
- 1 cup cottage cheese
- 1/2 cup half and half cream
- 1 tsp salt
- 1 cup shredded swiss cheese

Directions:
1. Preheat your Ninja Foodi for 5 minutes at 350 °F (175°C) on Saute Mode.
2. Add bacon, and onion to the Foodi and saute for 10 minutes until crispy.
3. Stir in spinach and stir cook for 3 minutes.
4. Whisk eggs with cottage cheese, salt and half and half cream in a bowl.
5. Pour this mixture into the Ninja Foodi cooking pot.
6. Drizzle swiss cheese over the egg mixture.
7. Secure the Ninja Foodi lid and switch the Foodi to Bake/Roast mode for 20 minutes at 350 °F (175°C).
8. Serve warm.

Nutrition:
- InfoCalories 139; Total Fat 10.1g; Total Carbs 2.3g; Protein 10.1 g

Butternut Breakfast Squash

Servings: 4
Cooking Time: 15 Minutes
Ingredients:
- 1 tbsp. coconut oil
- 12 oz. butternut squash, cubed
- 1 tbsp. peanut butter
- ¼ tsp cinnamon
- ¼ tsp all-spice
- 2 tsp maple syrup

Directions:
1. Select sauté function on medium heat and add the coconut oil to the cooking pot.
2. Add the squash and cook until it starts to soften, about 8-10 minutes.
3. Add remaining ingredients and mix well. Cook 2-3 minutes longer until heated through. Serve warm.

Nutrition:
- InfoCalories 201,Total Fat 11g,Total Carbs 26g,Protein 3g,Sodium 9mg.

Ham & Broccoli Frittata

Servings: 6
Cooking Time: 30 Minutes
Ingredients:
- 1 tbsp. butter, soft
- 1 cup red pepper, seeded & sliced
- 1 cup ham, cubed
- 2 cups broccoli florets
- 4 eggs
- 1 cup half-n- half
- 1 cup cheddar cheese, grated
- 1 tsp salt
- 2 tsp pepper
- 2 cups water

Directions:
1. Use the soft butter to grease a 6x3-inch baking dish.
2. Place the peppers in an even layer on the bottom of the dish. Top with ham then broccoli.
3. In a mixing bowl, whisk together eggs, half-n-half, salt, and pepper.
4. Stir in cheese and pour mixture over ingredients in the baking dish. Cover with foil.
5. Pour 2 cups water into the cooking pot and place the rack inside.
6. Place the baking dish on the rack and secure the lid. Select pressure cooking on high and set the timer for 20 minutes.
7. When the timer goes off, release pressure naturally for 10 minutes, then quick release.
8. Remove the baking dish and let cool at least 5 minutes. With a sharp knife, loosen the sides of the frittata then invert onto serving plate. Serve immediately.

Nutrition:
- InfoCalories 401,Total Fat 29g,Total Carbs 9g,Protein 26g,Sodium 1487mg.

Savory Custards With Ham And Cheese

Servings: 4
Cooking Time: 40 Min
Ingredients:
- 4 large eggs
- 1 ounce cottage cheese; at room temperature /30g
- 2 serrano ham slices; halved widthwise
- ¼ cup caramelized white onions /32.5g
- ¼ cup half and half /62.5ml
- ¼ cup grated Emmental cheese /32.5g
- ¼ tsp salt /1.25g
- Ground black pepper to taste

Directions:
1. Preheat the inner pot by choosing Sear/Sauté and adjust to Medium; press Start. Put the serrano ham in the pot and cook for 3 to 4 minutes or until browned, turning occasionally.
2. Remove the ham onto a paper towel-lined plate. Next, use a brush to coat the inside of four 1- cup ramekins with the ham fat. Set the cups aside, then, empty and wipe out the inner pot with a paper towel, and return the pot to the base.
3. Crack the eggs into a bowl and add the cottage cheese, half and half, salt, and several grinds of black pepper. Use a hand mixer to whisk the Ingredients until co cheese lumps remain.
4. Stir in the grated emmental cheese and mix again to incorporate the cheese. Lay a piece of ham in the bottom of each custard cup. Evenly share the onions among the cups as well as the egg mixture. Cover each cup with aluminum foil.
5. Pour 1 cup or 250ml of water into the inner pot and fix the reversible rack in the pot. Arrange the ramekins on top. Lock the pressure lid in Seal position; choose Pressure, adjust to High, and set the timer to 7 minutes. Press Start.
6. After cooking, perform a quick pressure release. Use tongs to remove the custard cups from the pressure cooker. Cool for 1 to 2 minutes before serving.

Deviled Eggs[1]

Servings: 4
Cooking Time: 10 Minutes
Ingredients:
- 8 large eggs
- 1 cup of water
- Guacamole
- Sliced Radishes
- Mayonnaise
- Furikake

Directions:
1. Add water to the inner insert of your Ninja Foodi.
2. Place the steamer rack inside the pot and set the eggs on top of the rack.
3. Lock pressure lid and cook on "HIGH" pressure for 6 minutes.
4. Release Pressure naturally over 10 minutes and transfer the eggs to a suitable full of icy water.
5. Peel after 5 minutes.
6. Cut in half and decorate with guacamole, sliced radish, mayo and enjoy.

Nutrition:
- InfoCalories: 70; Fat: 6g; Carbohydrates: 1g; Protein: 3g

Strawberry Muffins

Servings: 12
Cooking Time: 25 Minutes
Ingredients:
- 1 ¼ cups white whole wheat flour
- 1/3 cup oats
- ½ tsp cinnamon
- ½ tsp baking soda
- 1 tsp baking powder
- ½ tsp salt
- 2/3 cup Stevia
- 3/4 cup Greek yogurt
- 1 egg
- 1/3 cup coconut oil, melted
- 1 cup strawberries, chopped

Directions:
1. Set to air fryer function on 375°F (190°C). Line 2 6-cup muffin tins with paper liners.
2. In a large bowl, combine dry ingredients.
3. In a medium bowl, whisk together yogurt, egg, and oil. Stir in berries and add to dry ingredients. Stir just until combined.
4. Fill prepared muffin tins 2/3 full. Place pans, one at a time, in the cooker and secure the tender-crisp lid. Bake 25 minutes, or until muffins pass the toothpick test. Repeat.
5. Let cool in the pan 10 minutes, then transfer to wire rack to cool completely.

Nutrition:
- InfoCalories 131,Total Fat 8g,Total Carbs 27g,Protein 4g,Sodium 163mg.

Cranberry And Toasted Almond Grits

Servings: 5
Cooking Time: 17 Minutes
Ingredients:
- ¾ cup stone-ground grits or polenta (not instant)
- ½ cup unsweetened dried cranberries
- 1 tbsp. half-and-half
- ¼ cup sliced almonds, toasted
- Pinch kosher salt
- 1 tbsp. unsalted butter (optional)

Directions:
1. Stir together the grits, salt, cranberries, and 3 cups of water in the electric pressure cooker.
2. Close the pressure lid. Set the steamer valve to Seal.
3. Select Pressure and the time to 10 minutes.
4. Once cooking is complete, press Stop and quick release the pressure.
5. When the pin drops, unlock and remove the lid.
6. Add the butter and half-and-half. Stir until it is creamy, adding more half-and-half if necessary.
7. Spoon into serving bowls and sprinkle with toasted almonds.

Curried Chickpea And Roasted Tomato Shakshuka

Servings: 6
Cooking Time: 30 Minutes
Ingredients:
- 2 tablespoons extra-virgin olive oil
- 2 red bell peppers, diced
- 1 small onion, diced
- 2 garlic cloves, minced
- 1 tablespoon red curry paste
- 1 tablespoon tomato paste
- 1 can crushed fire-roasted tomatoes
- 1 can chickpeas, rinsed and drained
- Kosher salt
- Freshly ground black pepper
- 6 large eggs
- 2 tablespoons chopped cilantro

Directions:
1. Select SEAR/SAUTÉ and set to HI. Select START/STOP to begin. Add the olive oil and let preheat for 5 minutes.
2. Add the bell peppers, onion, and garlic and cook for 3 minutes, stirring occasionally.
3. Add the curry and tomato pastes and cook for 2 minutes, stirring occasionally.
4. Add the crushed tomatoes, chickpeas, and season with salt and pepper and stir. Assemble pressure lid, making sure the pressure release valve is in the SEAL position.
5. Select PRESSURE and set to HI. Set time to 10 minutes. Select START/STOP to begin.
6. When pressure cooking is complete, quick release the pressure by turning the pressure release valve to the VENT position. Carefully remove the lid when the unit has finished releasing pressure.
7. With the back of a spoon, make six indents in the sauce. Crack an egg into each indent. Close crisping lid.
8. Select BAKE/ROAST, set temperature to 350°F (175°C), and set time to 10 minutes (or until eggs are cooked to your liking). Select START/STOP to begin.
9. When cooking is complete, open lid. Let cool 5 to 10 minutes, then garnish with the cilantro and serve. If desired,

serve with crusty bread, chopped scallions, feta cheese, and/or pickled jalapeños.

Nutrition:
- InfoCalories: 258,Total Fat: 12g,Sodium: 444mg,Carbohydrates: 27g,Protein: 11g.

Very Berry Puffs

Servings: 3
Cooking Time: 20 Min
Ingredients:
- 3 pastry dough sheets
- 2 cups cream cheese /260g
- 1 tbsp honey /15ml
- 2 tbsp mashed raspberries /30g
- 2 tbsp mashed strawberries /30g
- ¼ tsp vanilla extract /1.25ml

Directions:
1. Divide the cream cheese between the dough sheets and spread it evenly. In a small bowl, combine the berries, honey, and vanilla. Divide the mixture between the pastry sheets. Pinch the ends of the sheets, to form puff.
2. You can seal them by brushing some water onto the edges, or even better, use egg wash. Lay the puffs into a lined baking dish.
3. Place the dish into the Ninja Foodi, close the crisping lid and cook for 15 minutes on Air Crisp mode at 370 °F or 185°C. Once the timer beeps, check the puffs to ensure they're puffed and golden. Serve warm.

Cranberry Lemon Quinoa

Servings: 6
Cooking Time: 20 Minutes
Ingredients:
- 16 oz. quinoa
- 4 ½ cups water
- ½ cup brown sugar, packed
- 1 tsp lemon extract
- ½ tsp salt
- ½ cup cranberries, dried

Directions:
1. Add all ingredients, except the cranberries, to the cooker and stir to mix.
2. Secure the lid and select pressure cooking on high. Set timer for 20 minutes.
3. When timer goes off, use natural release for 10 minutes. Then use quick release and remove the lid.
4. Stir in cranberries and serve.

Nutrition:
- InfoCalories 284,Total Fat 4g,Total Carbs 56g,Protein 8g,Sodium 152mg.

Breakfast Egg Pizza

Servings: 8
Cooking Time: 28 Minutes
Ingredients:
- 12 eggs
- 1/2 cup heavy cream
- 1/2 tsp salt
- 1/4 tsp pepper
- 8 oz sausage
- 2 cups peppers sliced
- 1 cup cheese shredded

Directions:
1. Heat peppers in a bowl for 3 minutes in the microwave.
2. Place air crisper basket in the Ninja Foodi and place the bacon in it.
3. Secure the Ninja Foodi lid and Air Fry them for 10 minutes.
4. Transfer the cooked crispy bacon to a plate and keep them aside.
5. Whisk eggs with salt, pepper, and cream in a bowl.
6. Pour this mixture in a greased baking pan.
7. Place the trivet in the Ninja Food cooking pot and set the baking pan over it.
8. Secure the Ninja Foodi lid and turn the pressure valve to 'closed' position.
9. Select 'Bake/Roast' for 15 minutes at 350 °F (175°C).
10. Once done, top the egg bake with cheese and peppers.
11. Broil this pizza for 3 minutes in the broiler until the cheese melts.
12. Serve warm.

Nutrition:
- InfoCalories 489; Total Fat 43.3g; Total Carbs 5g; Protein 22.2 g

Pumpkin Breakfast Bread

Servings: 14
Cooking Time: 3 Hours
Ingredients:
- Nonstick cooking spray
- 2 cups whole wheat pastry flour
- 1 ½ tsp baking soda
- 2 tsp pumpkin pie spice
- ½ cup coconut oil, melted
- ¾ cup honey
- 2 eggs
- 3 cups pumpkin puree
- 1 tsp. vanilla extract
- 1 banana, mashed
- ½ cup walnuts, chopped & divided

Directions:
1. Spray the cooking pot with cooking spray.
2. In a large bowl, combine flour, baking soda, and pumpkin spice.
3. Make a "well" in the middle of the dry ingredients and add oil, honey, eggs, pumpkin, vanilla, and banana, and ¼ cup of the walnuts. Mix well to thoroughly combine all ingredients.
4. Pour batter into cooking pot and sprinkle remaining walnuts over the top. Place two paper towels over the top of the pot and secure the lid. Select slow cooking function on high. Set timer for 2 hours.
5. When timer goes off check bread, it should pass the toothpick test. If it is not done, continue cooking another 30-60 minutes.
6. When bread is done, transfer to a wire rack to cool.

Nutrition:
- InfoCalories 207,Total Fat 9g,Total Carbs 30g,Protein 4g,Sodium 130mg.

Hanging Bacon

Servings: 24
Cooking Time: 12 Minutes
Ingredients:
- 1 pound (454 g) bacon strips
- Cooking spray

Directions:
1. Cut the bacon in half crosswise to make shorter strips. Coat the reversible rack with cooking spray and fold the bacon strips over every other rung of the rack.
2. Add ½ cup water to the Foodi's inner pot, then set the rack in the inner pot in the high position. Lock on the Pressure Lid, making sure the valve is set to Seal, and set to Pressure on High for 2 minutes. When timer reaches 0, quick-release the pressure and carefully remove the lid.
3. Drop the Crisping Lid and set the Foodi to Air Crisp at 390°F(200°C) for 10 to 15 minutes, depending on your preferred crispness. The bacon is actually fully cooked at this point—all you are doing now is crisping it up; I like my bacon crisp with a little chew here and there, so 13 minutes is my sweet spot.

Easy Homemade Yogurt

Servings: 8
Cooking Time: 12 Hours
Ingredients:
- ½ gallon whole milk
- 2 tbsps. plain yogurt with active live cultures
- ½ cup honey (optional)
- 1 tbsp. vanilla extract (optional)

Directions:
1. In the pot, add the milk. Assemble the Pressure Lid, set the steamer valve to Seal. Select Sear/Sauté. Select Start/Stop to begin.
2. Bring the milk to 180°F (80°C), checking the temperature often and stirring frequently to avoid burning at the bottom. Select Start/Stop to turn off Sear/Sauté.
3. Let the milk cool to 110°F (45°C), continuing to often check the temperature and stirring frequently. Skim off the "skin" on the milk and discard.
4. Add the yogurt and whisk until incorporated.
5. Assemble the Pressure Lid, set the steamer valve to Vent. Allow to incubate for 8 hours.
6. After 8 hours, place the yogurt into a glass container and chill in the refrigerator for 4 hours.
7. Mix in the honey and vanilla to the yogurt and combine well. Cover and return the glass bowl into the refrigerator, or divide the yogurt among airtight glass jars.

Pancetta Hash With Baked Eggs

Servings: 4
Cooking Time: 50 Min
Ingredients:
- 6 slices pancetta; chopped
- 2 potatoes, peeled and diced
- 4 eggs
- 1 white onion; diced
- 1 tsp freshly ground black pepper /5g
- 1 tsp garlic powder /5g
- 1 tsp sweet paprika /5g
- 1 tsp salt /5g

Directions:
1. Choose Sear/Sauté, set to Medium High, and choose Start/Stop to preheat the pot for 5 minutes.
2. Once heated, lay the pancetta in the pot, and cook, stirring occasionally; for 5 minutes, or until the pancetta is crispy.
3. Stir in the onion, potatoes, sweet paprika, salt, black pepper, and garlic powder. Close the crisping lid; choose Bake/Roast, set the temperature to 350°F or 175°C, and the time to 25 minutes. Cook until the turnips are soft and golden brown while stirring occasionally.
4. Crack the eggs on top of the hash, close the crisping lid, and choose Bake/Roast. Set the temperature to 350°F or 175°C, and the time to 10 minutes.
5. Cook the eggs and check two or three times until your desired crispiness has been achieved. Serve immediately.

Butternut Squash Apple Soup With Cinnamon

Servings: 4
Cooking Time: 6 Minutes
Ingredients:
- 3 cups (430 g) seeded, peeled and cut butternut squash (½" [1.3-cm] chunks)
- 1 apple, peeled, cored and cut into ½" (1.3-cm) chunks
- 1 (13.5-oz [400-ml, 383 g]) can full-fat coconut milk
- 2 tsps. (5 g) ground cinnamon
- 1 tbsp. (15 ml) pure maple syrup
- Pinch of salt
- ½ cup (55 g) roasted and chopped pecans

Directions:
1. Add the butternut squash, apple pieces, coconut milk, cinnamon, maple syrup and salt into the Ninja pressure cooker, combine them together.
2. Lock the pressure lid, set the steamer vent to Seal. Select Pressure, and cook for 6 minutes.
3. Release with a quick release. Remove the lid once the steam has been completely released. Blend with an immersion blender or high-powered blender until smooth.
4. Top with pecans and serve.

Cinnamon Sugar Donuts

Servings: 4
Cooking Time: 10 Minutes
Ingredients:
- ⅔ cup all-purpose flour, plus additional for dusting
- 3 tablespoons granulated sugar, divided
- ½ teaspoon baking powder
- ¼ teaspoon, plus ½ tablespoon cinnamon
- ¼ teaspoon sea salt
- 2 tablespoons cold unsalted butter, cut into small pieces
- ¼ cup plus 1½ tablespoons whole milk
- Cooking spray

Directions:
1. In a medium bowl, mix together the flour, 1 tablespoon of sugar, baking powder, ¼ teaspoon of cinnamon, and salt.
2. Use a pastry cutter or two forks to cut in the butter, breaking it up into little pieces until the mixture resembles

coarse cornmeal. Add the milk and continue to mix together until the dough forms a ball.
3. Place the dough on a lightly floured work surface and knead it until a smooth ball forms, about 30 seconds. Divide the dough into 8 equal pieces and roll each piece into a ball.
4. Place the Cook & Crisp Basket in the pot. Close crisping lid. Select AIR CRISP, set temperature to 350°F (175°C), and set time to 3 minutes. Press START/STOP to begin.
5. Once preheated, coat the basket with cooking spray. Place the dough balls in the basket, leaving room between each. Spray them with cooking spray. Close crisping lid.
6. Select AIR CRISP, set temperature to 350°F (175°C), and set time to 10 minutes. Press START/STOP to begin.
7. In a medium bowl, combine the remaining 2 tablespoons of sugar and ½ tablespoon of cinnamon.
8. When cooking is complete, open lid. Place the dough balls in the bowl with the cinnamon sugar and toss to coat. Serve immediately.

Nutrition:
- InfoCalories: 192,Total Fat: 7g,Sodium: 126mg,Carbohydrates: 31g,Protein: 3g.

Apricot Oatmeal

Servings: 8
Cooking Time: 8 Hours
Ingredients:
- 2 cups steel-cut oats
- 1/3 cup dried apricots, chopped
- ½ cup dried cherries
- 1 teaspoon ground cinnamon
- 4 cups milk
- 4 cups water
- ¼ teaspoon liquid stevia

Directions:
1. In the Ninja Foodi's insert, place all ingredients and stir to combine.
2. Close the Ninja Foodi's lid with a crisping lid and select "Slow Cooker."
3. Set on "Low" for 6-8 hours.
4. Press the "Start/Stop" button to initiate cooking.
5. Open the Ninja Foodi's lid and serve warm.

Nutrition:
- InfoCalories: 148; Fat: 3.5g; Carbohydrates: 4.2 g; Protein: 5.9 g

Sweet Potato Hash And Eggs

Servings:6
Cooking Time: 35 Minutes
Ingredients:
- 3 pounds sweet potatoes, diced
- 2 cups water
- 2 tablespoons unsalted butter
- 1 yellow onion, diced
- 3 garlic cloves, minced
- 1 red bell pepper, diced
- 1 green bell pepper, diced
- 1 bunch scallions, sliced
- 2 teaspoons smoked paprika
- Kosher salt
- Freshly ground black pepper
- 6 brown eggs

Directions:
1. Place the sweet potatoes in the Cook & Crisp Basket. Pour the water in pot and insert basket. Assemble the pressure lid, making sure the pressure release valve is in the SEAL position.
2. Select PRESSURE and set to HI. Set timer for 2 minutes. Select START/STOP to begin.
3. When pressure cooking is complete, quick release the pressure by turning the pressure release valve to the VENT position. Carefully remove lid when the unit has finished releasing pressure.
4. Remove basket with sweet potatoes. Pour out any remaining water from the pot.
5. Select SEAR/SAUTÉ and set to MED. Let preheat for 3 minutes.
6. Add the butter, onion, garlic, and bell peppers. Cook for 5 minutes. Add the sweet potatoes, scallions, and paprika and stir. Cook for 5 minutes, stirring occasionally. Season with salt and pepper. Crack the eggs on top of the hash, equally spaced apart. Close crisping lid.
7. Select AIR CRISP, set temperature to 325°F (160°C), and set time to 10 minutes. Select START/STOP to begin.
8. When cooking is complete, open lid and serve immediately.

Nutrition:
- InfoCalories: 376,Total Fat: 13g,Sodium: 304mg,Carbohydrates: 51g,Protein: 16g.

Maple Giant Pancake

Servings: 6
Cooking Time: 30 Min
Ingredients:
- 3 cups flour /390g
- ⅓ cup olive oil /84ml
- ⅓ cup sparkling water /84ml
- ¾ cup sugar /98g
- 5 eggs
- 2 tbsp maple syrup /30ml
- ⅓ tsp salt /1.67g
- 1 ½ tsp baking soda /7.5g
- A dollop of whipped cream to serve

Directions:
1. Start by pouring the flour, sugar, eggs, olive oil, sparkling water, salt, and baking soda into a food processor and blend until smooth. Pour the batter into the Ninja Foodi and let it sit in there for 15 minutes. Close the lid and secure the pressure valve.
2. Select the Pressure mode on Low pressure for 10 minutes. Press Start/Stop.
3. Once the timer goes off, press Start/Stop, quick-release the pressure valve to let out any steam and open the lid.
4. Gently run a spatula around the pancake to let loose any sticking. Once ready, slide the pancake onto a serving plate and drizzle with maple syrup. Top with the whipped cream to serve

Spinach Casserole

Servings: 4
Cooking Time: 5 Minutes
Ingredients:
- 4 whole eggs
- 1 tablespoons milk
- 1 tomato, diced
- ½ cup spinach
- ¼ teaspoon salt
- ¼ teaspoon black pepper

Directions:
1. Take a baking pan small enough to fit Ninja Foodi and grease it with butter.
2. Take a medium bowl and whisk in eggs, milk, salt, pepper, add veggies to the bowl and stir.
3. Pour egg mixture into the baking pan and lower the pan into the Ninja Foodi.
4. Close Air Crisping lid and Air Crisp for 325 degrees for 7 minutes.
5. Remove the pan from eggs, and enjoy hot.

Nutrition:
- InfoCalories: 78; Fat: 5g; Carbohydrates: 1 g; Protein: 7 g

Prosciutto Egg Bake

Servings: 4
Cooking Time: 45 Min
Ingredients:
- 8 ounces prosciutto; chopped /240g
- 1 cup shredded Monterey Jack cheese /130g
- 1 cup water /250ml
- 1 cup whole milk /250ml
- 1 orange bell pepper, seeded and chopped
- 4 eggs
- 1 tsp salt /5g
- 1 tsp freshly ground black pepper /5g

Directions:
1. Break the eggs into a bowl, pour in the milk, salt, and black pepper and whisk until combined. Stir in the Monterey Jack Cheese.
2. Put the bell pepper and prosciutto in the cake pan. Then, pour over the egg mixture, cover the pan with aluminum foil and put on the reversible rack.
3. Put the rack in the pot and pour in the water. Seal the pressure lid, choose pressure and set to High. Set the time to 20 minutes and choose Start/Stop.
4. When done cooking, do a quick pressure release and carefully remove the lid that is after the pressure has completely escaped.
5. When baking is complete, take the pan out of the pot and set it on a heatproof surface, and cool for 5 minutes.

Cheesy Tex-mex Breakfast Egg Bake Casserole

Servings: 4
Cooking Time: 10 Minutes
Ingredients:
- 8 ounces (227 g) corn tortilla chips, divided
- 1 cup green salsa, plus more for serving
- 2 cups shredded pepper Jack cheese, divided
- ¼ cup whole milk
- 3 large eggs
- 1 tsp. Mexican/Southwestern Seasoning Mix, or a store-bought mix
- ¼ cup heavy (whipping) cream
- ½ tsp. kosher salt (or ¼ tsp. fine salt)

Directions:
1. In a 1-to 5-quart heat-proof dish, add about half of the chips. Pour over the chips with the salsa and gently toss to distribute the salsa. Sprinkle over the top with about half the cheese.
2. Whisk the milk, eggs, seasonings, heavy cream, and salt in a medium bowl. Pour over the chips and cheese with the egg mixture. Use aluminum foil to cover the dish.
3. In the inner pot, add 1 cup of water. Place the dish on the Reversible Rack, then put in the pot.
4. Lock the Pressure Lid into place, set the steamer valve to Seal. Select Pressure and set the cook time to 10 minutes. Press Start.
5. When the cooking is complete, naturally release the pressure for 5 minutes, then quick release any remaining pressure. Open and remove the Pressure Lid carefully.
6. Remove the foil from the casserole. Over the top arrange with about half the remaining chips and sprinkle with half the remaining cheese. Repeat the layers with the remaining chips and cheese.
7. Close the Crisping Lid. Select Broil and adjust the time to 7 minutes. Press Start. Broil until the chips are browned in spots and the cheese is melted.
8. Take the dish out from the pot and allow to cool for several minutes. Serve with additional salsa.

Walnut Orange Coffee Cake

Servings: 8
Cooking Time: 25 Minutes
Ingredients:
- Butter flavor cooking spray
- 1 cup Stevia
- 1/4 cup butter, unsalted, soft
- 1 egg
- 2 tsp orange zest, grated
- ½ tsp vanilla
- 1/8 tsp cinnamon
- 2 cups whole wheat flour
- 1 tsp baking soda
- ½ cup orange juice, fresh squeezed
- ½ cup water
- ½ cup walnuts, chopped

Directions:
1. Select bake function and heat cooker to 350°F (175°C). Spray a 7-inch round pan with cooking spray.
2. In a medium bowl, beat Stevia and butter until smooth.
3. Add egg, zest, vanilla, and cinnamon and mix until combined.
4. In a separate bowl, combine dry ingredients. Add to butter mixture and mix until thoroughly combined. Stir in nuts.
5. Spread batter in prepared pan and place in the cooker. Secure the tender-crisp lid and bakke 20-25 minutes, or until it passes the toothpick test.
6. Let cool in pan 10 minutes, then invert onto wire rack. Serve warm.

Nutrition:
- InfoCalories 203,Total Fat 10g,Total Carbs 53g,Protein 6g,Sodium 170mg.

Bacon And Gruyère Cheese Quiche

Servings: 1
Cooking Time: 40 Minutes
Ingredients:
- 1 (9-inch) frozen piecrust (the kind that comes fitted into a tin pan)
- 6 large eggs
- ½ cup heavy cream
- Kosher salt, to taste
- Freshly ground black pepper to taste
- 8 ounces (227 g) Gruyère cheese, grated (about 1 cup)
- 1 cup cooked and crumbled bacon

Directions:
1. Let the piecrust thaw for 15 minutes at room temperature. Prick the piecrust all over with the tines of a fork. Place the crust on the Foodi's reversible rack in the low position, then set the rack into the inner pot, drop the Crisping Lid, and set to Bake/Roast at 375°F(190°C) for 10 minutes, or until golden brown. Lift the lid and carefully remove the rack and piecrust from the Foodi; the crust won't be cooked all the way through—just slightly browned.
2. In a large bowl, whisk together the eggs and cream. Add a few pinches of salt and pepper, the grated cheese, and the bacon, and stir to combine.
3. Place the parbaked crust on the rack as before, place the rack in the Foodi's inner pot, and then carefully pour the egg filling into the crust. Drop the Crisping Lid and set the Foodi to Bake/Roast at 325°F(160°C) for 30 minutes, or until the center is set and the top is golden brown.
4. Lift the lid and carefully remove the rack and quiche, then set aside to cool. Serve warm or at room temperature.

Butter Cookies

Servings: 6
Cooking Time: 15 Minutes
Ingredients:
- 2 cups self-rising flour, plus extra as needed
- ½ cup (1 stick) cold unsalted butter, cut into small cubes, plus 3 tablespoons, melted
- ¾ cup buttermilk
- Cooking spray
- ¼ teaspoon kosher salt

Directions:
1. Remove the inner pot from the Foodi and add the flour and cold butter cubes. Use a silicone-coated potato masher to mash the butter and flour together until there aren't any pieces of butter larger than a small pea.
2. Add the buttermilk to the flour-butter mixture and use a silicone spatula to stir until it makes a sticky dough.
3. Coat your hands in some flour and work the dough in the Foodi pot, adding more flour as needed to prevent sticking to the pot, until the dough is just barely holding together. Turn the dough out onto a lightly floured work surface, lightly flour the top of the dough, and use the underside of the Foodi pot to flatten the dough into a ¾-inch-thick disk. Then use your hands to press the dough until it is about ½ inch thick. Wipe off the bottom and the inside of the pot, and lightly coat the inside of the pot with cooking spray. Insert the pot back into the Foodi.
4. Dip the rim of a drinking glass or biscuit cutter into a bit of flour and then cut 6 biscuits from the dough, flouring the cutter after each cut. Arrange the biscuits in the pot, brush with the melted butter, and sprinkle with salt.
5. Drop the Crisping Lid and set the Foodi to Broil for 15 minutes, or until the biscuits are golden brown. Let the biscuits cool for 5 minutes before lifting the lid and removing them from the pot.

Pecan Steel-cut Oats

Servings: 4
Cooking Time: 20 Minutes
Ingredients:
- 2 cups (320 g) steel-cut oats
- 3 cups (710 ml) water
- 1 (13.5-oz [400-ml, 383 g]) can full-fat coconut milk, divided
- ⅓ cup (80 ml) pure maple syrup, plus more to taste
- ½ tsp. sea salt
- ½ cup (56 g) toasted pecan pieces
- 2 tsps. (5 g) ground cinnamon (optional)

Directions:
1. Add the oats, water, 1 cup of the coconut milk, and the maple syrup and salt into the Ninja pressure cooker, combine them by quickly stirring the mixture. Lock the pressure lid and set the steamer vent to seal.
2. Choose Pressure, and cook for 4 minutes.
3. Use a natural release for 15 minutes, then release any remaining steam before removing the lid.
4. Once removing the lid, add the remaining coconut milk and additional maple syrup to taste.
5. Serve with the toasted pecans and sprinkle the cinnamon over if using.

Cinnamon Bun Oatmeal

Servings: 6
Cooking Time: 26 Minutes
Ingredients:
- 1 cup gluten-free steel-cut oats
- 3½ cups water
- ¼ teaspoon sea salt
- 1 teaspoon nutmeg
- 2 teaspoons cinnamon, divided
- ½ cup all-purpose flour
- ½ cup rolled oats
- ⅔ cup brown sugar
- ⅓ cup cold unsalted butter, cut into pieces
- 2 tablespoons granulated sugar
- ¾ cup raisins
- 2 ounces cream cheese, at room temperature
- 2 tablespoons confectioners' sugar
- 1 teaspoon whole milk

Directions:
1. Place the steel-cut oats, water, salt, nutmeg, and 1 teaspoon of cinnamon in the pot. Assemble pressure lid, making sure the pressure release valve is in the SEAL position.
2. Select PRESSURE and set to HI. Set time to 11 minutes. Select START/STOP to begin.

3. In a medium bowl, combine the flour, rolled oats, brown sugar, butter, remaining 1 teaspoon of cinnamon, and granulated sugar until a crumble forms.
4. When pressure cooking is complete, allow pressure to naturally release for 5 minutes. After 5 minutes, quick release any remaining pressure by moving the pressure release valve to the VENT position. Carefully remove lid when unit has finished releasing pressure.
5. Stir the raisins into the oatmeal. Cover and let sit 5 minutes to thicken.
6. Evenly spread the crumble topping over the oatmeal. Close crisping lid.
7. Select AIR CRISP, set temperature to 400°F (205°C), and set time to 10 minutes. Select START/STOP to begin.
8. In a small bowl, whisk together the cream cheese, confectioners' sugar, and milk. Add more milk or sugar, as needed, to reach your desired consistency.
9. When crumble topping is browned, cooking is complete. Open lid and serve the oatmeal in individual bowls topped with a swirl of cream cheese topping.

Nutrition:
- InfoCalories: 454, Total Fat: 16g, Sodium: 117mg, Carbohydrates: 73g, Protein: 8g.

Chili Cheese Quiche

Servings: 4
Cooking Time: 30 Minutes
Ingredients:
- Nonstick cooking spray
- 4 eggs
- 1 cup half-n-half
- 10 oz. green chilies, diced
- ½ tsp salt
- ½ tsp cumin
- 1 cup Mexican blend cheese, grated
- ¼ cup cilantro, chopped

Directions:
1. Spray a 6-inch baking pan with cooking spray.
2. In a mixing bowl, beat eggs then stir in half-n-half, chilies, salt, cumin, and half the cheese.
3. Pour into prepared pan and cover with foil.
4. Add 2 cups water to the cooking pot and add the rack. Place the pan on the rack and secure the lid.
5. Select pressure cooking on high and set timer for 20 minutes.
6. When timer goes off, release pressure naturally for 10 minutes, then use quick release.
7. Remove the foil and sprinkle remaining cheese over the top. Secure the tender-crisp lid and set to 375°F (190°C). Cook another 3-5 minutes or until cheese is melted and starts to brown. Serve garnished with cilantro.

Nutrition:
- InfoCalories 300, Total Fat 23g, Total Carbs 7g, Protein 16g, Sodium 1172mg.

Stuffed Baked Potatoes

Servings: 4
Cooking Time: 20 Minutes
Ingredients:
- 4 large baked potatoes
- 2 tbsp. butter, melted
- 1 tsp salt
- 1 tsp black pepper
- 1 cup cheddar cheese, grated
- 6 slices bacon, cook crisp & chop
- 4 large eggs
- 2 tbsp. chives, chop

Directions:
1. Select bake function and heat cooker to 350°F (175°C).
2. Cut an opening in the top of the potatoes. With a spoon, scoop out most of the center.
3. Brush with melted butter and sprinkle with salt and pepper.
4. Divide ¾ of the cheese evenly among the potatoes. Top with ¾ of the bacon.
5. Crack one egg into each potato then top with remaining bacon, cheese and chives.
6. Place on the rack of the cooker and secure the tender-crisp lid. Set the timer for 20 minutes. Egg whites should be cooked completely but the yolk should still be soft. Serve immediately.

Nutrition:
- InfoCalories 389, Total Fat 31g, Total Carbs 6g, Protein 20g, Sodium 1052mg.

Mediterranean Quiche

Servings: 6
Cooking Time: 45 Minutes
Ingredients:
- Nonstick cooking spray
- 2 cups potatoes, grated
- ¾ cup feta cheese, fat free, crumbled
- 1 tbsp. olive oil
- 1 cup grape tomatoes, halved
- 3 cups baby spinach
- 2 eggs
- 2 egg whites
- ¼ cup skim milk
- ½ tsp salt
- ¼ tsp pepper

Directions:
1. Select bake function and heat to 375°F (190°C). Spray an 8-inch round pan with cooking spray.
2. Press the potatoes on the bottom and up sides of the prepared pan. Place in the cooker. Secure the tender-crisp lid and bake 10 minutes.
3. Remove pan from the cooker and sprinkle half the feta cheese over the bottom of the crust.
4. Set cooker to sauté function on medium heat. Add the oil and heat until hot.
5. Add the tomatoes and spinach and cook until spinach has wilted, about 2-3 minutes. Place over the feta cheese.
6. In a medium bowl, whisk together eggs, milk, salt, and pepper. Pour over spinach mixture and top with remaining feta cheese.
7. Place the pan back in the cooking pot and secure the tender-crisp lid. Set temperature to 375°F (190°C) and bake 30 minutes or until eggs are completely set and starting to brown. Let cool 10 minutes before serving.

Nutrition:
- InfoCalories 145, Total Fat 8g, Total Carbs 12g, Protein 7g, Sodium 346mg.

Bbq Chicken Sandwiches

Servings: 4
Cooking Time: 45 Min
Ingredients:
- 4 chicken thighs, boneless and skinless
- 1½ cups iceberg lettuce, shredded /195g
- 2 cups barbecue sauce /500ml
- 1 onion, minced
- 2 garlic cloves, minced
- 4 burger buns
- 2 tbsp minced fresh parsley /30g
- 1 tbsp lemon juice /15ml
- 1 tbsp mayonnaise /15ml
- Salt to taste

Directions:
1. Season the chicken with salt, and transfer into the inner pot. Add in garlic, onion and barbeque sauce. Coat the chicken by turning in the sauce. Seal the pressure lid, choose Pressure, set to High, and set the timer to 15 minutes. Press Start.
2. When ready, do a natural pressure release for 10 minutes. Use two forks to shred the chicken and mix into the sauce. Press Sear/Sauté and let the mixture to simmer for 15 minutes to thicken the sauce, until desired consistency.
3. Meanwhile, using a large bowl, mix the lemon juice, mayonnaise, salt, and parsley; toss lettuce into the mixture to coat.
4. Separate the chicken in equal parts to match the sandwich buns; apply lettuce for topping and complete the sandwiches.

Applesauce Pumpkin Muffins

Servings: 8
Cooking Time: 15 Minutes
Ingredients:
- 4 eggs
- ½ cup applesauce, unsweetened
- ½ cup pumpkin
- ½ cup coconut flour
- 2 tbsp. cinnamon
- ¼ tsp cloves
- ¼ tsp ginger
- 1/8 tsp nutmeg
- ¼ tsp salt
- 1 tsp baking soda
- 2 tsp vanilla
- 4 tbsp. coconut oil, melted
- 1 tbsp. honey

Directions:
1. Set cooker to air fryer function on 375°F (190°C). Line 2 6-cup muffin tins with paper liners.
2. Add all ingredients to a blender or food processor and blend on low just until combined.
3. Pour batter evenly into prepared tins. Place muffin pans, one at a time, in the cooker and secure the tender-crisp lid. Bake 12-15 minutes or until muffins pass the toothpick test.
4. Let cool in pans 10 minutes, then transfer to wire rack to cool completely.

Nutrition:
- InfoCalories 122,Total Fat 9g,Total Carbs 11g,Protein 3g,Sodium 264mg.

Cheddar Shrimp And Grits

Servings:4
Cooking Time: 22 Minutes
Ingredients:
- 3 tablespoons unsalted butter
- 1 cup Quaker Oats Quick 5-Minute Grits
- 2 garlic cloves, minced
- 1 teaspoon kosher salt, plus more as needed
- Freshly ground black pepper, to taste
- 2 cups whole milk
- ½ cup shredded cheddar cheese
- 2 tablespoons minced pickled jalapeño
- 12 ounces (340 g) frozen, peeled, and deveined raw extra jumbo shrimp (16–20 count)
- Cooking spray
- Chopped fresh chives, for garnish

Directions:
1. Set the Foodi to Sear/Saute on High. Add the butter to the inner pot and cook until melted, stirring the butter occasionally with a silicone spatula, about 4 minutes.
2. Add the grits, garlic, 1 teaspoon salt, and the pepper and allow to cook until the garlic begins to soften, about 3 minutes, stirring occasionally. Add 2 cups water and stir the grits once. Lock on the Pressure Lid, making sure the valve is set to Seal, and set to Pressure on High for 0 minutes. When the timer reaches 0, quick-release the pressure and carefully remove the lid.
3. Stir in the milk, cheese, and jalapeño. Insert the reversible rack in the high position.
4. In a bowl, spray both sides of the shrimp with cooking spray. Season with salt and pepper, then place the shrimp on the rack. Drop the Crisping Lid and set the Foodi to Broil for 10 minutes. After 5 minutes, lift the lid and flip the shrimp. Drop the lid and continue to cook until the shrimp are pink, about another 5 minutes. Set the shrimp aside.
5. Stir the grits and divide among 4 bowls. Top each bowl with a few shrimp, then sprinkle with chives and serve immediately.

Southern Grits Casserole

Servings:8
Cooking Time: 45 Minutes
Ingredients:
- 3 cups water
- 2 cups milk or heavy (whipping) cream, divided
- 2 cups stone ground grits
- Kosher salt
- Freshly ground black pepper
- 4 tablespoons unsalted butter
- 1 pound cooked breakfast sausage, casing removed and chopped
- 6 eggs
- 2 cups shredded Cheddar cheese

Directions:
1. Pour the water, 1½ cups of milk, and grits in the pot. Season with salt and pepper. Stir well. Assemble pressure lid,

making sure the pressure release valve is in the SEAL position.
2. Select PRESSURE and set to HI. Set time to 10 minutes. Select START/STOP to begin.
3. When pressure cooking is complete, allow pressure to naturally release for 15 minutes. Then quick release remaining pressure by moving the pressure release valve to the VENT position. Carefully remove lid when unit has finished releasing pressure.
4. Stir in the butter and sausage.
5. In a large bowl, whisk together the eggs and remaining ½ cup of milk. Fold the eggs and cheese into the grits. Close crisping lid.
6. Select BAKE/ROAST, set temperature to 375°F (190°C), and set time to 25 minutes. Select START/STOP to begin.
7. Once cooking is complete, open lid. Let cool for 10 minutes before slicing to serve.

Nutrition:
- InfoCalories: 551,Total Fat: 36g,Sodium: 692mg,Carbohydrates: 31g,Protein: 27g.

Homemade Vanilla Yogurt

Servings:6
Cooking Time: 8 Hours
Ingredients:
- ½ gallon whole milk
- 3 tablespoons plain yogurt with active live cultures
- ½ tablespoon vanilla extract
- ½ cup honey

Directions:
1. Pour the milk into the pot. Assemble pressure lid, making sure the pressure release valve is in the VENT position.
2. Select YOGURT and set time to 8 hours. Select START/STOP to begin.
3. After the milk has boiled, the display will read COOL.
4. Once cooled, the unit will beep and display ADD & STIR. Remove pressure lid. Add the plain yogurt and whisk until fully incorporated. Reassemble pressure lid, making sure the pressure release valve is still in the VENT position.
5. When incubating is complete after 8 hours, transfer the yogurt to a glass container or bowl, cover, and refrigerate for a minimum of 8 hours.
6. Once the yogurt has chilled, stir in the vanilla and honey until well combined. Cover and place the glass bowl back in the refrigerator or divide the yogurt into airtight glass jars. The yogurt may be refrigerated up to 2 weeks.

Nutrition:
- InfoCalories: 286,Total Fat: 11g,Sodium: 133mg,Carbohydrates: 38g,Protein: 11g.

Cinnamon Oatmeal With Cream Cheese

Servings: 6
Cooking Time: 26 Minutes
Ingredients:
- 1 cup gluten-free steel-cut oats
- 1 tsp. nutmeg
- 2 tsps. cinnamon, divided
- 3½ cups water
- ¼ tsp. sea salt
- ½ cup rolled oats
- ½ cup all-purpose flour
- ⅔ cup brown sugar
- 2 tbsps. granulated sugar
- ⅓ cup cold unsalted butter, cut into pieces
- ¾ cup raisins
- 2 ounces (57 g) cream cheese, at room temperature
- 1 tsp. whole milk
- 2 tbsps. confectioners'sugar

Directions:
1. In the pot, combine the steel-cut oats, nutmeg, 1 teaspoon of cinnamon, water, and salt. Assemble pressure lid, set the steamer valve to Seal.
2. Set PRESSUR and the time 11 minutes.
3. Mix the rolled oats, flour, brown sugar, granulated sugar, butter, and the remaining 1 tsp. of cinnamon in a medium bowl until a crumble forms.
4. After the cooking is completed, let the pressure release for 5 minutes. Then move pressure release valve to quickly release any remaining pressure. Carefully remove lid.
5. Add raisins to the oatmeal, stir well. Cover, sit for 5 minutes.
6. Top the oatmeal with crumbles.
7. Select AIR CRISP, set the temperature to 400°F (205°C), and the time to 10 minutes.
8. Whisk the cream cheese, milk and confectioners sugar in a small bowl.
9. When the crumbs turn brown, open the crisping lid and place the oatmeal in individual bowls. Top with a swirl of cream cheese.

Japanese Pancake

Servings:4
Cooking Time: 22 Minutes
Ingredients:
- 2 cups all-purpose flour
- 3 tablespoons granulated sugar
- 2 teaspoons baking powder
- ½ teaspoon baking soda
- ½ teaspoon kosher salt
- 1½ cups whole milk
- 1 large egg
- 1 tablespoon fresh lemon juice
- 4 tablespoons unsalted butter, melted, plus extra for serving
- Cooking spray
- Confectioners' sugar or cocoa powder, for garnish
- Warm maple syrup, for garnish

Directions:
1. In a medium bowl, whisk together the flour, granulated sugar, baking powder, baking soda, and salt. In another medium bowl, whisk together the milk, egg, and lemon juice, and then whisk the melted butter into the milk mixture. Pour the wet ingredients into the dry ingredients, and whisk until completely combined and there aren't any flour streaks remaining in the batter .
2. Thoroughly spray the Foodi's inner pot with cooking spray. Add the batter. Lock on the Pressure Lid, making sure the valve is set to Seal, and set to Pressure on Low for 7

minutes. When the timer reaches 0, quick-release the pressure and carefully remove the lid.

3. Drop the Crisping Lid and set the Foodi to Air Crisp at 390°F(200°C) for 15 minutes, or until the pancake is golden brown and a toothpick inserted into the center comes out clean. While it cooks, open the lid and spray the top with cooking spray every 5 minutes. Use a silicone spatula to remove the pancake from the pot and place it on a platter. Dust with confectioners' sugar and serve in wedges like a pie, with butter and warm maple syrup.

Chocolate Chip And Banana Bread Bundt Cake

Servings: 8
Cooking Time: 40 Minutes
Ingredients:
- 2 cups all-purpose flour
- 1 teaspoon baking soda
- ¼ teaspoon cinnamon
- ¼ teaspoon sea salt
- 1 stick (½ cup) unsalted butter, at room temperature
- ½ cup dark brown sugar
- ¼ cup granulated sugar
- 2 eggs, beaten
- 1 teaspoon vanilla extract
- 3 ripe bananas, mashed
- 1 cup semisweet chocolate chips
- Cooking spray

Directions:
1. Close crisping lid. Select BAKE/ROAST, set temperature to 325°F (160°C), and set time to 5 minutes. Select START/STOP to begin preheating.
2. In a medium bowl, stir together the flour, baking soda, cinnamon, and salt.
3. In a large bowl, beat together the butter, brown sugar, and granulated sugar. Stir in the eggs, vanilla, and bananas.
4. Slowly add the dry mixture to wet mixture, stirring until just combined. Fold in chocolate chips.
5. Use cooking spray to grease the Ninja Tube Pan or a 7-inch Bundt pan. Pour the batter into the pan.
6. Once preheated, place pan on the Reversible Rack in the lower position. Close crisping lid.
7. Select BAKE/ROAST, set temperature to 325°F (160°C), and set time to 40 minutes. Select START/STOP to begin.
8. After 30 minutes, open lid and check doneness by inserting a toothpick into the cake. If it comes out clean, it is done. If not, continue baking until done.
9. When cooking is complete, remove pan from pot and place on a cooling rack for 30 minutes before serving.

Nutrition:
- InfoCalories: 484,Total Fat: 21g,Sodium: 238mg,Carbohydrates: 70g,Protein: 6g.

Ninja Foodi Hard-boiled Eggs

Servings: 2 To 12 Eggs
Cooking Time: 15 Minutes
Ingredients:
- 2 to 12 eggs
- 1 cup water

Directions:
1. Put the Reversible Rack in the pot. Pour in the water and arrange the eggs on the rack in a single layer.
2. Assemble the Pressure Lid, set the steamer valve to Seal. Select Pressure. Set the time to 8 minutes. Select Start/Stop to begin.
3. Meanwhile, prepare a large bowl of ice water.
4. After pressure cooking is finish, move the pressure release valve to the Vent position to quick release the pressure. Remove the lid when the unit has finished releasing pressure carefully.
5. Immediately transfer the eggs to the ice water bath with a slotted spoon and let cool for 5 minutes.

Strawberry Oat Breakfast Bars

Servings: 16
Cooking Time: 25 Minutes
Ingredients:
- 2 cups oats
- ¼ cup oat flour
- 1 cup coconut flakes, unsweetened
- 2 tbsp. chia seeds, ground
- ½ cup almonds, chopped
- ¼ salt
- 2 bananas, mashed
- 2 tbsp. honey
- ¼ cup coconut oil, melted
- 1 cup strawberries, chopped
- 1 tsp vanilla

Directions:
1. Set to bake function on 350°F (175°C). Line an 8-inch baking dish with parchment paper.
2. In a large bowl, combine dry ingredients.
3. Stir in remaining ingredients until thoroughly combined.
4. Press mixture into prepared pan and place in cooker. Add the tender-crisp lid and bake 25 minutes until golden brown.
5. Let cool before slicing into 2-inch squares.

Nutrition:
- InfoCalories 179,Total Fat 8g,Total Carbs 24g,Protein 5g,Sodium 53mg.

Paprika Hard-boiled Eggs

Servings: 3
Cooking Time: 25 Min
Ingredients:
- 6 eggs
- 1 cup water /250ml
- 1 tsp sweet paprika /5g
- Salt and ground black pepper, to taste

Directions:
1. In the Foodi, add water and place a reversible rack on top. Lay your eggs on the rack. Seal the pressure lid, choose Pressure, set to High, and set the timer to 5 minutes. Press Start.
2. Once ready, do a natural release for 10 minutes. Transfer the eggs to ice cold water to cool completely. When cooled, peel and slice. Season with salt and pepper. Sprinkle with sweet paprika before serving.

Vegan & Vegetable

Green Squash Gruyere

Servings: 4
Cooking Time: 70 Min
Ingredients:
- 1 large green squash; sliced
- 2 cups tomato sauce /500ml
- 1 cup shredded mozzarella cheese /130g
- 1½ cups panko breadcrumbs /195g
- ⅓ cup grated Gruyere cheese /44g
- 3 tbsps melted unsalted butter /45ml
- 2 tsp s salt /10g

Directions:
1. Season the squash slices on both sides with salt and place the slices on a wire rack to drain liquid for 5 to 10 minutes. In a bowl, combine the melted butter, breadcrumbs, and Gruyere cheese and set aside.
2. Rinse the squash slices with water and blot dry with paper towel. After, arrange the squash in the inner pot in a single layer as much as possible and pour the tomato sauce over the slices.
3. Seal the pressure lid, choose Pressure, set to High, and the time to 5 minutes. Press Start to commence cooking. When the timer has read to the end, perform a quick pressure release. Sprinkle the squash slices with the mozzarella cheese.
4. Close the crisping lid. Choose Bake/Roast; adjust the temperature to 375°F or 190°C and the cook time to 2 minutes. Press Start to broil.
5. After, carefully open the lid and sprinkle the squash with the breadcrumb mixture. Close the crisping lid again, choose Bake/Roast, adjust the temperature to 375°F (190°C), and the cook time to 8 minutes. Press Start to continue broiling. Serve immediately.

Quinoa Stuffed Peppers With Pesto

Servings: 4
Cooking Time: 30 Minutes
Ingredients:
- 4 red bell peppers, halved lengthwise and cored
- 1 (15-ounce, 425 g) can no-salt-added diced tomatoes
- 1 cup no-sodium vegetable broth
- 8 ounces (227 g) fresh baby spinach
- ¾ cup dried quinoa, rinsed
- 2 tbsps. everyday pesto

Directions:
1. Use parchment paper to line the inner pot.
2. Place the bell pepper halves on Crisp Plate, skin-side up.
3. Press Broil and cook at 350°F (175°C) until the pepper skins begin to blister and slightly blacken, about 2 to 5 minutes. Remove from the Ninja Foodi.
4. Add the tomatoes and vegetable broth into the inner pot, press Sear/Sauté on High. Stir in the spinach and quinoa. Adjust to Low, cover and cook for 10 minutes, stirring occasionally.
5. Fill the quinoa mixture into the pepper halves.
6. Bake for 10 minutes. Top with the pesto and serve warm.

Sesame Radish

Servings: 4
Cooking Time: 15 Minutes
Ingredients:
- 2 leeks, sliced
- ½ pound radishes, sliced
- 2 scallions, chopped
- 2 tablespoons black sesame seeds
- 1/3 cup chicken stock
- 1 tablespoon ginger, grated
- 1 tablespoon chives, minced

Directions:
1. In your Ninja Foodi, combine the leeks with the radishes and the other ingredients.
2. Put the Ninja Foodi's lid on and cook on High for 15 minutes more.
3. Release the pressure quickly for 5 minutes, divide everything between plates and serve.

Nutrition:
- InfoCalories: 112; Fat: 2g; Carbohydrates: 4.2g; Protein: 2g

Mushroom Goulash

Servings: 6
Cooking Time: 40 Minutes
Ingredients:
- 2 tbsp. olive oil, divided
- ½ onion, sliced thin
- 1 red bell pepper, chopped
- 2 lbs. mushrooms, chopped
- ½ tsp salt
- ¼ tsp pepper
- 14 oz. tomatoes, diced
- 2 cups vegetable broth, low sodium
- 1 tsp garlic powder
- 1 ½ tbsp. paprika
- 5 -6 sprigs fresh thyme

Directions:
1. Add half the oil to the cooking pot and set to sauté on med-high.
2. Add the onion and cook until they start to get soft, about 4 minutes. Add the red pepper and cook 3-5 minutes or until onions start to caramelize. Transfer to a plate.
3. Add the remaining oil to the pot and let it get hot. Add the mushrooms and cook until liquid is almost evaporated, stirring occasionally. Season with salt and pepper.

4. Add the peppers and onions back to the pot along with tomatoes, broth, garlic powder, paprika, and thyme, stir to mix well. Bring to a boil, cover, reduce heat to med-low and let simmer 20 minutes. Serve.
Nutrition:
- InfoCalories 115, Total Fat 5g, Total Carbs 14g, Protein 6g, Sodium 544mg.

Eggplant Casserole
Servings: 8
Cooking Time: 1 Hour
Ingredients:
- Nonstick cooking spray
- 1 lb. eggplant, peeled, cubed
- ½ cup seasoned bread crumbs, divided
- 2 eggs
- ¼ tsp Italian seasoning
- ½ tsp garlic powder
- 1/8 tsp salt
- 1/8 tsp pepper
- 2 tomatoes, sliced

Directions:
1. Spray an 8x8-inch baking dish with cooking spray.
2. Add enough water to the cooking pot to come 2 inches up the sides. Set to sauté on high heat and bring to a boil.
3. Add the eggplant, reduce heat to medium, cover and cook 20-30 minutes until soft. Drain.
4. Add the eggplant to a large bowl and mash with a fork. Stir in ¼ cup bread crumbs, eggs, Italian seasoning, garlic, salt, and pepper and mix well.
5. Add the rack to the cooking pot. Spread the eggplant mixture in the prepared dish. Top with sliced tomatoes. Sprinkle tomatoes with remaining bread crumbs and spray with cooking spray. Place the dish on the rack.
6. Add the tender-crisp lid and set to bake on 350°F (175°C). Bake 25-30 minutes or until tomatoes are tender and starting to brown around the edges. Serve.

Nutrition:
- InfoCalories 67, Total Fat 2g, Total Carbs 10g, Protein 3g, Sodium 181mg.

Broccoli & Pesto Penne
Servings: 4
Cooking Time: 35 Minutes
Ingredients:
- 8 oz. whole wheat penne
- 2 cups baby broccoli
- 1 cup oven roasted tomatoes
- 1 tsp garlic, chopped fine
- ¼ cup pesto
- ¼ cup feta cheese, crumbled
- ½ tbsp. lemon juice
- 2 tbsp. fresh basil, chopped

Directions:
1. Add enough water to the cooking pot to cook the pasta. Set to sauté on high and bring to a boil.
2. Add the penne and cook according to package directions. Add the broccoli to the pot in the last 2 minutes of cooking time. Drain and return to the pot.
3. Reduce heat to med-high. Add tomatoes and garlic and cook 2 minutes, stirring frequently.
4. Stir in the pesto, half the feta, and lemon juice. Toss to combine. Spoon onto serving plates and top with remaining feta and basil before serving.

Nutrition:
- InfoCalories 338, Total Fat 12g, Total Carbs 52g, Protein 11g, Sodium 267mg.

Artichoke With Mayo
Servings: 4
Cooking Time: 20 Min
Ingredients:
- 2 large artichokes
- 2 garlic cloves, smashed
- ½ cup mayonnaise /125ml
- 2 cups water /500ml
- Juice of 1 lime
- Salt and black pepper to taste

Directions:
1. Using a serrated knife, trim about 1 inch from the artichokes' top. Into the pot, add water and set trivet over. Lay the artichokes on the trivet. Seal lid and cook for 14 minutes. Press Start.
2. When ready, release the pressure quickly. Mix the mayonnaise with garlic and lime juice; season with salt and pepper. Serve artichokes in a platter with garlic mayo on the side.

Mushroom Brown Rice Pilaf
Servings: 4
Cooking Time: 15 Min
Ingredients:
- 2 cups brown rice, rinsed /260g
- 1 cup Portobello mushrooms, thinly sliced /130g
- ¼ cup Romano cheese, grated /32.5g
- 2 sprigs parsley, to garnish
- 4 cups vegetable broth /1000ml
- 3 tsp s olive oil /15ml
- Salt to taste

Directions:
1. Heat the oil on Sear/Sauté on Medium, and stir-fry the mushrooms for 3 minutes until golden. Season with salt, and add rice and broth.
2. Close the lid, secure the pressure valve, and select Pressure mode on High pressure for 5 minutes. Press Start/Stop to start cooking.
3. Once the timer has ended, do a quick pressure release and open the lid.
4. Spread the cheese over and close the crisping lid. Select Bake/Roast, adjust to 375°F or 190°C and the timer to 2 minutes. Press Start/Stop to start cooking. To serve, plate the pilaf and top with freshly chopped parsley.

Southern Pineapple Casserole

Servings: 8
Cooking Time: 35 Minutes
Ingredients:
- Nonstick cooking spray
- 1/3 cup butter, soft
- 1/4 cup Stevia
- 2 eggs
- 2 egg whites
- 1 tsp vanilla
- 2 tbsp. flour
- 20 oz. crushed pineapple in juice, drained; reserve 1 cup liquid
- 5 slices whole-wheat bread, cubed

Directions:
1. Spray the cooking pot with cooking spray.
2. In a large bowl, beat butter and Stevia until smooth and creamy.
3. Beat in eggs, egg whites, and vanilla until combined.
4. Stir in flour, pineapple, and reserved juice and mix well.
5. Add bread and toss to coat. Pour into cooking pot.
6. Add tender-crisp lid and set to bake on 350°F (175°C). Bake 30-35 minutes or until a knife inserted in center comes out clean. Serve warm.

Nutrition:
- InfoCalories 191,Total Fat 10g,Total Carbs 29g,Protein 5g,Sodium 183mg.

Rustic Veggie Tart

Servings: 6
Cooking Time: 40 Minutes
Ingredients:
- 1 tbsp. olive oil
- 3 cups cherry tomatoes
- ½ tsp salt, divided
- 1/8 tsp red pepper flakes
- 1 cup fresh corn kernels
- 1 zucchini, chopped
- 5-6 green onions, sliced thin
- 1 ¼ cups flour
- 8 tbsp. butter, sliced
- ¼ cup sour cream
- 2 tsp fresh lemon juice
- ¼ cup ice water
- ½ cup parmesan cheese
- 1 egg yolk
- 1 tsp water

Directions:
1. In a large bowl, combine flour and ¼ tsp salt. Cut in butter until mixture resembles coarse crumbs.
2. In a small bowl, whisk together sour cream, lemon juice, and water until combined. Add to flour mixture and stir until it forms a soft dough. Form dough into a ball and wrap with plastic wrap, refrigerate at least 1 hour.
3. Add oil to the cooking pot and set to sauté on med-high heat.
4. Add tomatoes, remaining salt, and red pepper flakes, cover and cook until tomatoes burst, turning tomatoes frequently.
5. Reduce heat to medium and add zucchini. Cook 2 minutes until they soften. Add corn and cook 1 minute more. Stir in scallions and turn off the heat. Transfer to a large plate and let cool.
6. Wipe out the cooking pot and add the rack.
7. On a floured surface, roll out dough to a 12-inch circle. Transfer to a piece of parchment paper.
8. Sprinkle vegetables with half the parmesan cheese and spoon into the center of the dough, leaving a 2-inch border. Sprinkle most of the remaining parmesan over the vegetables.
9. Fold edges over the filling, pleating as you go.
10. In a small bowl, beat together egg yolk and teaspoon of water. Brush the crust with egg yolk glaze and sprinkle with the last of the parmesan.
11. Carefully pick up the parchment paper and transfer to the rack in the cooking pot. Add the tender-crisp lid and set to bake on 400°F (205°C). Bake 30-40 minutes until golden brown. Transfer to wire rack to cool 5 minutes before serving.

Nutrition:
- InfoCalories 159,Total Fat 10g,Total Carbs 14g,Protein 4g,Sodium 170mg.

Worthy Caramelized Onion

Servings:6
Cooking Time: 30-35 Minutes
Ingredients:
- 2 tablespoons unsalted butter
- 3 large onions sliced
- 2 tablespoons water
- 1 teaspoon salt

Directions:
1. Set your Ninja Foodi to Sauté mode and add set temperature to medium heat, pre-heat the inner pot for 5 minutes. Add butter and let it melt, add onions, water, and stir
2. Lock lid and cook on HIGH pressure for 30 minutes. Quick release the pressure
3. Remove lid and set the pot to sauté mode, let it sear in Medium-HIGH mode for 15 minutes until all liquid is gone. Serve and enjoy!

Cauliflower Chunks With Lemon Sauce

Servings: 4
Cooking Time: 15 Minutes
Ingredients:
- 1-pound cauliflower, cut into chunks
- 1 tablespoon dill, chopped
- 1 tablespoon lemon zest, grated
- Juice of ½ lemon
- 2 tablespoons butter, melted
- Black pepper and salt to the taste

Directions:
1. Set the Foodi on Sauté mode, stir in the butter, melt it, add the cauliflower chunks and brown for 5 minutes.

2. Add the lemon zest and the other ingredients set the machine on Air Crisp and cook at 390 °F (200°C) for 10 minutes.
3. Divide everything between plates and serve.
Nutrition:
- InfoCalories: 122; Fat: 3.3g; Carbohydrates: 3g; Protein: 2g

Cheesy Spicy Pasta

Servings: 6
Cooking Time: 40 Minutes
Ingredients:
- 1 ½ cups cottage cheese, low fat
- ½ cup ricotta cheese
- ½ cup Greek yogurt
- 2 cups mozzarella cheese, grated, divided
- ¼ cup fresh parsley, chopped
- 2 cups baby spinach
- 1 tbsp. butter
- 1 onion, chopped
- 2 tbsp. garlic, chopped fine
- 14 ½ oz. fire-roasted tomatoes
- 8 oz. tomato sauce
- ½ tsp red pepper flakes
- 1 ½ tsp oregano
- 1 tsp rosemary
- ½ tsp salt
- ½ tsp pepper
- ¾ lb. whole grain pasta, cooked & drained
- 6 tbsp. parmesan cheese

Directions:
1. In a medium bowl, combine cottage cheese, ricotta, yogurt, 1 cup mozzarella, parsley, and spinach, mix well.
2. Add the butter to the cooking pot and set to sauté on med-high. Once the butter melts, add the onion and cook until translucent. Add the garlic and cook 1 minute more.
3. Stir in tomatoes, tomato sauce, and seasonings, reduce heat to low and simmer 5 minutes.
4. Stir in the pasta and the ricotta mixture, mix well. Top with remaining mozzarella and the parmesan cheese.
5. Add the tender-crisp lid and set to bake on 400°F (205°C). Bake 25-30 minutes until hot and bubbly. Serve.

Nutrition:
- InfoCalories 282,Total Fat 7g,Total Carbs 30g,Protein 28g,Sodium 522mg.

Cheesy Green Beans With Nuts

Servings: 6
Cooking Time: 15 Min
Ingredients:
- 2 pounds green beans, trimmed /900g
- 1 cup chopped toasted pine nuts /130g
- 1 cup feta cheese, crumbled /130g
- 1½ cups water /375ml
- Juice from 1 lemon
- 6 tbsp olive oil /90ml
- ½ tsp salt /2.5g
- freshly ground black pepper to taste

Directions:
1. Add water to the pot. Set the reversible rack over the water. Loosely heap green beans into the reversible rack.
2. Seal lid and cook on High Pressure for 5 minutes. Press Start. When the cooking cycle is complete, When ready, release pressure quickly. Drop green beans into a salad bowl; top with the olive oil, feta cheese, pepper, and pine nuts.

Caramelized Sweet Potatoes

Servings: 4
Cooking Time: 20 Minutes
Ingredients:
- 1 cup water
- 2 large sweet potatoes
- 2 tbsp. butter
- ½ tsp salt
- ¼ tsp pepper

Directions:
1. Add the trivet and water to the cooking pot.
2. Prick the potatoes with a fork and place on the trivet. Add the lid and set to pressure cook on high. Set timer for 15 minutes. Once timer goes off, use natural release to remove the pressure.
3. Transfer potatoes to a cutting board and slice ½-inch thick.
4. Remove the trivet and add butter to the pot. Set to sauté on med-high heat.
5. Add the potatoes and cook, turning occasionally, until potatoes are nicely browned on both sides. Season with salt and pepper and serve.

Nutrition:
- InfoCalories 107,Total Fat 6g,Total Carbs 14g,Protein 1g,Sodium 227mg.

Veggie Loaded Pasta

Servings: 8
Cooking Time: 2 Minutes
Ingredients:
- 1 box dry pasta, such as rigatoni or penne
- 4 cups water
- 2 tablespoons extra-virgin olive oil, divided
- 2 teaspoons kosher salt, divided
- 3 avocados
- Juice of 2 limes
- 2 tablespoons minced cilantro
- 1 red onion, chopped
- 1 cup cherry tomatoes, halved
- 4 heaping cups spinach, half an 11-ounce container
- ¼ cup shredded Parmesan cheese, divided
- Freshly ground black pepper, for serving

Directions:
1. Place the pasta, water, 1 tablespoon of olive oil, and 1 teaspoon of salt in the pot. Stir to incorporate. Assemble pressure lid, making sure the pressure release valve is in the SEAL position.
2. Select PRESSURE and set to LO. Set time to 2 minutes. Select START/STOP to begin.
3. While pasta is cooking, place the avocados in a medium-sized mixing bowl and mash well with a wooden spatula until a thick paste forms. Add all remaining ingredients to the bowl and mix well to combine.

4. When pressure cooking is complete, allow pressure to naturally release for 10 minutes. After 10 minutes, quick release remaining pressure by moving the pressure release valve to the VENT position. Carefully remove lid when unit has finished releasing pressure.
5. If necessary, strain pasta to remove any residual water and return pasta to pot. Add avocado mixture to pot and stir.
6. Garnish pasta with Parmesan cheese and black pepper, as desired, then serve.

Nutrition:
- InfoCalories: 372,Total Fat: 16g,Sodium: 149mg,Carbohydrates: 49g,Protein: 11g.

Potato Filled Bread Rolls

Servings: 4
Cooking Time: 25 Min
Ingredients:
- 8 slices of bread
- 2 green chilies, deseeded; chopped
- 5 large potatoes, boiled, mashed
- 2 sprigs curry leaf
- 1 medium onion; chopped
- 1 tbsp olive oil /15ml
- ½ tsp mustard seeds /2.5g
- ½ tsp turmeric /2.5g
- Salt, to taste

Directions:
1. Combine the olive oil, onion, curry leaves, and mustard seed, in the Ninja Foodi basket. Cook for 5 minutes. Mix the onion mixture with the mashed potatoes, chilies, turmeric, and some salt. Divide the dough into 8 equal pieces.
2. Trim the sides of the bread, and wet it with some water. Make sure to get rid of the excess water. Take one wet bread slice in your palm and place one of the potato pieces in the center.
3. Roll the bread over the filling, sealing the edges. Place the rolls onto a prepared baking dish, close the crisping lid and cook for 12 minutes on Air Crisp at 350 °F or 175°C.

Aloo Gobi With Cilantro

Servings: 4
Cooking Time: 40 Min
Ingredients:
- 1 head cauliflower, cored and cut into florets
- 1 potato, peeled and diced
- 4 garlic cloves, minced
- 1 tomato, cored and chopped
- 1 jalapeño pepper, deseeded and minced
- 1 onion, minced
- 1 cup water /250ml
- 1 tbsp curry paste /15g
- 1 tbsp vegetable oil /15ml
- 1 tbsp ghee /15g
- 2 tsp cumin seeds /10g
- 1 tsp ground turmeric /5g
- ½ tsp chili pepper /2.5g
- salt to taste
- A handful of cilantro leaves; chopped

Directions:
1. Warm oil on Sear/Sauté. Add in potato and cauliflower and cook for 8 to 10 minutes until lightly browned; add salt for seasoning. Set the vegetables to a bowl.
2. Add ghee to the pot. Mix in cumin seeds and cook for 10 seconds until they start to pop; add onion and cook for 3 minutes until softened. Mix in garlic; cook for seconds.
3. Add in tomato, curry paste, chili pepper, jalapeño pepper, curry paste, and turmeric; cook for 3 to 5 minutes until the tomato starts to break down.
4. Return potato and cauliflower to the pot. Add water over the vegetables, add more salt if need be, and stir. Seal the pressure lid, choose Pressure, set to High, and set the timer to 4 minutes. Press Start. Release pressure naturally. Top with cilantro and serve.

Ritzy Vegetable Mix

Servings: 4
Cooking Time: 5 Minutes
Ingredients:
- 1 tablespoon butter, at room temperature
- 1 clove garlic, minced
- ½ pound (227 g) broccoli, cut into florets
- 2 medium waxy potatoes, peeled and cubed
- 2 cups (500 mL) acorn squash
- 1 parsnip, cut into 1-inch pieces
- 1 carrot, cut into 1-inch pieces
- 1 cup (250 mL) roasted vegetable broth

Directions:
1. Press the Sauté button and melt the butter in the cooking pot.
2. Add and sauté the garlic for 1 minute or until fragrant. Stir in the remaining ingredients.
3. Assemble pressure lid, making sure the pressure release valve is in the Seal position. Select Pressure and set to high. Set time to 4 minutes. Press Start to begin.
4. Once cooking is complete, perform a quick pressure release. Carefully open the lid.
5. Serve warm.

Roasted Vegetable Salad

Servings: 1
Cooking Time: 25 Min
Ingredients:
- 1 potato, peeled and chopped
- 1 cup cherry tomatoes/130g
- 1 carrot; sliced diagonally
- ½ small beetroot; sliced
- ¼ onion; sliced
- Juice of 1 lemon
- A handful of rocket salad
- A handful of baby spinach
- 2 tbsp olive oil /30ml
- 3 tbsp canned chickpeas /45g
- ½ tsp cumin /2.5g
- ½ tsp turmeric /2.5g
- ¼ tsp sea salt /1.25g
- Parmesan shavings

Directions:
1. Combine the onion, potato, cherry tomatoes, carrot, beetroot, cumin, seas salt, turmeric, and 1 tbsp olive oil, in a

bowl. Place in the Ninja Foodi, close the crisping lid and cook for 20 minutes on Air Crisp mode at 370 °F or 185°C; let cool for 2 minutes.
2. Place the rocket, salad, spinach, lemon juice, and 1 tbsp olive oil, into a serving bowl. Mix to combine; stir in the roasted veggies. Top with chickpeas and Parmesan shavings.

Stuffed Manicotti

Servings: 4
Cooking Time: 50 Minutes
Ingredients:
- Nonstick cooking spray
- 8 manicotti shells, cooked & drained
- ½ onion, chopped
- 1 cloves garlic, chopped fine
- 1 cup mushrooms, chopped
- 16 oz. ricotta cheese, fat free
- ½ cup mozzarella cheese, grated
- 1 egg
- 1 cup spinach, chopped
- ¾ tsp Italian seasoning
- ¼ tsp pepper
- 1 cups light spaghetti sauce
- 1 tbsp. parmesan cheese, grated

Directions:
1. Spray the cooking pot and an 8x8-inch baking pan with cooking spray.
2. Set cooker to sauté on med-high heat. Add onion and garlic and cook until tender, about 3-4 minutes.
3. Add mushrooms and cook until browned. Turn off the heat.
4. In a large bowl, combine ricotta and mozzarella cheeses, egg, spinach, Italian seasoning, and pepper, mix well.
5. Add the mushroom mixture to the cheese mixture and stir to combine. Spoon into manicotti shells and lay in the prepared pan.
6. Pour the spaghetti sauce over the top and sprinkle with parmesan cheese. Cover with foil.
7. Place the rack in the cooking pot and add the manicotti. Add the tender-crisp lid and set to bake on 400°F (205°C). Bake 30-35 minutes or until heated through. Serve immediately.

Nutrition:
- InfoCalories 367, Total Fat 19g, Total Carbs 27g, Protein 24g, Sodium 308mg.

Slowly Cooked Lemon Artichokes

Servings: 4
Cooking Time: 5 Hours
Ingredients:
- 5 large artichokes
- 1 teaspoon of sea salt
- 2 stalks celery, sliced
- 2 large carrots, cut into matchsticks
- Juice from ½ a lemon
- ¼ teaspoon black pepper
- 1 teaspoon dried thyme
- 1 tablespoon dried rosemary
- Lemon wedges for garnish

Directions:
1. Remove the stalk from your artichokes and remove the tough outer shell
2. Transfer the chokes to your Ninja Foodi and add 2 cups of boiling water
3. Add celery, lemon juice, salt, carrots, black pepper, thyme, rosemary
4. Cook on Slow Cook mode for 4-5 hours
5. Serve the artichokes with lemon wedges. Serve and enjoy!

The Veggie Lover's Onion And Tofu Platter

Servings: 4
Cooking Time: 12 Minutes
Ingredients:
- 4 tablespoons butter
- 2 tofu blocks, pressed and cubed into 1-inch pieces
- Salt and pepper to taste
- 1 cup cheddar cheese, grated
- 2 medium onions, sliced

Directions:
1. Take a bowl and add tofu, season with salt and pepper
2. Set your Foodi to Saute mode and add butter, let it melt
3. Add onions and Saute for 3 minutes. Add seasoned tofu and cook for 2 minutes more
4. Add cheddar and gently stir
5. Lock the lid and bring down the Air Crisp mode, let the dish cook on "Air Crisp" mode for 3 minutes at 340 degrees F. Once done, take the dish out, serve and enjoy!

Cheesy Chilies

Servings: 4
Cooking Time: 25 Minutes
Ingredients:
- Nonstick cooking spray
- 2 poblano chilies, halved, seeded, stems on
- 1 cup cottage cheese, drained
- ¼ cup green onion, chopped
- ½ cup Colby-Jack cheese, grated

Directions:
1. Spray the fryer basket with cooking spray.
2. Place the chilies in the basket and add the tender-crisp lid. Set to broil. Cook chilies until skin is charred on all sides. Transfer to a bag and let cool. When cool, remove the skin.
3. Spray an 8x8-inch baking pan with cooking spray.
4. Place chilies in the prepared pan. Spoon cottage cheese in the chilies and sprinkle with green onion and Colby Jack cheese.
5. Place the rack in the cooking pot and add the baking pan. Add the tender-crisp lid and set to bake on 350°F (175°C). Bake 15-20 minutes until hot and cheese is melted. Serve immediately.

Nutrition:
- InfoCalories 119, Total Fat 7g, Total Carbs 5g, Protein 10g, Sodium 313mg.

Green Cream Soup

Servings: 4
Cooking Time: 22 Min
Ingredients:
- ½ lb. kale leaves; chopped /225g
- ½ lb. Swiss chard leaves; chopped /225g
- ½ lb. spinach leaves; chopped /225g
- 1 onion; chopped
- 4 cloves garlic, minced
- 4 cups vegetable broth /1000ml
- 1 ¼ cup heavy cream /312.5ml
- 1 tbsp olive oil /15ml
- 1 ½ tbsp white wine vinegar/ 22.5ml
- Salt and pepper, to taste
- Chopped Peanuts to garnish

Directions:
1. Turn on the Ninja Foodi and select Sear/Sauté mode on Medium. Add the olive oil, once it has heated add the onion and garlic and sauté for 2-3 minutes until soft. Add greens and vegetable broth.
2. Close the lid, secure the pressure valve, and select Pressure mode on High pressure for 10 minutes. Press Start/Stop. Once the timer has ended, do a quick pressure release.
3. Add the white wine vinegar, salt, and pepper. Use a stick blender to puree the Ingredients in the pot. Close the crisping lid and cook for 3 minutes on Broil mode. Stir in the heavy cream. Spoon the soup into bowls, sprinkle with peanuts, and serve.

Okra Bhindi Masala

Servings: 2 To 4
Cooking Time: 8 Minutes
Ingredients:
- 1 tablespoon coconut oil, at room temperature
- ½ yellow onion, sliced
- 1 teaspoon ginger garlic paste
- ½ pound (227 g) okra, cut into small pieces
- ½ cup (125 mL) tomato purée
- ⅓ teaspoon cumin seeds
- ⅓ teaspoon ground turmeric
- ½ teaspoon Gram masala
- ½ teaspoon mango powder
- ½ teaspoon Sriracha sauce
- Himalayan salt, to taste

Directions:
1. Press the Sauté button and heat the coconut oil until shimmering.
2. Add and sauté the onion for 3 minutes or until translucent.
3. Stir in the ginger-garlic paste and cook for 1 minute. Stir the remaining ingredients into the pot.
4. Assemble pressure lid, making sure the pressure release valve is in the Seal position. Select Pressure and set to high. Set time to 4 minutes. Press Start to begin.
5. Once cooking is complete, perform a quick pressure release. Carefully open the lid.
6. Serve warm.

Spanish Rice

Servings: 4
Cooking Time: 50 Min
Ingredients:
- 1 small onion; chopped
- 1 can pinto beans, drained and rinsed /480g
- 2 garlic cloves, minced
- 1 banana pepper, seeded and chopped
- ¼ cup stewed tomatoes /32.5g
- ½ cup vegetable stock /125ml
- 1 cup jasmine rice /130g
- ⅓ cup red salsa /88g
- 3 tbsps ghee /45g
- 1 tbsp chopped fresh parsley /15g
- 1 tsp Mexican Seasoning Mix /5g
- 1 tsp salt /5g

Directions:
1. On your Foodi, choose Sear/Sauté and adjust to Medium. Press Start to preheat the inner pot. Add the ghee to melt until no longer foaming and cook the onion, garlic, and banana pepper in the ghee. Cook for 2 minutes or until fragrant.
2. Stir in the rice, salsa, tomato sauce, vegetable stock, Mexican seasoning, pinto beans, and salt. Seal the pressure lid, choose Pressure and adjust the pressure to High and the cook time to 6 minutes; press Start.
3. After cooking, do a natural pressure release for 10 minutes. Stir in the parsley, dish the rice, and serve.

Tomato And Poblano Stuffed Squash

Servings: 3
Cooking Time: 50 Min
Ingredients:
- ½ butternut squash
- 6 grape tomatoes, halved
- ¼ cup grated mozzarella, optional /32.5g
- 1 poblano pepper, cut into strips
- 2 tsp olive oil divided /10ml
- Salt and pepper, to taste

Directions:
1. Meanwhile, cut trim the ends and cut the squash lengthwise. You will only need one half for this recipe. Scoop the flash out, so you make room for the filling. Brush 1 tsp oil over the squash. Place in the Ninja Foodi and roast for 30 minutes.
2. Combine the other tsp of olive oil with the tomatoes and poblanos. Season with salt and pepper, to taste. Place the peppers and tomatoes into the squash. Close the crisping lid and cook for 15 more minutes on Air Crisp mode at 350 °F or 175°C. If using mozzarella, add it on top of the squash, two minutes before the end.

Mushroom And Swiss Cheese Tarts

Servings: 4
Cooking Time: 27 Minutes
Ingredients:
- 5 ounces (142 g) oyster mushrooms, sliced
- 1 small white onion, sliced
- 2 tablespoons melted butter, divided
- Salt and black pepper, to taste
- ¼ cup (63 mL) dry white wine
- 1 sheet puff pastry

- 1 cup (250 mL) shredded Swiss cheese, divided
- 1 cup (250 mL) water
- 1 tablespoon sliced green onions

Directions:
1. Press the Sauté button, then add the mushrooms, onion, and 1 tablespoon of butter in cooking pot. Sauté for 5 minutes or until tender.
2. Season with salt and pepper, pour in white wine and cook for 2 minutes or until evaporated. Set aside.
3. Unwrap the puff pastry and cut into 4 squares. Pierce the dough with a fork and brush both sides with the remaining butter.
4. Scatter half of the Swiss cheese evenly over the puff pastry squares. Spread the mushroom mixture over the pastry squares and top with the remaining cheese. Place in a baking pan.
5. Pour the water in the pot, then arrange a reversible rack in the pot. Lay the pan on the rack.
6. Assemble pressure lid, making sure the pressure release valve is in the Seal position. Select Pressure and set to high. Set time to 20 minutes. Press Start to begin.
7. Once cooking is complete, do a natural release for 10 minutes, then release any remaining pressure. Carefully open the lid.
8. Transfer the tart to a plate. Garnish with the green onions and serve.

Creamy Polenta & Mushrooms

Servings: 2
Cooking Time: 40 Minutes

Ingredients:
- 3 tbsp. olive oil
- 1 lb. assorted mushrooms, rinsed & chopped
- 1 clove garlic, chopped fine
- 1 tsp salt, divided
- 3/8 tsp pepper, divided
- 2 ½ cups water, divided
- 3 tbsp. butter
- 1 ½ tbsp. fresh lemon juice
- 1 tbsp. fresh parsley, chopped
- ½ cup stone-ground white grits
- 1/8 cup heavy cream
- 3 tbsp. parmesan cheese, grated, divided
- ¼ cup mascarpone

Directions:
1. Add oil to the cooking pot and set to sauté on medium heat.
2. Add mushrooms, garlic, ½ teaspoon salt, and ¼ teaspoon pepper and cook, stirring occasionally, until mushrooms are nicely browned and liquid has evaporated, about 6-8 minutes.
3. Add ¼ cup water, butter, lemon juice, and parsley and cook, stirring, until butter melts. Cook 1-2 minutes. Transfer to a large bowl and keep warm.
4. Add the remaining water to the pot and increase heat to med-high. Bring just to a boil.
5. Whisk in grits slowly until combined. Reduce heat to med-low and simmer, stirring occasionally, about 30 minutes, or until liquid is absorbed. Turn off the heat.
6. Stir in cream, 1 tablespoon cheese, and remaining salt and pepper and mix well. Ladle polenta onto serving plates. Top with mushrooms, mascarpone, and remaining parmesan cheese. Serve immediately.

Nutrition:
- InfoCalories 102,Total Fat 7g,Total Carbs 8g,Protein 2g,Sodium 215mg.

Mesmerizing Spinach Quiche

Servings: 4
Cooking Time: 33 Minutes

Ingredients:
- 1 tablespoon butter, melted
- 1 pack (10 ounces frozen spinach, thawed
- 5 organic eggs, beaten
- Salt and pepper to taste
- 3 cups Monterey Jack Cheese, shredded

Directions:
1. Set your Ninja Foodi to Saute mode and let it heat up, add butter and let the butter melt
2. Add spinach and Saute for 3 minutes, transfer the Sautéed spinach to a bowl
3. Add eggs, cheese, salt, and pepper to a bowl and mix it well
4. Transfer the mixture to greased quiche molds and transfer the mold to your Foodi
5. Close the lid and choose the "Bake/Roast" mode and let it cook for 30 minutes at 360 degrees F. Once done, open lid and transfer the dish out
6. Cut into wedges and serve. Enjoy!

Italian Spinach & Tomato Soup

Servings: 6
Cooking Time: 4 Hours

Ingredients:
- 1 tsp olive oil
- 1 onion, chopped
- 3 cloves garlic, chopped fine
- 3 large tomatoes, chopped
- 2 tsp Italian seasoning
- 28 oz. vegetable broth, low sodium
- 10 oz. fresh spinach, trimmed
- ½ tsp pepper
- 2 tbsp. parmesan cheese

Directions:
1. Add the oil to the cooking pot and set to sauté on med-high.
2. Add the onion and garlic and cook, stirring occasionally, 5 minutes or until onion starts to brown.
3. Stir in remaining ingredients, except spinach and parmesan, and mix well. Add the lid and set to slow cook on high. Cook 3-4 hours until tomatoes are tender. Stir occasionally.
4. Add the spinach and cook until it wilts. Ladle into bowls and sprinkle with parmesan. Serve.

Nutrition:
- InfoCalories 60,Total Fat 2g,Total Carbs 10g,Protein 3g,Sodium 602mg.

Risotto And Roasted Bell Peppers

Servings: 4
Cooking Time: 80 Min
Ingredients:
- 4 mixed bell peppers, seeds removed and chopped diagonally
- 1 garlic clove, minced
- 2 cups carnaroli rice /260g
- 1½ cups grated Parmesan cheese, plus more for garnish /195g
- 5 cups vegetable stock /1250ml
- ¼ cup freshly squeezed lemon juice /62.5ml
- 2 tbsps ghee; divided /30g
- 2 tbsps unsalted butter /30g
- 1 tsp grated lemon zest /15g
- 2 tsp s salt; divided /10g
- 1 tsp freshly ground black pepper /5g

Directions:
1. On the pot, choose Sear/Sauté and set to Medium High. Choose Start/Stop to preheat the pot. Melt the ghee and cook the garlic until fragrant, about 1 minute.
2. Then, pour the stock, lemon juice, lemon zest, and rice into the pot. Sprinkle with 1 tsp of salt and stir to combine well.
3. Seal the pressure lid, hit Pressure, set to High, and the timer to 7 minutes; press Start. While the rice cooks, in a bowl, toss the peppers with the remaining ghee, salt, and black pepper.
4. When the timer has ended, do a natural pressure release for 10 minutes, then a quick pressure release. Stir the butter into the rice until properly mixed.
5. Then, put the reversible rack inside the pot in the higher position, which will be over the risotto. Arrange the bell peppers on the rack.
6. Close the crisping lid. Choose Broil and set the time to 8 minutes; press Start/Stop.
7. When done cooking, take out the rack from the pot. Stir the Parmesan cheese into the risotto. To serve, spoon the risotto into serving plates, top with the bell peppers and garnish with extra Parmesan. Serve immediately.

Hawaiian Tofu

Servings: 6
Cooking Time: 3 Hours
Ingredients:
- 1 package extra firm tofu, cubed
- ¼ cup fresh pineapple, cubed
- ¼ cup tamari, low sodium
- 1 tbsp. sesame oil
- 1 tbsp. olive oil
- 1 tbsp. brown rice vinegar
- 2 cloves garlic, chopped
- 2 tsp fresh ginger, chopped
- 4 cups zucchini, chopped
- ¼ cup sesame seeds

Directions:
1. Add the tofu to the cooking pot.
2. Add the pineapple, soy sauce, sesame oil, olive oil, vinegar, garlic, and ginger to a food processor or blender. Process until smooth. Pour over tofu.
3. Add the lid and set to slow cook on low. Cook 3 hours, stirring occasionally.
4. During the last 15 minutes of cooking time, add the zucchini and sesame seeds to the pot and stir to combine. Serve over quinoa or rice.

Nutrition:
- InfoCalories 164,Total Fat 13g,Total Carbs 5g,Protein 10g,Sodium 680mg.

Hearty Veggie Soup

Servings: 12
Cooking Time: 15 Minutes
Ingredients:
- 2 cups water
- 3 ½ cups vegetable broth, low sodium
- 15 oz. red kidney beans, drained & rinsed
- 16 oz. cannellini beans, drained & rinsed
- 28 oz. tomatoes, crushed
- 10 oz. spinach, chopped
- 1 onion, chopped
- 10 oz. mixed vegetables, frozen
- 1 tsp garlic powder
- ½ tsp pepper
- 1 cup elbow macaroni

Directions:
1. Set the cooker to sauté on med-high heat.
2. Add all the ingredients, except macaroni, and stir to combine. Bring to a boil.
3. Stir in macaroni. Add the lid and set to pressure cook on high. Set timer for 10 minutes. When timer goes off, use natural release to remove the pressure. Stir well and serve.

Nutrition:
- InfoCalories 181,Total Fat 1g,Total Carbs 34g,Protein 10g,Sodium 478mg.

Chives And Radishes Platter

Servings: 4
Cooking Time: 7 Minutes
Ingredients:
- 2 cups radishes, quartered
- ½ cup chicken stock
- Salt and pepper to taste
- 2 tablespoons melted ghee
- 1 tablespoon chives, chopped
- 1 tablespoon lemon zest, grated

Directions:
1. Add radishes, stock, salt, pepper, zest to your Ninja Foodi and stir
2. Lock lid and cook on HIGH pressure for 7 minutes
3. Quick release pressure. Add melted ghee, toss well. Sprinkle chives and enjoy!

Complete Cauliflower Zoodles

Servings: 6
Cooking Time: 8 Minutes
Ingredients:
- 2 tablespoons butter
- 2 cloves garlic
- 7-8 cauliflower florets
- 1 cup vegetable broth
- 2 teaspoons salt
- 2 cups spinach, coarsely chopped

- 2 green onions, chopped
- 1 pound of zoodles (Spiralized Zucchini)
- Garnish
- Chopped sun-dried tomatoes
- Balsamic vinegar
- Gorgonzola cheese

Directions:
1. Set your Ninja Foodi to Saute mode and add butter, allow the butter to melt
2. Add garlic cloves and Saute for 2 minutes
3. Add cauliflower, broth, salt and lock up the lid and cook on HIGH pressure for 6 minutes
4. Prepare the zoodles. Perform a naturally release over 10 minutes
5. Use an immersion blender to blend the mixture in the pot to a puree
6. Pour the sauce over the zoodles
7. Serve with a garnish of cheese, sun-dried tomatoes and a drizzle of balsamic vinegar. Enjoy!

Cauliflower Cakes

Servings: 6
Cooking Time: 15 Minutes
Ingredients:
- 1 cup water
- 1 head cauliflower, cut in florets
- ¼ cup onion, chopped
- ½ cup cheddar cheese, low fat, grated
- ½ cup panko bread crumbs
- 2 eggs, lightly beaten
- ½ tsp salt
- ¼ tsp cayenne pepper
- Nonstick cooking spray

Directions:
1. Add water, cauliflower and onion to the cooking pot. Add the lid and set to pressure cook on high. Set the timer for 6 minutes. When the timer goes off, use quick release to remove the pressure. Drain and add the vegetables to a large bowl.
2. Mash the cauliflower with an electric mixer beating until smooth.
3. Stir in remaining ingredients. Form into 12 patties.
4. Spray the fryer basket with cooking spray. Place the patties in a single layer in the basket. Add the tender-crisp lid and set to air fry on 375°F (190°C). Cook cauliflower 4-5 minutes per side until golden brown. Serve immediately.

Nutrition:
- InfoCalories 102,Total Fat 3g,Total Carbs 12g,Protein 8g,Sodium 395mg.

Zucchini Cream Soup

Servings: 6
Cooking Time: 40 Minutes
Ingredients:
- Nonstick cooking spray
- 1 cup onion, chopped
- ½ red bell pepper, chopped
- 3 cloves garlic, chopped fine
- 1 ½ lb. zucchini, cut in ½-inch cubes
- 28 oz. vegetable broth, low sodium
- 1 tbsp. fresh dill, chopped
- ½ tsp salt
- ¼ tsp pepper
- 1 cup skim milk
- 3 tbsp. cornstarch

Directions:
1. Spray the cooking pot with cooking spray. Set to sauté on med-high heat.
2. Add onion, bell pepper, and garlic and cook 4-5 minutes, stirring frequently, until soft.
3. Add zucchini, broth, dill, salt, and pepper and bring to a boil. Reduce heat to low, cover and cook 25-30 minutes until zucchini is soft.
4. In a small bowl, whisk together milk and cornstarch until smooth. Stir into soup and cook another 2-3 minutes until thickened. Serve.

Nutrition:
- InfoCalories 72,Total Fat 1g,Total Carbs 14g,Protein 5g,Sodium 764mg.

Veggie And Quinoa Stuffed Peppers

Servings: 1
Cooking Time: 16 Min
Ingredients:
- ¼ cup cooked quinoa /32.5g
- ½ diced tomato, plus one tomato slice
- 1 bell pepper
- ½ tbsp diced onion /7.5g
- 1 tsp olive oil /5ml
- ¼ tsp smoked paprika/1.25g
- ¼ tsp dried basil /1.25g
- Salt and pepper, to taste

Directions:
1. Core and clean the bell pepper to prepare it for stuffing. Brush the pepper with half of the olive oil on the outside.
2. In a small bowl, combine all of the other Ingredients, except the tomato slice and reserved half-tsp olive oil. Stuff the pepper with the filling. Top with the tomato slice.
3. Brush the tomato slice with the remaining half-tsp of oil and sprinkle with basil. Close the crisping lid and cook for 10 minutes on Air Crisp mode at 350 °F or 175°C.

Zucchini And Artichoke Platter

Servings:4
Cooking Time: 10 Minutes
Ingredients:
- 2 tablespoon coconut oil
- 1 bulb garlic, minced
- 1 large artichoke heart, cleaned sliced
- 2 medium zucchinis, sliced
- ½ cup vegetable broth
- Salt and pepper as needed

Directions:
1. Set your Ninja Foodi to Saute mode and add oil, allow the oil the heat up
2. Add garlic and Saute until nicely fragrant. Add rest of the and stir
3. Lock lid and cook on HIGH pressure for 10 minutes. Quick release, serve and enjoy!

Green Lasagna Soup

Servings: 4
Cooking Time: 30 Min
Ingredients:
- ½ pound broccoli; chopped /225g
- 3 lasagna noodles
- 1 carrot; chopped
- 2 garlic cloves minced
- 1 cup tomato paste /250ml
- 1 cup tomatoes; chopped /130g
- ¼ cup dried green lentils /32.5g
- 2 cups vegetable broth /500ml
- 1 cup leeks; chopped /130g
- 1 tsp olive oil /5ml
- 2 tsp Italian seasoning /10g
- salt to taste

Directions:
1. Warm oil on Sear/Sauté. Add garlic and leeks and cook for 2 minutes until soft; add tomato paste, carrot, Italian seasoning, broccoli, tomatoes, lentils, and salt. Stir in vegetable broth and lasagna pieces.
2. Seal the pressure lid, choose Pressure, set to High, and set the timer to 3 minutes. Press Start.
3. Release pressure naturally for 10 minutes, then release the remaining pressure quickly. Divide soup into serving bowls and serve.

Minestrone With Pancetta

Servings: 6
Cooking Time: 40 Min
Ingredients:
- 2 ounces pancetta; chopped /60g
- 1 can diced tomatoes/450g
- 1 can chickpeas, rinsed and drained /450g
- 1 onion; diced
- 1 parsnip, peeled and chopped
- 2 carrots, peeled and sliced into rounds
- 2 celery stalks,
- 2 garlic cloves, minced
- 6 cups chicken broth /1500ml
- ½ cup grated Parmesan cheese/65g
- 2 cups green beans, trimmed and chopped /260g
- 1½ cups small shaped pasta /195g
- 1 tbsp dried basil/ 15g
- 1 tbsp dried oregano/15g
- 2 tbsp olive oil /30ml
- 1 tbsp dried thyme /15g
- salt and ground black pepper to taste

Directions:
1. Warm oil on Sear/Sauté. Add onion, carrots, garlic, pancetta, celery, and parsnip, and cook for 5 minutes until they become soft.
2. Stir in basil, oregano, green beans, broth, tomatoes, pepper, salt, thyme, vegetable broth, chickpeas, and pasta.
3. Seal the pressure lid, choose Pressure, set to High, and set the timer to 6 minutes. Press Start.
4. Release pressure naturally for 10 minutes then release the remaining pressure quickly. Ladle the soup into bowls and serve garnished with grated parmesan cheese.

Italian Sausage With Garlic Mash

Servings: 6
Cooking Time: 30 Min
Ingredients:
- 6 Italian sausages
- 4 large potatoes, peeled and cut into 1½-inch chunks
- 2 garlic cloves, smashed
- ⅓ cup butter, melted /44ml
- ¼ cup milk; at room temperature, or more as needed /62.5ml
- 1 ½ cups water /375ml
- 1 tbsp olive oil /15ml
- 1 tbsp chopped chives/15g
- salt and ground black pepper to taste

Directions:
1. Select Sear/Sauté, set to Medium High, and choose Start/Stop to preheat the pot and heat olive oil. Cook for 8-10 minutes, turning periodically until browned. Set aside. Wipe the pot with paper towels. Add in water and set the reversible rack over water. Place potatoes onto the reversible rack.
2. Seal the pressure lid, choose Pressure, set to High, and set the timer to 12 minutes. Press Start.
3. When ready, release the pressure quickly. Remove reversible rack from the pot. Drain water from the pot. Return potatoes to pot. Add in salt, butter, pepper, garlic, and milk and use a hand masher to mash until no large lumps remain.
4. Using an immersion blender, blend potatoes on Low for 1 minute until fluffy and light. Avoid over-blending to ensure the potatoes do not become gluey!
5. Transfer the mash to a serving plate, top with sausages and scatter chopped chives over to serve.

Pineapple Appetizer Ribs

Servings: 4
Cooking Time: 30 Min
Ingredients:
- 2 lb. cut spareribs /900g
- 2 cups water /500ml
- 5 oz. canned pineapple juice /150ml
- 7 oz. salad dressing /210g
- Garlic salt
- Salt and black pepper

Directions:
1. Sprinkle the ribs with salt and pepper and place them in a saucepan. Pour water and cook the ribs for around 12 minutes on high heat. Drain the ribs and arrange them in the Ninja Foodi.
2. Sprinkle with garlic salt. Close the crisping lid and cook for 15 minutes at 390 °F or 200°C on Air Crisp mode.
3. Meanwhile, prepare the sauce by combining the salad dressing and the pineapple juice. Serve the ribs with this delicious dressing sauce!

Ninja Foodi Cookbook

Soups & Stews

Creamy Italian Sausage, Potato, And Kale Soup

Servings: 8
Cooking Time: 18 Minutes
Ingredients:
- 1½ pounds (680 g) hot Italian sausage, ground
- 1 pound (455 g) sweet Italian sausage, ground
- 4 large Russet potatoes, cut in ½-inch thick quarters
- 6 cups kale, chopped
- 1 large yellow onion, diced
- 5 cups chicken stock
- 1 tbsp. extra-virgin olive oil
- 2 tbsps. minced garlic
- 2 tbsps. Italian seasoning
- 2 tsps. crushed red pepper flakes
- Freshly ground black pepper
- ½ cup heavy (whipping) cream
- Salt

Directions:
1. Select the Saute mode to preheat for 5 minutes.
2. Put the olive oil and hot and sweet Italian sausage in the pot. Cook 5 minutes, breaking up the sausage with a spatula.
3. Combine onion, garlic, potatoes, chicken stock, Italian seasoning, and crushed red pepper flakes, salt and pepper in the pot, mix well. Assemble pressure lid, set the steamer valve to Seal.
4. Select Pressure, set the time 10 minutes.
5. After cooking is complete, move pressure release valve to VENT position to quickly release the pressure. Carefully remove lid.
6. Add kale and heavy cream. Stir and serve warm.

Creamy Pumpkin And Squash Bisque With Apple

Servings: 4 To 5
Cooking Time: 25 Minutes
Ingredients:
- 2 tbsps. (30 ml) avocado oil or extra-virgin olive oil
- 1 (3- to 4-lb [1.4- to 1.8-kg]) butternut squash
- 1 (2- to 3-lb [1- to 1.4-kg]) pie pumpkin
- 1 large apple
- 1 medium white onion, diced
- 2 cloves garlic, minced
- 3 to 4 cups (710 to 946 ml) vegetable or chicken stock
- 2 tbsps. (30 ml) cider vinegar
- 2 tsps. (3 g) dried basil
- 2 tsps. (2 g) dried sage
- 1 tsp. salt, plus more to taste
- ½ cup (120 ml) coconut milk, coconut cream, or light or heavy dairy cream
- ½ cup (70 g) pumpkin seeds, for garnish
- 2 tbsps. (3 g) fresh rosemary or thyme

Directions:
1. Prepare your butternut squash, peel the skin off, cut in half vertically and remove the seeds, then cut into 1-inch chunks. Cut the pumpkin in half and remove the seeds, then carve out the inside flesh of the pumpkin. Cut the pumpkin into 1-inch chunks.
2. Select sauté on the Ninja pressure cooker, when hot, use the oil to coat the bottom. Add the onion and cook for 2 to 3 minutes, then add the garlic and cook for 1 to 2 minutes.
3. Place the squash, pumpkin and apple into the pot. Cover with 3 cups of the stock and the vinegar, basil, sage and salt.
4. Secure the lid with the steam vent in the sealed position. Select Pressure, and cook for 14 minutes.
5. Use a natural release for 15 minutes, then release the remaining steam before opening the lid.
6. Stir in the coconut milk, and use an immersion blender to blend your soup or blend in batches in a regular blender. Add an additional ½ to 1 cup of stock if needed.
7. Garnish with pumpkin seeds and fresh herbs.

Delicious Hungarian Goulash Soup

Servings: 6
Cooking Time: 55 Minutes
Ingredients:
- 1½ pounds (680 g) small Yukon Gold potatoes, halved
- 2 pounds (907 g) beef stew meat
- ½ cup all-purpose flour
- 2 cups beef broth
- ½ tsp. freshly ground black pepper
- 1 medium red bell pepper, seeded and chopped
- 4 garlic cloves, minced
- 1 large yellow onion, diced
- 2 tbsps. canola oil
- 2 tbsps. smoked paprika
- 2 tbsps. tomato paste
- ¼ cup sour cream
- 1 tbsp. kosher salt
- Fresh parsley for garnish

Directions:
1. Select Saute mode. Preheat for 5 minutes.
2. In a small bowl, combine the flour, salt, and pepper. Dip the beef pieces into the flour mixture and shake off the excess flour.
3. Add oil, beef to pot, cook 10 minutes, until all sides browned.
4. Add bell pepper, garlic, onion, and smoked paprika. Sauté until the onion is translucent.
5. Add the potatoes, beef broth, and tomato paste and stir. Assemble pressure lid, set the steamer valve to Seal.
6. Select Pressure, set the time 30 minutes. Press START to begin.
7. After cooking is complete, move pressure release valve to VENT position to quickly release the pressure. Carefully remove lid.
8. Stir with sour cream. Add parsley for decoration, if desired. Serve warm.

Pho Tom

Servings: 6
Cooking Time: 36 Minutes
Ingredients:
- 2 tablespoons canola oil
- 1 onion, peeled and halved
- 1 piece fresh ginger, peeled
- 2 tablespoons brown sugar
- 2 tablespoons kosher salt
- 1½ tablespoons Chinese five-spice powder
- ¼ cup fish sauce
- 4 cups beef bone broth
- 8 cups water
- 1 package rice noodles, cooked according to the package directions
- 1 pound peeled cooked shrimp
- Bean sprouts, for topping (optional)
- Lime wedges, for serving (optional)
- Fresh basil, for topping (optional)
- Sriracha, for topping (optional)

Directions:
1. Select SEAR/SAUTÉ and set temperature to HI. Select START/STOP to begin. Allow to preheat for 5 minutes.
2. Add oil to the pot and allow to heat for 1 minute. Add the onion and ginger and sear on all sides, about 6 minutes. Select START/STOP to end the function.
3. Add the sugar, salt, five-spice powder, fish sauce, bone broth, and water. Stir for 1 minute to combine.
4. Assemble the pressure lid, making sure the pressure release valve is in the SEAL position.
5. Select PRESSURE and set to HI. Set the time to 30 minutes. Select START/STOP to begin.
6. When pressure cooking is complete, quick release the pressure by turning the pressure release valve to the VENT position. Carefully remove the lid when the unit has finished releasing pressure.
7. Add the desired amount of noodles to a bowl and top with 5 or 6 shrimp and some sliced onion. Ladle the pho broth to cover the noodles, shrimp, and onion. Top as desired.

Nutrition:
- InfoCalories: 242, Total Fat: 7g, Sodium: 2419mg, Carbohydrates: 25g, Protein: 22g.

Garlicy Roasted Cauliflower And Potato Soup

Servings: 6
Cooking Time: 30 Minutes
Ingredients:
- 8 garlic cloves, peeled
- 1 large cauliflower head, cut into small florets
- 2 russet potatoes, peeled and chopped into 1-inch pieces
- 1 yellow onion, coarsely chopped
- 1 celery stalk, coarsely chopped
- 1 tablespoon water, plus more as needed
- 6 cups no-sodium vegetable broth
- 2 thyme sprigs
- 2 teaspoons paprika
- ¼ teaspoon freshly ground black pepper
- 1 tablespoon chopped fresh rosemary leaves

Directions:
1. Use parchment paper to line the inner pot.
2. Use the aluminum foil to wrap the garlic cloves or place in a garlic roaster.
3. In Ninja Foodi, evenly spread with the potatoes and cauliflower. Place the wrapped garlic on the inner pot.
4. Press Roast and cook at 450°F (230°C) for 15 to 20 minutes, or until the cauliflower is lightly browned.
5. Combine the onion and celery in Ninja Foodi, press Sear/Sauté and cook at 390°F(200°C) for 4 to 5 minutes, adding water, 1 tablespoon at a time, to prevent burning, until the onion starts to brown.
6. Pour in the vegetable broth and bring the soup to a simmer.
7. Add the roasted vegetables and thyme, garlic, paprika, and pepper. Bring the soup to a simmer, cover pressure lid and press Pressure and cook at 390°F(200°C) . for 10 minutes.
8. Remove and discard the thyme. Puree the soup with an immersion blender until smooth. Add some water if the soup is too thick, to the desired consistency.
9. Stir in the rosemary and serve.

Vegetable And Lamb Stew

Servings: 6
Cooking Time: 33 Minutes
Ingredients:
- 2 pounds (907 g) boneless lean lamb shoulder, cut into cubes
- ¼ teaspoon salt
- ¼ teaspoon ground black pepper
- 2 tablespoons olive oil
- 1 large onion, peeled and chopped
- 1 clove garlic, minced
- ¼ cup (63 mL) dry white wine
- 4 cups (1 L) chicken stock
- 1 bay leaf
- 1 teaspoon dried thyme
- 2 pounds (907 g) small red potatoes, scrubbed and quartered
- 16 ounces (454 g) sliced button mushrooms
- 8 ounces (227 g) baby-cut carrots
- 8 ounces (227 g) frozen peas, thawed

Directions:
1. In a bowl, season the lamb shoulder with salt and pepper. Cover in plastic and set in a refrigerator for 15 minutes.
2. Press the Sauté button and heat the oil. Arrange half the lamb in an even layer in the pot, making sure there is space between pieces to prevent steam from forming. Sear the lamb for 3 minutes on each side, or until lightly browned. Transfer the lamb to a plate. Repeat with the remaining lamb.
3. Add the onion and garlic to the pot and cook for 1 minute. Pour in the wine and scrape any bits from bottom of the pot. Stir in the lamb along with the remaining ingredients, except for the peas.
4. Assemble pressure lid, making sure the pressure release valve is in the Seal position. Select Pressure and set to high . Set time to 20 minutes. Press Start to begin. When the timer goes off, do a natural pressure release for 20 minutes, then release any remaining pressure. Open the lid.
5. Remove and discard the bay leaf. Whisk in the peas and let it sit in the residual heat for 10 minutes. Serve warm.

Coconut Shrimp And Pea Bisque

Servings: 4
Cooking Time: 15 Minutes
Ingredients:
- ¼ cup red curry paste
- 2 tablespoons water
- 1 tablespoon extra-virgin olive oil
- 1 bunch scallions, sliced
- 1 pound (454 g) medium (21-30 count) shrimp, peeled and deveined
- 1 cup frozen peas
- 1 red bell pepper, diced
- 1 (14-ounce / 397-g) can full-fat coconut milk
- Kosher salt

Directions:
1. In a small bowl, whisk together the red curry paste and water. Set aside.
2. Select SEAR/SAUTÉ and set to MED. Select START/STOP to begin. Let preheat for 3 minutes.
3. Add the oil and scallions. Cook for 2 minutes.
4. Add the shrimp, peas, and bell pepper. Stir well to combine. Stir in the red curry paste. Cook for 5 minutes, until the peas are tender.
5. Stir in coconut milk and cook for an additional 5 minutes until shrimp is cooked through and the bisque is thoroughly heated.
6. Season with salt and serve immediately.

English Pub Split Pea Soup

Servings: 8
Cooking Time: 15 Minutes
Ingredients:
- 1 meaty ham bone
- 4 cups (1 L) water
- 1 (12-ounce / 340-g) bottle light beer
- 1⅓ cups dried green split peas, rinsed
- 2 celery ribs, chopped
- 1 large carrot, chopped
- 1 sweet onion, chopped
- 1 tablespoon prepared English mustard
- ½ cup (125 mL) 2% milk
- ¼ cup (63 mL) minced fresh parsley
- ½ teaspoon salt
- ¼ teaspoon pepper
- ¼ teaspoon ground nutmeg

Directions:
1. Place ham bone in cooking pot. Add water, beer, peas, celery, carrot, onion and mustard. Assemble pressure lid, making sure the pressure release valve is in the Seal position. Select Pressure and set to high. Set time to 15 minutes. Press Start. When pressure cooking is complete, allow pressure to natural release.
2. Remove bone from soup. Cool slightly, trim away fat and remove meat from bone; discard fat and bone. Cut meat into bite-sized pieces; return to pressure cooker. Stir in remaining ingredients. If desired, top with additional minced parsley.

Spanish Chorizo And Lentil Soup

Servings: 6 To 8
Cooking Time: 30 Minutes
Ingredients:
- 8 ounces (227 g) Spanish-style chorizo sausage, quartered lengthwise and sliced thin
- 1 large onion, peeled
- 1 tbsp. extra-virgin olive oil, plus extra for drizzling
- 2 carrots, peeled and halved crosswise
- 4 garlic cloves, minced
- 1½ tsp. smoked paprika
- 5 cups (1200 ml) water
- 1 pound (2¼ cups, 455 g) French green lentils, picked over and rinsed
- 4 cups (960 ml) chicken broth
- 1 tbsp. sherry vinegar, plus extra for seasoning
- 2 bay leaves
- 1 tsp. table salt
- ½ cup slivered almonds, toasted
- ½ cup minced fresh parsley
- salt and pepper to taste

Directions:
1. In Ninja pressure cooker, select sauté function, heat oil until shimmering. Add chorizo and cook 3 to 5 minutes until lightly browned. Stir in garlic and paprika and cook about 30 seconds until fragrant. Add water, scraping up any browned bits, then stir in lentils, bay leaves, vinegar, broth, and salt. Nestle carrots and onion into pot.
2. Lock lid and close pressure release valve. Choose pressure function and cook for 14 minutes. Turn off and quick-release pressure. Carefully remove lid, letting steam escape away from you.
3. Throw away bay leaves. Transfer onion and carrots to food processor with a slotted spoon and process about 1 minute until smooth, scraping down sides of bowl if you like. Stir vegetable mixture into lentils and season with pepper, salt, and extra vinegar. Drizzle each portion with extra oil, sprinkle with almonds and parsley and serve.

Italian Sausage Soup

Servings: 8
Cooking Time: 18 Minutes
Ingredients:
- 1 tablespoon extra-virgin olive oil
- 1½ pounds (680 g) hot Italian sausage, ground
- 1 pound (454 g) sweet Italian sausage, ground
- 1 large yellow onion, diced
- 2 tablespoons minced garlic
- 4 large Russet potatoes, cut in ½-inch thick quarters
- 5 cups chicken stock
- 2 tablespoons Italian seasoning
- 2 teaspoons crushed red pepper flakes
- Salt
- Freshly ground black pepper
- 6 cups kale, chopped
- ½ cup heavy (whipping) cream

Directions:

1. Select SEAR/SAUTÉ. Set temperature to MD:HI. Select START/STOP to begin. Let preheat for 5 minutes.
2. Add the olive oil and hot and sweet Italian sausage. Cook, breaking up the sausage with a spatula, until the meat is cooked all the way through, about 5 minutes.
3. Add the onion, garlic, potatoes, chicken stock, Italian seasoning, and crushed red pepper flakes. Season with salt and pepper. Stir to combine. Assemble pressure lid, making sure the pressure release valve is in the SEAL position.
4. Select PRESSURE and set to HI. Set time to 10 minutes. Select START/STOP to begin.
5. When pressure cooking is complete, quick release the pressure by turning the pressure release valve to the VENT position. Carefully remove lid when the unit has finished releasing pressure.
6. Stir in the kale and heavy cream. Serve.

Haddock And Biscuit Chowder

Servings: 8
Cooking Time: 30 Minutes
Ingredients:
- 5 strips bacon, sliced
- 1 white onion, chopped
- 3 celery stalks, chopped
- 4 cups chicken stock
- 2 Russet potatoes, rinsed and cut in 1-inch pieces
- 4 (6-ounce / 170-g) frozen haddock fillets
- Kosher salt
- ½ cup clam juice
- ⅓ cup all-purpose flour
- 2 (14-ounce / 397-g) cans evaporated milk
- 1 (14-ounce / 397-g) tube refrigerated biscuit dough

Directions:
1. Select SEAR/SAUTÉ and set to HI. Select START/STOP to begin. Let preheat for 5 minutes.
2. Add the bacon and cook, stirring frequently, for 5 minutes. Add the onion and celery and cook for an additional 5 minutes, stirring occasionally.
3. Add the chicken stock, potatoes, and haddock filets. Season with salt. Assemble pressure lid, making sure the pressure release valve is in the SEAL position.
4. Select PRESSURE and set to HI. Set time to 5 minutes. Select START/STOP to begin.
5. Whisk together the clam juice and flour in a small bowl, ensuring there are no flour clumps in the mixture.
6. When pressure cooking is complete, quick release the pressure by moving the pressure release valve to the VENT position. Carefully remove lid when unit has finished releasing pressure.
7. Select SEAR/SAUTÉ and set to MED. Select START/STOP to begin. Add the clam juice mixture, stirring well to combine. Add the evaporated milk and continue to stir frequently for 3 to 5 minutes, until chowder has thickened to your desired texture.
8. Place the Reversible Rack in the pot in the higher position. Place the biscuits on the rack; it may be necessary to tear the last biscuit or two into smaller pieces in order to fit them all on the rack. Close crisping lid.
9. Select BAKE/ROAST, set temperature to 350°F(175°C), and set time to 12 minutes. Select START/STOP to begin.
10. After 10 minutes, check the biscuits for doneness. If desired, cook for up to an additional 2 minutes.
11. When cooking is complete, open lid and remove rack from pot. Serve the chowder and top each portion with biscuits.

Beef And Pork Chili

Servings: 4
Cooking Time: 40 Minutes
Ingredients:
- 1 tablespoon olive oil
- ½ pound (227 g) ground beef
- ½ pound (227 g) ground pork
- 1 medium onion, peeled and diced
- 1 (28-ounce / 794-g) can puréed tomatoes, undrained
- 1 large carrot, peeled and diced
- 1 small green bell pepper, deseeded and diced
- 1 small jalapeño, deseeded and diced
- 3 cloves garlic, minced
- 2 tablespoons chili powder
- 1 teaspoon sea salt
- 2 teaspoons ground black pepper

Directions:
1. Press the Sauté button and heat the olive oil. Add the ground beef, ground pork and onion to the pot and sauté for 5 minutes, or until the pork is no longer pink.
2. Stir in the remaining ingredients.
3. Assemble pressure lid, making sure the pressure release valve is in the Seal position. Select Pressure and set to high. Set time to 35 minutes. Press Start to begin. Once cooking is complete, use a natural pressure release for 15 minutes, then release any remaining pressure. Open the lid.
4. Serve warm.

Butternut Squash And Orzo Soup

Servings: 8
Cooking Time: 28 Minutes
Ingredients:
- 4 slices uncooked bacon, cut into ½-inch pieces
- 12 ounces (340 g) butternut squash, peeled and cubed
- 1 green apple, cut into small cubes
- Kosher salt
- Freshly ground black pepper
- 1 tablespoon minced fresh oregano
- 2 quarts (1.8 kg) chicken stock
- 1 cup orzo

Directions:
1. Select SEAR/SAUTÉ and set temperature to HI. Select START/STOP to begin. Let preheat for 5 minutes.
2. Place the bacon in the pot and cook, stirring frequently, about 5 minutes, or until fat is rendered and the bacon starts to brown. Using a slotted spoon, transfer the bacon to a paper towel-lined plate to drain, leaving the rendered bacon fat in the pot.
3. Add the butternut squash, apple, salt, and pepper and sauté until partially soft, about 5 minutes. Stir in the oregano.
4. Add the bacon back into the pot along with the chicken stock. Bring to a boil for about 10 minutes, then add the orzo. Cook for about 8 minutes, until the orzo is tender. Serve.

Chicken And Black Bean Enchilada Soup

Servings: 8
Cooking Time: 30 Minutes
Ingredients:
- 1 tablespoon extra-virgin olive oil
- 1 small red onion, diced
- 2 (10-ounce / 283-g) cans fire-roasted tomatoes with chiles
- 1 (15-ounce / 425-g) can corn
- 1 (15-ounce / 425-g) can black beans, rinsed and drained
- 1 (10-ounce / 283-g) can red enchilada sauce
- 1 (10-ounce / 283-g) can tomato paste
- 3 tablespoons taco seasoning
- 2 tablespoons freshly squeezed lime juice
- 2 (8-ounce / 227-g) boneless, skinless chicken breasts
- Salt
- Freshly ground black pepper

Directions:
1. Select SEAR/SAUTÉ and set temperature to MD:HI. Select START/STOP to begin. Let preheat for 5 minutes.
2. Place the olive oil and onion in the pot. Cook until the onions are translucent, about 2 minutes.
3. Add the tomatoes, corn, beans, enchilada sauce, tomato paste, taco seasoning, lime juice, and chicken. Season with salt and pepper and stir. Assemble pressure lid, making sure the pressure release valve is in the SEAL position.
4. Select PRESSURE and set to HI. Set time to 9 minutes. Select START/STOP to begin.
5. When pressure cooking is complete, allow pressure to naturally release for 10 minutes. After 10 minutes, quick release remaining pressure by moving the pressure release valve to the VENT position. Carefully remove lid when unit has finished releasing pressure.
6. Transfer the chicken breasts to a cutting board. Using two forks, shred the chicken. Return the chicken back to the pot and stir. Serve in a bowl with toppings of choice, such as shredded cheese, crushed tortilla chips, sliced avocado, sour cream, cilantro, and lime wedges, if desired.

Lasagna Soup

Servings: 8
Cooking Time: 16 Minutes
Ingredients:
- 1 tablespoon extra-virgin olive oil
- 16 ounces Italian sausage
- 1 small onion, diced
- 4 garlic cloves, minced
- 1 jar marinara sauce
- 2 cups water
- 1 cup vegetable broth
- 1 teaspoon dried basil
- 1 teaspoon dried oregano
- ½ teaspoon dried thyme
- Freshly ground black pepper
- 8 ounces lasagna noodles, broken up
- 1 cup ricotta cheese
- ½ cup grated Parmesan cheese
- 1 teaspoon dried parsley
- ½ cup heavy (whipping) cream
- 1 cup shredded mozzarella cheese

Directions:
1. Select SEAR/SAUTÉ and set to HI. Select START/STOP to begin. Let preheat for 5 minutes.
2. Add the oil and sausage and cook for about 5 minutes. Using a wooden spoon, break apart the sausage and stir.
3. Add the onions and cook, stirring occasionally, for 3 minutes. Add the garlic and cook for 2 minutes, or until the meat is no longer pink.
4. Add the marinara sauce, water, vegetable broth, basil, oregano, thyme, pepper, and lasagna noodles. Assemble pressure lid, making sure the pressure release valve is in the SEAL position.
5. Select PRESSURE and set to HI. Set time to 6 minutes. Select START/STOP to begin.
6. In a medium bowl, combine the ricotta cheese, Parmesan cheese, and parsley. Cover and refrigerate.
7. When pressure cooking is complete, quick release the pressure by turning the pressure release valve to the VENT position. Carefully remove lid when unit has finished releasing pressure.
8. Stir in the heavy cream. Add the cheese mixture and stir. Top the soup with the mozzarella. Close crisping lid.
9. Select BROIL and set time to 5 minutes. Select START/STOP to begin.
10. When cooking is complete, serve immediately.

Nutrition:
- InfoCalories: 398, Total Fat: 22g, Sodium: 892mg, Carbohydrates: 29g, Protein: 23g.

Chicken Potpie Soup

Servings: 6
Cooking Time: 1 Hour
Ingredients:
- 4 chicken breasts
- 2 cups chicken stock
- 2 tablespoons unsalted butter
- 1 yellow onion, diced
- 16 ounces frozen mixed vegetables
- 1 cup heavy (whipping) cream
- 1 can condensed cream of chicken soup
- 2 tablespoons cornstarch
- 2 tablespoons water
- Salt
- Freshly ground black pepper
- 1 tube refrigerated biscuit dough

Directions:
1. Place the chicken and stock in the pot. Assemble pressure lid, making sure the pressure release valve is in the SEAL position.
2. Select PRESSURE and set to HI. Set time to 15 minutes. Select START/STOP to begin.
3. Once pressure cooking is complete, quick release the pressure by turning the pressure release valve to the VENT position. Carefully remove lid when the unit has finished releasing pressure.
4. Using a silicone-tipped utensil, shred the chicken.

5. Select SEAR/SAUTÉ and set to MED. Add the butter, onion, mixed vegetables, cream, and condensed soup and stir. Select START/STOP to begin. Simmer for 10 minutes.
6. In a small bowl, whisk together the cornstarch and water. Slowly whisk the cornstarch mixture into the soup. Set temperature to LO and simmer for 10 minutes more. Season with salt and pepper.
7. Carefully arrange the biscuits on top of the simmering soup. Close crisping lid.
8. Select BAKE/ROAST, set temperature to 325°F (160°C), and set time to 15 minutes. Select START/STOP to begin.
9. When cooking is complete, remove the biscuits. To serve, place a biscuit in a bowl and ladle soup over it.

Nutrition:
- InfoCalories: 731,Total Fat: 26g,Sodium: 1167mg,Carbohydrates: 56g,Protein: 45g.

Roasted Red Pepper And Caramelized Onion Soup With Grilled Cheese

Servings: 4
Cooking Time: 25 Minutes
Ingredients:
- ⅔ cup dry or medium-dry sherry
- 3 large roasted red peppers (about 16 ounces jarred peppers, 455 g), cut into chunks, blotted dry if using jarred
- 1 recipe Caramelized Onions
- 2 cups Roasted Vegetable Stock or low-sodium vegetable broth
- 8 Italian or French bread slices
- 8 ounces (227 g) grated aged Cheddar or Gouda cheese
- 4 tbsps. (½ stick) unsalted butter, at room temperature
- ¼ cup heavy (whipping) cream

Directions:
1. On your Foodi, preheat the inner pot by selecting Sear/Sauté. Press Start. Preheat for 5 minutes. Add the sherry the roasted peppers and caramelized onions. Bring to a boil. Cook until the sherry has mostly evaporated, about 5 minutes. Pour in the vegetable stock.
2. Lock the Pressure Lid into place, set the valve to Seal. Select Pressure, adjust the cook time to 6 minutes. Press Start.
3. Meanwhile, on a cutting board, lay out 4 slices of bread and evenly divide the cheese among them. Place the remaining bread slices on the top. Butter one side of each sandwich, then carefully turn them over and butter the other side.
4. When the soup is complete cooking, quick release the pressure. Open and remove the Pressure Lid carefully. Add the cream and stir well.
5. Transfer the sandwiches to the Reversible Rack, and then in the pot.
6. Close the Crisping Lid and select Bake/Roast, adjust the temperature to 390°F (200°C) and the cook time to 6 minutes. Press Start. After 3 minutes, open the lid and check the sandwiches. The tops should be golden brown and crisp. If not, continue to cook for another minute. When the tops are browned, flip the sandwiches. Close the lid and continue cooking until the other side is browned. Remove the rack.
7. Ladle into bowls with the soup and serve with the sandwiches.

Curry Acorn Squash Soup

Servings: 6
Cooking Time: About 1 Hour
Ingredients:
- 1 acorn squash
- 2 garlic cloves, chopped
- 1 yellow onion, chopped
- 2 celery stalks, coarsely chopped
- 1 tbsp. water, plus more as needed
- 2 tbsps. whole wheat flour
- 2 cups no-sodium vegetable broth
- ½ tsp. dill
- 1 tsp. curry powder, plus more for seasoning
- ⅛ tsp. cayenne pepper
- 1 (14-ounce, 397 g) can full-fat coconut milk
- Chopped scallions, green parts only, for serving

Directions:
1. Cut the acorn squash in half lengthwise and scoop out the seeds and stringy center. Put the squash halves in the Ninja Foodi, cut-side down, and add enough water to come up about 1 inch all around.
2. Press Bake and cook at 350°F (175°C) for 30 to 45 minutes, or until the squash can be easily pierced with a fork. Take the squash out from the inner pot and allow to cool for 10 minutes. Scoop out the soft flesh and set aside in a bowl.
3. Combine the garlic, onion, and celery in the Ninja Foodi, press Sear/Sauté on HIGH for 2 to 3 minutes, add the water, 1 tablespoon at a time, to prevent burning, until the onion is translucent but not browned.
4. Sprinkle over with the flour and stir to coat the vegetables.
5. Add the roasted squash, vegetable broth, dill, curry powder and cayenne pepper. Bring the mixture to a boil. Adjust to LOW, cover and cook for 10 minutes.
6. Pour in the coconut milk. Blend the soup until smooth with an immersion blender. Serve immediately or place in an airtight container and refrigerate for up to 1 week.
7. Place the scallions and a sprinkle of curry powder on the top and serve.

Italian Sausage, Potato, And Kale Soup

Servings: 8
Cooking Time: 18 Minutes
Ingredients:
- 1 tablespoon extra-virgin olive oil
- 1½ pounds hot Italian sausage, ground
- 1 pound sweet Italian sausage, ground
- 1 large yellow onion, diced
- 2 tablespoons minced garlic
- 4 large Russet potatoes, cut in ½-inch thick quarters
- 5 cups chicken stock
- 2 tablespoons Italian seasoning
- 2 teaspoons crushed red pepper flakes
- Salt
- Freshly ground black pepper
- 6 cups kale, chopped

- ½ cup heavy (whipping) cream

Directions:
1. Select SEAR/SAUTÉ. Set temperature to MD:HI. Select START/STOP to begin. Let preheat for 5 minutes.
2. Add the olive oil and hot and sweet Italian sausage. Cook, breaking up the sausage with a spatula, until the meat is cooked all the way through, about 5 minutes.
3. Add the onion, garlic, potatoes, chicken stock, Italian seasoning, and crushed red pepper flakes. Season with salt and pepper. Stir to combine. Assemble pressure lid, making sure the pressure release valve is in the SEAL position.
4. Select PRESSURE and set to HI. Set time to 10 minutes. Select START/STOP to begin.
5. When pressure cooking is complete, quick release the pressure by turning the pressure release valve to the VENT position. Carefully remove lid when the unit has finished releasing pressure.
6. Stir in the kale and heavy cream. Serve.

Nutrition:
- InfoCalories: 689,Total Fat: 45g,Sodium: 1185mg,Carbohydrates: 38g,Protein: 33g.

Whole Farro And Leek Soup

Servings: 6 To 8
Cooking Time: 30 Minutes

Ingredients:
- 1 cup whole farro
- 1 tbsp. extra-virgin olive oil, plus extra for drizzling
- 3 ounces (85 g) pancetta, chopped fine
- 1 pound (455 g) leeks, ends trimmed, chopped, and washed thoroughly
- 1 celery rib, chopped
- 2 carrots, peeled and chopped
- ½ cup minced fresh parsley
- 8 cups (1920 ml) chicken broth, plus extra as needed
- salt and pepper to taste
- Grated Parmesan cheese

Directions:
1. Pulse farro in blender for about 6 pulses until about half of grains are broken into smaller pieces, set aside.
2. In Ninja pressure cooker, select sauté function, heat oil until shimmering. Add pancetta and cook 3 to 5 minutes until lightly browned. Stir in carrots, leeks, and celery and cook about 5 minutes until softened. Add broth, scraping up any browned bits, then stir in farro.
3. Lock lid and close pressure release valve. Choose pressure function and cook for 8 minutes. Turn off and quick-release pressure. Carefully remove lid, letting steam escape away from you.
4. Adjust consistency with extra hot broth if you like. Stir in parsley and season with salt and pepper. Drizzle each portion with extra oil and top with Parmesan. Serve.

Coconut And Shrimp Bisque

Servings:4
Cooking Time: 15 Minutes

Ingredients:
- ¼ cup red curry paste
- 2 tablespoons water
- 1 tablespoon extra-virgin olive oil
- 1 bunch scallions, sliced
- 1 pound medium shrimp, peeled and deveined
- 1 cup frozen peas
- 1 red bell pepper, diced
- 1 can full-fat coconut milk
- Kosher salt

Directions:
1. In a small bowl, whisk together the red curry paste and water. Set aside.
2. Select SEAR/SAUTÉ and set to MED. Select START/STOP to begin. Let preheat for 3 minutes.
3. Add the oil and scallions. Cook for 2 minutes.
4. Add the shrimp, peas, and bell pepper. Stir well to combine. Stir in the red curry paste. Cook for 5 minutes, until the peas are tender.
5. Stir in coconut milk and cook for an additional 5 minutes until shrimp is cooked through and the bisque is thoroughly heated.
6. Season with salt and serve immediately.

Nutrition:
- InfoCalories: 460,Total Fat: 32g,Sodium: 902mg,Carbohydrates: 16g,Protein: 29g.

Tomatillo Chicken Thigh Stew

Servings:4
Cooking Time: 46 Minutes

Ingredients:
- 3 medium onions, quartered
- 3 garlic cloves, whole
- 2 poblano peppers, seeded and quartered
- ½ pound (227 g) tomatillos
- 2 small jalapeño peppers, seeded and quartered (optional)
- 2 tablespoons canola oil, divided
- Kosher salt
- Freshly ground black pepper
- 2½ pounds (1.1 kg) boneless, skinless chicken thighs (6 to 8 pieces)
- 1 cup chicken stock
- 1 teaspoon cumin
- 1 tablespoon oregano
- 1 tablespoon all-purpose flour
- 1 cup water

Directions:
1. Place Cook & Crisp Basket in pot and close crisping lid. Select AIR CRISP and set to HIGH. Set time to 25 minutes. Select START/STOP to begin. Let preheat for 5 minutes.
2. Place the onions, garlic, poblano peppers, tomatillos, jalapeños, 1 tablespoon of canola oil, salt, and pepper in a medium-sized bowl and mix until vegetables are evenly coated.
3. Once unit has preheated, open lid and place the vegetables in the basket. Close lid and cook for 20 minutes.
4. After 10 minutes, open lid, then lift basket and shake the vegetables or toss them with silicone-tipped tongs. Lower basket back into pot and close lid to continue cooking.
5. When cooking is complete, remove basket and vegetables and set aside.
6. Select SEAR/SAUTÉ and set to HI. Select START/STOP to begin. Let preheat for 5 minutes.

7. Season the chicken thighs with salt and pepper.
8. After 5 minutes, add the remaining 1 tablespoon of oil and chicken. Sear the chicken, about 3 minutes on each side.
9. Add the chicken stock, cumin, and oregano. Scrape the pot with a rubber or wooden spoon to release any pieces that are sticking to the bottom. Assemble pressure lid, making sure the pressure release valve is in the SEAL position.
10. Select PRESSURE and set to HI. Set time to 10 minutes. Select START/STOP to begin.
11. Remove the vegetables from the basket and roughly chop.
12. In a small bowl, add the flour and water and stir.
13. When pressure cooking is complete, quick release the pressure by turning the pressure release valve to the VENT position. Carefully remove lid when unit has finished releasing pressure.
14. Remove the chicken and shred it using two forks.
15. Select SEAR/SAUTÉ and set to MED. Select START/STOP to begin. Return the chicken and vegetables and stir with a rubber or wooden spoon, being sure to scrape the bottom of the pot. Slowly stir in the flour mixture. Bring to a simmer and cook for 10 minutes, or until the broth becomes clear and has thickened.
16. When cooking is complete, serve as is or garnish with sour cream, lime, cilantro, and a flour tortilla for dipping.

Roasted Tomato And Seafood Stew

Servings:6
Cooking Time: 46 Minutes
Ingredients:
- 2 tablespoons extra-virgin olive oil
- 1 yellow onion, diced
- 1 fennel bulb, tops removed and bulb diced
- 3 garlic cloves, minced
- 1 cup dry white wine
- 2 cans fire-roasted tomatoes
- 2 cups chicken stock
- 1 pound medium shrimp, peeled and deveined
- 1 pound raw white fish (cod or haddock), cubed
- Salt
- Freshly ground black pepper
- Fresh basil, torn, for garnish

Directions:
1. Select SEAR/SAUTÉ and set to MED. Select START/STOP to begin. Let preheat for 3 minutes.
2. Add the olive oil, onions, fennel, and garlic. Cook for about 3 minutes, until translucent.
3. Add the white wine and deglaze, scraping any stuck bits from the bottom of the pot using a silicone spatula. Add the roasted tomatoes and chicken stock. Simmer for 25 to 30 minutes. Add the shrimp and white fish.
4. Select SEAR/SAUTÉ and set to MD:LO. Select START/STOP to begin.
5. Simmer for 10 minutes, stirring frequently, until the shrimp and fish are cooked through. Season with salt and pepper.
6. Ladle into bowl and serve topped with torn basil.
Nutrition:
- InfoCalories: 301,Total Fat: 8g,Sodium: 808mg,Carbohydrates: 21g,Protein: 26g.

Tex-mex Chicken Tortilla Soup

Servings:8
Cooking Time: 20 Minutes
Ingredients:
- 1 tablespoon extra-virgin olive oil
- 1 onion, chopped
- 1 pound boneless, skinless chicken breasts
- 6 cups chicken broth
- 1 jar salsa
- 4 ounces tomato paste
- 1 tablespoon chili powder
- 2 teaspoons cumin
- ½ teaspoon sea salt
- ½ teaspoon freshly ground black pepper
- 1 pinch of cayenne pepper
- 1 can black beans, rinsed and drained
- 2 cups frozen corn
- Tortilla strips, for garnish

Directions:
1. Select SEAR/SAUTÉ and set to temperature to HI. Select START/STOP to begin. Let preheat for 5 minutes.
2. Place the olive oil and onions into the pot and cook, stirring occasionally, for 5 minutes.
3. Add the chicken breast, chicken broth, salsa, tomato paste, chili powder, cumin, salt, pepper, and cayenne pepper. Assemble pressure lid, making sure the pressure release valve is in the SEAL position.
4. Select PRESSURE and set to HI. Set time to 10 minutes. Select START/STOP to begin.
5. When pressure cooking is complete, allow pressure to naturally release for 10 minutes. After 10 minutes, quick release remaining pressure by moving the pressure release valve to the VENT position. Carefully remove lid when unit has finished releasing pressure.
6. Transfer the chicken breasts to a cutting board and shred with two forks. Set aside.
7. Add the black beans and corn. Select SEAR/SAUTÉ and set to MD. Select START/STOP to begin. Cook until heated through, about 5 minutes.
8. Add shredded chicken back to the pot. Garnish with tortilla strips, serve, and enjoy!
Nutrition:
- InfoCalories: 186,Total Fat: 4g,Sodium: 783mg,Carbohydrates: 23g,Protein: 19g.

Spicy Pork Stew With Black Benas And Tomatoes

Servings: 8
Cooking Time: 30 Minutes
Ingredients:
- 2 pounds (907 g) boneless pork shoulder, cut into 1-inch pieces
- 1 (10-ounce (283 g)) can diced tomatoes with chiles
- 1 (15-ounce (425 g)) can black beans, rinsed and drained
- 1 (15-ounce (425 g)) can hominy, rinsed and drained

- 4 cups chicken stock
- ¼ cup all-purpose flour
- ¼ cup unsalted butter
- ½ small onion, diced
- 1 carrot, diced
- 1 celery stalk, diced
- 2 garlic cloves, minced
- 1 tbsp. tomato paste
- 1 tbsp. cumin
- 1 tbsp. smoked paprika
- Freshly ground black pepper
- Sea salt

Directions:
1. Coat the pork pieces with the flour in a large bowl.
2. Select the Saute mode, to preheat for 5 minutes.
3. Add butter. Once melted, add pork and sear for 5 minutes until all sides browned.
4. Put the onion, carrot, celery, garlic, tomato paste, cumin, and paprika in the pot. Cook 3 minutes, stirring occasionally.
5. Add chicken stock and tomatoes. Assemble pressure lid, set the pressure release valve to Seal.
6. Select PRESSURE, set the time 15 minutes.
7. After cooking is complete, move pressure release valve to VENT position to quickly release the pressure. Carefully remove lid.
8. Select SEAR/SAUTÉ and HI PRESSURE. Select START/STOP to begin.
9. Add beans, hominy, salt, and pepper. Whisk well. Cook 2 minutes. Serve warm.

Loaded Potato Soup

Servings:6
Cooking Time: 30 Minutes
Ingredients:
- 5 slices bacon, chopped
- 1 onion, chopped
- 3 garlic cloves, minced
- 4 pounds Russet potatoes, peeled and chopped
- 4 cups chicken broth
- 1 cup whole milk
- ½ teaspoon sea salt
- ½ teaspoon freshly ground black pepper
- 1½ cups shredded Cheddar cheese
- Sour cream, for serving (optional)
- Chopped fresh chives, for serving (optional)

Directions:
1. Select SEAR/SAUTÉ and set to HI. Select START/STOP to begin. Let preheat for 5 minutes.
2. Add the bacon, onion, and garlic. Cook, stirring occasionally, for 5 minutes. Set aside some of the bacon for garnish.
3. Add the potatoes and chicken broth. Assemble pressure lid, making sure the pressure release valve is in the SEAL position.
4. Select PRESSURE and set to HI. Set time to 10 minutes, then select START/STOP to begin.
5. When pressure cooking is complete, quick release the pressure by moving the pressure release valve to the VENT position. Carefully remove lid when unit has finished releasing pressure.
6. Add the milk and mash the ingredients until the soup reaches your desired consistency. Season with the salt and black pepper. Sprinkle the cheese evenly over the top of the soup. Close crisping lid.
7. Select BROIL and set time to 5 minutes. Select START/STOP to begin.
8. When cooking is complete, top with the reserved crispy bacon and serve with sour cream and chives (if using).

Nutrition:
- InfoCalories: 468,Total Fat: 19g,Sodium: 1041mg,Carbohydrates: 53g,Protein: 23g.

Chicken Enchilada Soup

Servings:8
Cooking Time: 30 Minutes
Ingredients:
- 1 tablespoon extra-virgin olive oil
- 1 small red onion, diced
- 2 cans fire-roasted tomatoes with chiles
- 1 can corn
- 1 can black beans, rinsed and drained
- 1 can red enchilada sauce
- 1 can tomato paste
- 3 tablespoons taco seasoning
- 2 tablespoons freshly squeezed lime juice
- 2 boneless, skinless chicken breasts
- Salt
- Freshly ground black pepper

Directions:
1. Select SEAR/SAUTÉ and set temperature to MD:HI. Select START/STOP to begin. Let preheat for 5 minutes.
2. Place the olive oil and onion in the pot. Cook until the onions are translucent, about 2 minutes.
3. Add the tomatoes, corn, beans, enchilada sauce, tomato paste, taco seasoning, lime juice, and chicken. Season with salt and pepper and stir. Assemble pressure lid, making sure the pressure release valve is in the SEAL position.
4. Select PRESSURE and set to HI. Set time to 9 minutes. Select START/STOP to begin.
5. When pressure cooking is complete, allow pressure to naturally release for 10 minutes. After 10 minutes, quick release remaining pressure by moving the pressure release valve to the VENT position. Carefully remove lid when unit has finished releasing pressure.
6. Transfer the chicken breasts to a cutting board. Using two forks, shred the chicken. Return the chicken back to the pot and stir. Serve in a bowl with toppings of choice, such as shredded cheese, crushed tortilla chips, sliced avocado, sour cream, cilantro, and lime wedges, if desired.

Nutrition:
- InfoCalories: 257,Total Fat: 4g,Sodium: 819mg,Carbohydrates: 37g,Protein: 20g.

Lentil Spinach Soup With Lemon

Servings: 4 To 6
Cooking Time: 12 Minutes
Ingredients:
- 1 tsp. extra-virgin olive oil
- 2 lb (905 g) dried red lentils
- Juice of 1½ lemons
- 3 cups (90 g) baby spinach
- 32 oz (946 ml, 896 g) vegetable stock
- 1 yellow onion, diced
- 1 tsp. salt
- 1 tsp. ground cumin
- ¼ tsp. ground turmeric
- ¼ tsp. freshly ground black pepper
- ¼ tsp. ground coriander
- Croutons, for topping (optional)

Directions:
1. Press sauté on the Ninja pressure cooker. Add oil into the pot and heat for 1 minute, then add the onion. Sauté for 2 minutes, or until translucent.
2. Press Stop and stir in the salt, cumin, turmeric, pepper, coriander, stock and lentils. Combine them well.
3. Secure the lid with the steam vent in the sealed position. Press Pressure. Adjust the time to 12 minutes.
4. Once the timer sounds, release the pressure quickly. Remove the lid. Mix in the lemon juice. Puree the soup with an immersion blender until smooth.
5. Add the fresh spinach and top with croutons, if using. When the spinach slightly wilts, adjust the salt and pepper. Serve hot.

Goulash (hungarian Beef Soup)

Servings: 6
Cooking Time: 55 Minutes
Ingredients:
- ½ cup all-purpose flour
- 1 tablespoon kosher salt
- ½ teaspoon freshly ground black pepper
- 2 pounds beef stew meat
- 2 tablespoons canola oil
- 1 medium red bell pepper, seeded and chopped
- 4 garlic cloves, minced
- 1 large yellow onion, diced
- 2 tablespoons smoked paprika
- 1½ pounds small Yukon Gold potatoes, halved
- 2 cups beef broth
- 2 tablespoons tomato paste
- ¼ cup sour cream
- Fresh parsley, for garnish

Directions:
1. Select SEAR/SAUTÉ and set to HI. Select START/STOP to begin. Let preheat for 5 minutes.
2. Mix together the flour, salt, and pepper in a small bowl. Dip the pieces of beef into the flour mixture, shaking off any extra flour.
3. Add the oil and let heat for 1 minute. Place the beef in the pot and brown it on all sides, about 10 minutes.
4. Add the bell pepper, garlic, onion, and smoked paprika. Sauté for about 8 minutes or until the onion is translucent.
5. Add the potatoes, beef broth, and tomato paste and stir. Assemble pressure lid, making sure the pressure release valve is in the SEAL position.
6. Select PRESSURE and set to LO. Set time to 30 minutes. Select START/STOP to begin.
7. When pressure cooking is complete, quick release the pressure by moving the pressure release valve to the VENT position. Carefully remove lid when unit has finished releasing pressure.
8. Add the sour cream and mix thoroughly. Garnish with parsley, if desired, and serve immediately.

Nutrition:
- InfoCalories: 413,Total Fat: 13g,Sodium: 432mg,Carbohydrates: 64g,Protein: 37g.

Vegetable Wild Rice Soup

Servings: 6
Cooking Time: 30 Minutes
Ingredients:
- 8 ounces (227 g) fresh mushrooms, sliced
- 5 medium carrots, chopped
- 5 celery stalks, chopped
- 1 cup wild rice
- 6 cups vegetable broth
- 1 onion, chopped
- 3 garlic cloves, minced
- 1 tsp. poultry seasoning
- ½ tsp. dried thyme
- 1 tsp. kosher salt

Directions:
1. Add all the ingredients to the pot. Assemble pressure lid, set the pressure release valve to Seal.
2. Select PRESSURE, set the time 30 minutes.
3. After cooking is complete, move pressure release valve to VENT position to quickly release the pressure. Carefully remove lid.
4. Serve Warm.

Fish & Seafood

Mackerel En Papillote With Vegetables

Servings: 6
Cooking Time: 25 Min + 2 H For Marinating
Ingredients:
- 3 large whole mackerel, cut into 2 pieces
- 1 pound asparagus, trimmed /450g
- 1 carrot, cut into sticks
- 1 celery stalk, cut into sticks
- 3 cloves garlic, minced
- 2 lemons, cut into wedges
- 6 medium tomatoes, quartered
- 1 large brown onion; sliced thinly
- 1 Orange Bell pepper, seeded and cut into sticks
- ½ cup butter; at room temperature/65g
- 1 ½ cups water /375ml
- 2 ½ tbsp Pernod /37.5g
- Salt and black pepper to taste

Directions:
1. Cut out 6 pieces of parchment paper a little longer and wider than a piece of fish with kitchen scissors. Then, cut out 6 pieces of foil slightly longer than the parchment papers.
2. Lay the foil wraps on a flat surface and place each parchment paper on each aluminium foil.
3. In a bowl, add tomatoes, onions, garlic, bell pepper, pernod, butter, asparagus, carrot, celery, salt, and pepper. Use a spoon to mix them.
4. Place each fish piece on the layer of parchment and foil wraps. Spoon the vegetable mixture on each fish. Then, wrap the fish and place the fish packets in the refrigerator to marinate for 2 hours. Remove the fish to a flat surface.
5. Open the Ninja Foodi, pour the water in, and fit the reversible rack at the bottom of the pot. Put the packets on the trivet.
6. Seal the lid and select Steam mode on High pressure for 3 minutes. Press Start/Stop to start cooking.
7. Once the timer has ended, do a quick pressure release, and open the lid.
8. Remove the trivet with the fish packets onto a flat surface. Carefully open the foil and using a spatula. Return the packets to the pot, on top of the rack.
9. Close the crisping lid and cook on Air Crisp for 3 minutes at 300 °F or 150°C. Then, remove to serving plates. Serve with lemon wedges.

The Great Poached Salmon

Servings: 4
Cooking Time: 5 Minutes
Ingredients:
- 16-ounce salmon fillet, skin on
- 4 scallions, chopped
- Zest of 1 lemon
- ½ a teaspoon of fennel seeds
- 1 teaspoon white wine vinegar
- 1 bay leaf
- ½ cup dry white wine
- 2 cups chicken broth
- ¼ cup fresh dill
- Salt and pepper

Directions:
1. Add the listed to your Ninja Foodi, stir well
2. Lock lid and cook on HIGH pressure for 4 minutes. Release pressure naturally over 10 minutes
3. Serve and enjoy!

Curried Salmon & Sweet Potatoes

Servings: 4
Cooking Time: 20 Minutes
Ingredients:
- Nonstick cooking spray
- 2 sweet potatoes, peeled & cubed
- 1 tbsp. + 1 tsp olive oil, divided
- ½ tsp salt
- 1 tsp thyme
- 1 tsp curry powder
- 1 tsp honey
- ½ tsp lime zest
- 1/8 tsp crushed red pepper flakes
- 4 salmon filets

Directions:
1. Spray the cooking pot with cooking spray.
2. In a large bowl, combine potatoes, 1 tablespoon oil, salt, and thyme and toss to coat the potatoes. Place in the cooking pot.
3. Add the tender-crisp lid and set to roast on 400°F (205°C). Cook potatoes 10 minutes.
4. In a small bowl, whisk together remaining oil, curry powder, honey, zest, and pepper flakes. Lay the salmon on a sheet of foil and brush the curry mixture over the top.
5. Open the lid and stir the potatoes. Add the rack to the cooking pot and place the salmon, with the foil, on the rack. Close the lid and continue to cook another 10-15 minutes until potatoes are tender and fish flakes easily with a fork. Serve.

Nutrition:
- InfoCalories 239, Total Fat 8g, Total Carbs 15g, Protein 25g, Sodium 347mg.

Dijon Flavored Lemon Whitefish

Servings: 4
Cooking Time: 2 Minutes
Ingredients:
- 1 pound whitefish fillets
- 2 tablespoons Dijon mustard
- 1 teaspoon horseradish, grated
- 1 tablespoon fresh lemon juice

- 1 teaspoon fresh ginger, grated
- ½ teaspoon salt and black pepper (each)
- 1 lemon, sliced
- ½ tablespoon olive oil
- 1 cup of water

Directions:
1. Mix in Dijon mustard, lemon juice and horseradish in a bowl
2. Season white fish fillets with salt and pepper, add Dijon marinade
3. Let it marinate for 20 minutes. Add water to your Ninja Foodi and place a steamer rack inside
4. Put fillets on the rack and pour marinade on top
5. Lock lid and cook on HIGH pressure for 20 minutes
6. Release pressure naturally over 10 minutes. Enjoy!

Lemony Shrimp

Servings: 4 To 6
Cooking Time: 3 Minutes
Ingredients:
- 2 tablespoons butter
- 1 tablespoon lemon juice
- 1 tablespoon garlic, minced
- ½ cup (125 mL) chicken stock
- ½ cup (125 mL) white wine
- 2 pounds (907 g) shrimp
- Salt and ground black pepper, to taste
- 1 tablespoon parsley, for garnish

Directions:
1. Place the butter, lemon juice, and garlic in cooking pot.
2. Stir in the stock and wine.
3. Add the shrimp and sprinkle with the salt and pepper. Stir well.
4. Assemble pressure lid, making sure the pressure release valve is in the Seal position. Select Pressure and set to high. Set time to 3 minutes. Press Start to begin.
5. Once the timer beeps, do a quick pressure release. Carefully remove the lid.
6. Serve topped with the parsley.

Apricot Salmon With Potatoes

Servings: 4
Cooking Time: 25 Minutes
Ingredients:
- 20 ounces (567 g) baby potatoes, whole
- 1½ cups water
- 4 (6-ounce / 170-g) frozen skinless salmon fillets
- ¼ cup apricot preserves
- 2 teaspoons Dijon mustard
- 2 tablespoons extra-virgin olive oil
- ½ teaspoon kosher salt
- ½ teaspoon freshly ground black pepper

Directions:
1. Place the potatoes and water in the pot. Put Reversible Rack in pot, making sure it is in the higher position. Place salmon on the rack. Assemble pressure lid, making sure the pressure release valve is in the SEAL position.
2. Select PRESSURE and set to HI. Set time to 5 minutes. Select START/STOP to begin.
3. Mix together the apricot preserves and mustard in a small bowl.
4. When pressure cooking is complete, quick release the pressure by turning the pressure release valve to the VENT position. Carefully remove lid when unit has finished releasing pressure.
5. Carefully remove rack with salmon. Remove potatoes from pot and drain. Place the potatoes on a cutting board and, using the back of a knife, carefully press down to flatten each. Drizzle the flattened potatoes with the olive oil and season with salt and pepper.
6. Place Cook & Crisp Basket in the pot. Place the potatoes into the basket and close crisping lid.
7. Select AIR CRISP, set temperature to 390°F(200°C), and set time to 15 minutes. Select START/STOP to begin.
8. After 8 minutes, open lid, and using silicone-tipped tongs, gently flip the potatoes. Lower basket back into pot and close lid to resume cooking.
9. When cooking is complete, remove basket from pot. Return the rack with the salmon to the pot, making sure the rack is in the higher position. Gently brush the salmon with the apricot and mustard mixture.
10. Close crisping lid. Select BROIL and set time to 5 minutes. Select START/STOP to begin.
11. When cooking is complete, remove salmon and serve immediately with the potatoes.

Haddock With Sanfaina

Servings: 4
Cooking Time: 40 Min
Ingredients:
- 4 haddock fillets
- 1 can diced tomatoes, drained /435g
- ½ small onion; sliced
- 1 small jalapeño pepper, seeded and minced
- 2 large garlic cloves, minced
- 1 eggplant; cubed
- 1 bell pepper; chopped
- 1 bay leaf
- ⅓ cup sliced green olives /44g
- ¼ cup chopped fresh chervil; divided /32.5g
- 3 tbsps olive oil /45ml
- 3 tbsps capers; divided /45g
- ½ tsp dried basil /2.5g
- ¼ tsp salt /1.25g

Directions:
1. Season the fish on both sides with salt, place in the refrigerator, and make the sauce. Press Sear/Sauté and set to Medium. Press Start. Melt the butter until no longer foaming. Add onion, eggplant, bell pepper, jalapeño, and garlic; sauté for 5 minutes.
2. Stir in the tomatoes, bay leaf, basil, olives, half of the chervil, and half of the capers. Remove the fish from the refrigerator and lay on the vegetables in the pot.
3. Seal the pressure lid, choose Pressure; adjust the pressure to Low and the cook time to 3 minutes; press Start. After cooking, do a quick pressure release and carefully open the lid. Remove and discard the bay leaf.
4. Transfer the fish to a serving platter and spoon the sauce over. Sprinkle with the remaining chervil and capers. Serve.

Seafood Paella

Servings: 4
Cooking Time: 30 Minutes
Ingredients:
- 1 tbsp. extra-virgin olive oil
- 1 pound (455 g) chorizo, cut into ½-inch slices
- 4 garlic cloves, minced
- 1 yellow onion, chopped
- ½ cup dry white wine
- 4 cups chicken broth
- 2 cups long-grain white rice
- ½ tsp. sea salt
- 1 tsp. turmeric
- 1½ tsps. smoked paprika
- ½ tsp. freshly ground black pepper
- 1 pound (455 g) small clams, scrubbed
- 1 pound (455 g) fresh shrimp, peeled and deveined
- 1 red bell pepper, diced

Directions:
1. Preheat the pot by selecting Sear/Sauté. Select Start/Stop to begin. Preheat for 5 minutes.
2. In the preheated pot, add the oil and chorizo, cook for 3 minutes, until the meat is brown on both sides, stirring occasionally. Remove the chorizo from the pot and set aside.
3. Add the garlic and onion to the pot. Cook for 5 minutes, stirring occasionally. Add the wine and use a wooden spoon to stir, scraping up any brown bits from the bottom of the pot, and cook until the wine is reduced by half, about 2 minutes.
4. Add the broth and rice to the pot. Season with the salt, turmeric, paprika, and pepper. Assemble the Pressure Lid, set the pressure release valve to Seal.
5. Select Pressure and set the time to 5 minutes, then select Start/Stop to begin.
6. After pressure cooking is finish, set the pressure release valve to Vent, to quick release the pressure. Remove the lid when the pressure has finished releasing carefully.
7. Select Sear/Sauté. Select Start/Stop to begin. Add the clams and shrimp to the pot.
8. Assemble the Pressure Lid, set the pressure release valve to Vent. Cover and cook until the shrimp are pink and opaque and the clams have opened, about 6 minutes. Discard any unopened clams.
9. Place the chorizo back to the pot and add the bell pepper. Stir to combine and serve immediately.

Salmon With Dill Sauce

Servings: 4
Cooking Time: 20-25 Minutes
Ingredients:
- 4 salmon, each of 6 ounces
- 2 teaspoons olive oil
- 1 pinch salt
- Dill Sauce
- 1/2 cup non-Fat: Greek Yogurt
- 1/2 cup sour cream
- Pinch of salt
- 2 tablespoons dill, chopped

Directions:
1. Preheat Ninja Foodi by pressing the "AIR CRISP" option and setting it to "270 °F (130°C)" and timer to 25 minutes.
2. Wait until the appliance beeps.
3. Drizzle cut pieces of salmon with 1 teaspoon olive oil.
4. Season with salt.
5. Take the cooking basket out and transfer salmon to basket, cook for 20-23 minutes.
6. Take a suitable and stir in sour cream, salt, chopped dill, yogurt and mix well to prepare the dill sauce.
7. Serve cooked salmon by pouring the sauce all over.
8. Garnish with chopped dill and enjoy.

Nutrition:
- InfoCalories: 600; Fat: 45g; Carbohydrates: 5g; Protein: 60g

Steamed Shrimp With Asparagus

Servings: 2
Cooking Time: 2 Minutes
Ingredients:
- 1 pound (454 g) shrimp, frozen or fresh, peeled and deveined
- 1 cup (250 mL) water
- 6 ounces (170 g) asparagus
- 1 teaspoon olive oil
- ½ tablespoon Cajun seasoning (or your choice of seasoning)

Directions:
1. Pour the water in the cooking pot and place the reversible rack inside the pot.
2. Place the asparagus onto the reversible rack.
3. Arrange the shrimp on the asparagus and drizzle the olive oil over the top. Season with Cajun seasoning.
4. Assemble pressure lid, making sure the pressure release valve is in the Seal position. Select Steam and set time to 2 minutes. Press Start to begin.
5. Once the timer beeps, do a quick pressure release. Carefully remove the lid.
6. Transfer to a serving plate and serve immediately.

Tuscan Cod

Servings: 4
Cooking Time: 32 Minutes
Ingredients:
- 2 tablespoons canola oil, divided
- 1½ pounds baby red potatoes, cut into ½-inch pieces
- 2½ teaspoons kosher salt, divided
- 1 teaspoon freshly ground black pepper, divided
- 1 cup panko bread crumbs
- 6 tablespoons unsalted butter, divided
- 2 teaspoons poultry seasoning
- Juice of 1 lemon
- 1 medium onion, thinly sliced
- 1½ cups cherry tomatoes, halved
- 4 garlic cloves, quartered lengthwise
- ⅓ cup Kalamata olives, roughly chopped
- 4 fresh cod fillets
- 1 teaspoon fresh mint, finely chopped
- 1 lemon, cut into wedges

Directions:
1. Select SEAR/SAUTÉ and set to HI. Select START/STOP to begin. Let preheat for 5 minutes.
2. Add 1 tablespoon of oil and the potatoes. Season with 1½ teaspoons of salt and ½ teaspoon of pepper. Sauté for about 15 minutes, stirring occasionally, until the potatoes are golden brown.
3. While potatoes are cooking, combine the bread crumbs, 4 tablespoons of butter, poultry seasoning, the remaining 1 teaspoon of salt and ½ teaspoon of pepper, and lemon juice in a medium bowl. Stir well.
4. Once the potatoes are browned, carefully remove them from the pot and set aside. Add the remaining 1 tablespoon of oil, then the onion. Sauté for 2 to 3 minutes, until the onions are lightly browned. Add the tomatoes, garlic, and olives and cook for about 2 minutes more, stirring occasionally. Return the potatoes to the pot, stir. Select START/STOP to pause cooking. Close crisping lid to retain heat.
5. Coat the cod on both sides with the remaining 2 tablespoons of butter. Evenly distribute the breadcrumb mixture on top of the cod, pressing the crumbs down firmly.
6. Open lid and place the Reversible Rack in the pot over the potato mixture, making sure it is the higher position. Place the cod fillets on the rack, bread-side up. Close crisping lid.
7. Select BAKE/ROAST, set temperature to 375°F (190°C), and set time to 12 minutes. Select START/STOP to begin.
8. When cooking is complete, leave the cod in the pot with the crisping lid closed for 5 minutes to rest before serving. After resting, the internal temperature of the cod should be at least 145°F (60°C) and the bread crumbs should be golden brown. Serve with potato mixture and garnish with chopped mint and lemon wedges.

Nutrition:
- InfoCalories: 583,Total Fat: 28g,Sodium: 815mg,Carbohydrates: 48g,Protein: 37g.

Nawesome Cherry Tomato Mackerel

Servings: 4
Cooking Time: 7 Minutes
Ingredients:
- 4 Mackerel fillets
- ¼ teaspoon onion powder
- ¼ teaspoon lemon powder
- ¼ teaspoon garlic powder
- ½ teaspoon salt
- 2 cups cherry tomatoes
- 3 tablespoons melted butter
- 1 and ½ cups of water
- 1 tablespoon black olives

Directions:
1. Grease baking dish and arrange cherry tomatoes at the bottom of the dish
2. Top with fillets sprinkle all spices. Drizzle melted butter over
3. Add water to your Ninja Foodi
4. Lower rack in Ninja Foodi and place baking dish on top of the rack
5. Lock lid and cook on LOW pressure for 7 minutes. Quick release pressure. Serve and enjoy!

Sweet & Spicy Shrimp

Servings: 4
Cooking Time: 5 Minutes
Ingredients:
- ¾ cup pineapple juice, unsweetened
- 1 red bell pepper, sliced
- 1 ½ cups cauliflower, grated
- ¼ cup dry white wine
- ½ cup water
- 2 tbsp. soy sauce
- 2 tbsp. Thai sweet chili sauce
- 1 tbsp. chili paste
- 1 lb. large shrimp, frozen
- 4 green onions, chopped, white & green separated
- 1 ½ cups pineapple chunks, drained

Directions:
1. Add ¾ cup pineapple juice along with remaining ingredients, except the pineapple chunks and green parts of the onion, to the cooking pot. Stir to mix.
2. Add the lid and set to pressure cook on high. Set timer for 2 minutes. When the timer goes off, release pressure 10 minutes before opening the pot.
3. Add the green parts of the onions and pineapple chunks and stir well. Serve immediately.

Nutrition:
- InfoCalories 196,Total Fat 1g,Total Carbs 22g,Protein 26g,Sodium 764mg.

Basil Lemon Shrimp & Asparagus

Servings: 4
Cooking Time: 10 Minutes
Ingredients:
- 3 tbsp. water, divided
- 2 cloves garlic, chopped fine
- 2 tbsp. onion, chopped fine
- ½ tsp fresh ginger, grated
- ½ tsp salt
- ¼ tsp pepper
- ¼ tsp red pepper flakes
- 1 tbsp. fresh lemon juice
- 1 lb. asparagus, trimmed & cut in 1-inch pieces
- 1 lb. medium shrimp, peeled, deveined, tails removed
- 1 tsp lemon zest
- 3 tbsp. fresh basil, chopped

Directions:
1. Add 2 tablespoons water, garlic, and onion to the cooking pot and set to sauté on medium heat. Cook 1 minute, stirring.
2. Add remaining water, ginger, salt, pepper, red pepper flakes, lemon juice, and asparagus, stir to combine. Add the lid and cook 2-3 minutes until asparagus starts to turn bright green.
3. Add the shrimp and stir. Recover and cook another 3-5 minutes or until shrimp are pink and asparagus is fork-tender.
4. Stir in the lemon zest and basil and serve.

Nutrition:
- InfoCalories 110,Total Fat 1g,Total Carbs 7g,Protein 18g,Sodium 645mg.

Lemon Cod Goujons And Rosemary Chips

Servings: 4
Cooking Time: 100 Min
Ingredients:
- 4 cod fillets, cut into strips
- 2 potatoes, cut into chips
- 4 lemon wedges to serve
- 2 eggs
- 1 cup arrowroot starch /130g
- 1 cup flour /130g
- 2 tbsps olive oil /30ml
- 3 tbsp fresh rosemary; chopped /45g
- 1 tbsp cumin powder /15g
- ½ tbsp cayenne powder /7.5g
- 1 tsp black pepper, plus more for seasoning /5g
- 1 tsp salt, plus more for seasoning /5g
- Zest and juice from 1 lemon
- Cooking spray

Directions:
1. Fix the Crisping Basket in the pot and close the crisping lid. Choose Air Crisp, set the temperature to 375°F or 190°C, and the time to 5 minutes. Choose Start/Stop to preheat the pot.
2. In a bowl, whisk the eggs, lemon zest, and lemon juice. In another bowl, combine the arrowroot starch, flour, cayenne powder, cumin, black pepper, and salt.
3. Coat each cod strip in the egg mixture, and then dredge in the flour mixture, coating well on all sides. Grease the preheated basket with cooking spray. Place the coated fish in the basket and oil with cooking spray.
4. Close the crisping lid. Choose Air Crisp, set the temperature to 375°F or 190°C, and the time to 15 minutes; press Start/Stop. Toss the potatoes with oil and season with salt and pepper.
5. After 15 minutes, check the fish making sure the pieces are as crispy as desired. Remove the fish from the basket.
6. Pour the potatoes in the basket. Close the crisping lid; choose Air Crisp, set the temperature to 400°F or 205°C, and the time to 24 minutes; press Start/Stop.
7. After 12 minutes, open the lid, remove the basket and shake the fries. Return the basket to the pot and close the lid to continue cooking until crispy.
8. When ready, sprinkle with fresh rosemary. Serve the fish with the potatoes and lemon wedges.

The Ginger Flavored Tilapia

Servings: 4
Cooking Time: 5 Minutes
Ingredients:
- 1 pound Tilapia fish fillets
- 3 tablespoons low-sodium coconut aminos
- 2 tablespoons white vinegar
- 2 fresh garlic cloves, minced
- Pinch of salt and pepper
- 1 tablespoon olive oil
- 2 tablespoons fresh ginger, julienned
- ¼ cup fresh scallions, julienned
- ¼ cup fresh cilantro, chopped

Directions:
1. Take a bowl and add coconut aminos, white vinegar, minced garlic, salt, white pepper and mix well. Add tilapia fish and carefully spoon the sauce over and coat it
2. Marinate for 2 hours. Add 2 cups of water to the Ninja Foodi
3. Add steamer rack to the Ninja Foodi and remove fillets from marinade, transfer them to Steamer Rack. Lock lid and cook on LOW pressure for 2 minutes
4. Quick release pressure. Transfer fillets to serving the dish and discard water
5. Set your pot to Saute mode and add olive oil, let it heat up
6. Add julienned ginger and Saute for a few seconds
7. Add scallions, cilantro and Saute for 2 minutes. Stir in remaining marinade and let it heat up
8. Spoon the sauce over fish. Enjoy!

Crab Alfredo

Servings: 4
Cooking Time: 25 Minutes
Ingredients:
- ½ cup butter, unsalted
- ½ red bell pepper, seeded & chopped
- 2 tbsp. cream cheese, low fat
- 2 cups half and half
- ¾ cup parmesan cheese, reduced fat
- 1 tsp garlic powder
- 2 cups penne pasta, cooked & drained
- 6 oz. lump crab meat, cooked

Directions:
1. Add butter to the cooking pot and set to sauté on medium heat.
2. When butter has melted, add bell pepper and cook until it starts to soften, about 3-5 minutes.
3. Add the cream cheese and cook, stirring until it melts.
4. Stir in half and half and parmesan cheese, and garlic powder until smooth. Reduce heat to low and simmer 15 minutes.
5. Stir in cooked penne and crab meat and cook just until heated through. Serve immediately.

Nutrition:
- InfoCalories 388, Total Fat 23g, Total Carbs 26g, Protein 19g, Sodium 613mg.

Garlicky Shrimp With Broccoli

Servings: 4
Cooking Time: 5 Minutes
Ingredients:
- 2 tablespoons unsalted butter
- 1 shallot, minced
- 3 garlic cloves, minced
- ¼ cup white wine
- ½ cup chicken stock
- Juice of ½ lemon
- ½ teaspoon sea salt
- ½ teaspoon freshly ground black pepper
- 1½ pounds (680 g) frozen shrimp, thawed
- 1 large head broccoli, cut into florets

Directions:
1. Add the butter. Select SEAR/SAUTÉ and set to MED. Select START/STOP to begin.
2. Once the butter is melted, add the shallots and cook for 3 minutes. Add the garlic and cook for 1 minute.
3. Deglaze the pot by adding the wine and using a wooden spoon to scrape the bits of garlic and shallot off the bottom of the pot. Stir in the chicken stock, lemon juice, salt, pepper, and shrimp.
4. Place the broccoli florets on top of the shrimp mixture. Assemble pressure lid, making sure the pressure release valve is in the SEAL position.
5. Select PRESSURE and set to HI. Set time to 0 minutes. Select START/STOP to begin.
6. When pressure cooking is complete, quick release the pressure by moving the pressure release valve to the VENT position. Carefully remove lid when the unit has finished releasing pressure. Serve immediately.

Cod Over Couscous

Servings: 4
Cooking Time: 27–29 Minutes
Ingredients:
- 1 tablespoon extra-virgin olive oil
- 1 red bell pepper, diced
- 1 yellow bell pepper, diced
- 2 cups tricolor Israeli or pearl couscous
- 2½ cups chicken broth
- 1 cup panko bread crumbs
- 4 tablespoons (½ stick) unsalted butter, melted
- ¼ cup minced fresh parsley
- Juice of 1 lemon
- 1 teaspoon grated lemon zest
- 1 teaspoon sea salt
- 4 (5- to 6-ounce) cod fillets

Directions:
1. Select Sear/Sauté and set to Medium High. Select Start/Stop to begin. Allow the pot to preheat for 5 minutes.
2. Combine the oil, red and yellow bell peppers, and couscous in the preheated pot and cook for 1 minute. Stir in the chicken broth.
3. Assemble the Pressure Lid, making sure the pressure release valve is in the Seal position. Select Pressure and set to High. Set the time to 6 minutes, then select Start/Stop to begin.
4. Meanwhile, in a small mixing bowl, stir together the panko bread crumbs, butter, parsley, lemon juice, lemon zest, and salt. Press the panko mixture evenly on top of each cod fillet.
5. When pressure cooking the couscous is complete, quick release the pressure by moving the pressure release valve to the Vent position. Carefully remove the lid when the pressure has finished releasing.
6. Place the Reversible Rack in the pot over the couscous; making sure it is in the higher position. Place the cod fillets on the rack.
7. Close the Crisping Lid. Select Air Crisp, set the temperature to 350°F (175°C), and set the time to 12 minutes. Select Start/Stop to begin. Check the cod and cook for up to an additional 2 minutes if necessary. Cooking is complete when the internal temperature of the fillets reaches 145°F (60°C).

Great Seafood Stew

Servings: 4
Cooking Time: 10 Minutes
Ingredients:
- 3 tablespoons extra virgin olive oil
- 2 bay leaves
- 2 teaspoons paprika
- 1 small onion, sliced
- 1 small green bell pepper
- 2 garlic cloves, mashed
- Salt and pepper to taste
- 1 cup fish stock
- 1 and ½ pound meat fish
- 1 pound shrimp, cleaned and deveined
- 12 neck clams
- ¼ cup cilantro, garnish
- 1 tablespoon extra- virgin olive oil

Directions:
1. Set your Ninja Foodi to Saute mode and add olive oil
2. Add bay leaves and paprika and Saute for 30 seconds
3. Add onion, bell pepper, tomatoes, 2 tablespoons of cilantro, garlic and season with salt and pepper. Stir for a few minutes . Add fish stock
4. Season fish with salt and pepper and Nestle the clams and shrimp among the veggies in the Ninja Foodi. Add fish on top
5. Lock up the lid and cook on HIGH pressure for 10 minutes
6. Release the pressure over 10 minutes
7. Divide the stew amongst bowls and drizzle 1 tablespoon of olive oil
8. Sprinkle 2 tablespoon of cilantro and serve. Enjoy!

Shrimp Fried Rice

Servings: 6
Cooking Time: 15 Minutes
Ingredients:
- 2 tbsp. sesame oil
- 2 tbsp. olive oil
- 1 lb. medium shrimp, peeled & deveined
- 1 cup frozen peas & carrots
- 1/2 cup corn
- 3 cloves garlic, chopped fine
- ½ tsp ginger
- 3 eggs, lightly beaten
- 4 cups brown rice, cooked
- 3 green onions, sliced
- 3 tbsp. tamari
- ½ tsp salt
- ½ tsp pepper

Directions:
1. Add the sesame and olive oils to the cooking pot and set to sauté on med-high heat.
2. Add the shrimp and cook 3 minutes, or until they turn pink, turning shrimp over halfway through. Use a slotted spoon to transfer shrimp to a plate.

3. Add the peas, carrots, and corn to the pot and cook 2 minutes until vegetables start to soften, stirring occasionally. Add the garlic and ginger and cook 1 minute more.
4. Push the vegetables to one side and add the eggs, cook to scramble, stirring frequently. Add the shrimp, rice, and onions and stir to mix all ingredients together.
5. Drizzle with tamari and season with salt and pepper, stir to combine. Cook 2 minutes or until everything is heated through. Serve immediately.

Nutrition:
- InfoCalories 361,Total Fat 13g,Total Carbs 38g,Protein 24g,Sodium 1013mg.

Creamy Crab Soup

Servings: 4
Cooking Time: 45 Min
Ingredients:
- 2 lb. Crabmeat Lumps /900g
- 2 celery stalk; diced
- 1 white onion; chopped
- ¾ cup heavy cream /188ml
- ½ cup Half and Half cream /125ml
- 1 ½ cup chicken broth /375ml
- ¾ cup Muscadet /98g
- 6 tbsp butter /90g
- 6 tbsp flour /90g
- 3 tsp Worcestershire sauce /15ml
- 3 tsp old bay Seasoning /15ml
- 2 tsp Hot sauce /10ml
- 3 tsp minced garlic /15g
- Salt to taste
- Lemon juice to serve
- Chopped dill to serve

Directions:
1. Melt the butter on Sear/Sauté mode, and mix in the all-purpose flour, in a fast motion to make a rue. Add celery, onion, and garlic.
2. Stir and cook until soft and crispy; for 3 minutes. While stirring, gradually add the half and half cream, heavy cream, and broth.
3. Let simmer for 2 minutes. Add Worcestershire sauce, old bay seasoning, Muscadet, and hot sauce. Stir and let simmer for 15 minutes. Add the crabmeat and mix it well into the sauce.
4. Close the crisping lid and cook on Broil mode for 10 minutes to soften the meat.
5. Dish into serving bowls, garnish with dill and drizzle squirts of lemon juice over. Serve with a side of garlic crusted bread.

Classic Crab Imperial

Servings: 6
Cooking Time: 20 Minutes
Ingredients:
- 1 cup mayonnaise
- 2 eggs, lightly beaten
- 2 tsp sugar
- 2 tsp Old Bay seasoning
- 1 tsp lemon juice
- 2 tsp parsley, chopped fine
- 2 lb. jumbo lump crab meat

Directions:
1. In a medium bowl, combine mayonnaise, eggs, sugar, Old Bay, lemon juice, and parsley and mix well.
2. Gently fold in crab. Divide evenly between 6 ramekins and place in the cooking pot.
3. Add the tender-crisp lid and set to bake on 350°F (175°C). Bake 20-25 minutes until the top is golden brown. Let cool slightly before serving.

Nutrition:
- InfoCalories 382,Total Fat 18g,Total Carbs 10g,Protein 43g,Sodium 1201mg.

Very Low Carb Clam Chowder

Servings:6
Cooking Time: 4 Hours 20 Minutes
Ingredients:
- 13 slices bacon, thick cut
- 2 cups chicken broth
- 1 cup celery, chopped
- 1 cup onion, chopped
- 6 cups baby clams, with juice
- 2 cups heavy whipping cream
- 1 teaspoon salt
- 1 teaspoon ground thyme
- 1 teaspoon pepper

Directions:
1. Take a skillet and place it over medium heat, cook bacon until crispy
2. Drain and crumble the bacon. Chop onion, celery and add them to the pan
3. Once tender add veggies alongside remaining to your Ninja Foodi
4. Lock lid and cook on SLOW COOK MODE for 4-6 hours. Serve and enjoy!

Citrus Mahi Mahi

Servings: 4
Cooking Time: 4 Minutes
Ingredients:
- ½ cup (125 mL) filtered water
- 3 tablespoons grass-fed butter, softened
- 1 tablespoon grated ginger
- ½ lime, juiced
- ½ lemon, juiced
- ½ teaspoon dried basil
- ½ teaspoon garlic, minced
- ½ teaspoon kosher salt
- ½ teaspoon freshly ground black pepper
- 4 mahi mahi fillets
- Cooking spray

Directions:
1. Add the water to the cooking pot and place the reversible rack inside the pot.
2. Mix together the butter, ginger, lime juice, lemon juice, basil, garlic, salt, and black pepper in a large bowl. Stir well.
3. Add the mahi mahi filets to this mixture and stir to coat. Spray an pressure cooker-friendly dish with cooking spray and place the fillets in the dish.

4. Place the dish onto the rack and wrap loosely in aluminum foil.
5. Assemble pressure lid, making sure the pressure release valve is in the Seal position. Select Pressure and set to low. Set time to 4 minutes. Press Start to begin.
6. Once cook is complete, do a quick pressure release. Carefully open the lid.
7. Transfer the fillets to a serving plate and serve immediately.

Tuscan Cod With Red Potatoes

Servings: 4
Cooking Time: 32 Minutes
Ingredients:
- 2 tablespoons canola oil, divided
- 1½ pounds (680 g) baby red potatoes, cut into ½-inch pieces
- 2½ teaspoons kosher salt, divided
- 1 teaspoon freshly ground black pepper, divided
- 1 cup panko bread crumbs
- 6 tablespoons unsalted butter, divided
- 2 teaspoons poultry seasoning
- Juice of 1 lemon
- 1 medium onion, thinly sliced
- 1½ cups cherry tomatoes, halved
- 4 garlic cloves, quartered lengthwise
- ⅓ cup Kalamata olives, roughly chopped
- 4 (6-ounce / 170-g) fresh cod fillets
- 1 teaspoon fresh mint, finely chopped
- 1 lemon, cut into wedges

Directions:
1. Select SEAR/SAUTÉ and set to HI. Select START/STOP to begin. Let preheat for 5 minutes.
2. Add 1 tablespoon of oil and the potatoes. Season with 1½ teaspoons of salt and ½ teaspoon of pepper. Sauté for about 15 minutes, stirring occasionally, until the potatoes are golden brown.
3. While potatoes are cooking, combine the bread crumbs, 4 tablespoons of butter, poultry seasoning, the remaining 1 teaspoon of salt and ½ teaspoon of pepper, and lemon juice in a medium bowl. Stir well.
4. Once the potatoes are browned, carefully remove them from the pot and set aside. Add the remaining 1 tablespoon of oil, then the onion. Sauté for 2 to 3 minutes, until the onions are lightly browned. Add the tomatoes, garlic, and olives and cook for about 2 minutes more, stirring occasionally. Return the potatoes to the pot, stir. Select START/STOP to pause cooking. Close crisping lid to retain heat.
5. Coat the cod on both sides with the remaining 2 tablespoons of butter. Evenly distribute the breadcrumb mixture on top of the cod, pressing the crumbs down firmly.
6. Open lid and place the Reversible Rack in the pot over the potato mixture, making sure it is the higher position. Place the cod fillets on the rack, bread-side up. Close crisping lid.
7. Select BAKE/ROAST, set temperature to 375°F(190°C), and set time to 12 minutes. Select START/STOP to begin.
8. When cooking is complete, leave the cod in the pot with the crisping lid closed for 5 minutes to rest before serving. After resting, the internal temperature of the cod should be at least 145°F(60°C) and the bread crumbs should be golden brown. Serve with potato mixture and garnish with chopped mint and lemon wedges.

Cod Cornflakes Nuggets

Servings: 4
Cooking Time: 25 Min
Ingredients:
- 1 ¼ lb. cod fillets, cut into chunks /662.5g
- 1 egg
- 1 cup cornflakes /130g
- ½ cup flour /65g
- 1 tbsp olive oil/15ml
- 1 tbsp water /15ml
- Salt and pepper, to taste

Directions:
1. Add the oil and cornflakes in a food processor, and process until crumbed. Season the fish chunks with salt and pepper.
2. Beat the egg along with 1 tbsp or 15ml water. Dredge the chunks in flour first, then dip in the egg, and coat with cornflakes. Arrange on a lined sheet. Close the crisping lid and cook at 350 °F or 175°C for 15 minutes on Air Crisp mode.

Curry-flavored Shrimp

Servings: 2 To 4
Cooking Time: 4 Minutes
Ingredients:
- 2 cups (500 mL) water
- 1 pound (454 g) shrimp, peeled and deveined
- 8 ounces (227 g) unsweetened coconut milk
- 1 teaspoon curry powder
- 1 tablespoon garlic, minced
- Salt and ground black pepper, to taste

Directions:
1. Pour the water in the cooking pot and insert a reversible rack.
2. Mix together the shrimp, coconut milk, curry powder, and garlic in a large bowl. Sprinkle with the salt and pepper.
3. Add the mixture to the pan and place the dish onto the reversible rack, uncovered.
4. Assemble pressure lid, making sure the pressure release valve is in the Seal position. Select Pressure and set to high. Set time to 4 minutes. Press Start to begin.
5. Once cooking is complete, use a quick pressure release. Carefully open the lid.
6. Stir well and serve.

Parmesan Tilapia

Servings: 4
Cooking Time: 15 Min
Ingredients:
- ¾ cup grated Parmesan cheese /98g
- 4 tilapia fillets
- 1 tbsp olive oil /15ml
- 1 tbsp chopped parsley /15g
- ¼ tsp garlic powder /1.25g

- 2 tsp paprika /10g
- ¼ tsp salt /1.25g

Directions:
1. Mix parsley, Parmesan, garlic, salt, and paprika, in a shallow bowl. Brush the olive oil over the fillets, and then coat them with the Parmesan mixture.
2. Place the tilapia onto a lined baking sheet, and then into the Ninja Foodi.
3. Close the crisping lid and cook for about 4 to 5 minutes on all sides on Air Crisp mode at 350 °F or 175°C.

Buttery Scallops

Servings: 4
Cooking Time: 6 Minutes
Ingredients:
- 2 pounds sea scallops
- 12 cup butter
- 4 garlic cloves, minced
- 4 tablespoons rosemary, chopped
- Black pepper and salt to taste

Directions:
1. Select "Sauté" mode on your Ninja Foodi.
2. Add rosemary, garlic and butter, Sauté for 1 minute.
3. Stir in scallops, Black pepper and salt, Sauté for 2 minutes.
4. Close the crisping lid.
5. Cook for 3 minutes to 350°F (175°C).
6. Serve and enjoy.

Nutrition:
- InfoCalories: 278g; Fat: 15g; Carbohydrates: 5g; Protein: 25g

Shrimp And Sausage Paella

Servings: 4
Cooking Time: 70 Min
Ingredients:
- 1 pound andouille sausage; sliced /450g
- 1 pound baby squid, cut into ¼-inch rings /450g
- 1 pound jumbo shrimp, peeled and deveined /450g
- 1 white onion; chopped
- 4 garlic cloves, minced
- 1 red bell pepper; diced
- 2 cups Spanish rice /260g
- 4 cups chicken stock /1000ml
- ½ cup dry white wine /125ml
- 1 tbsp melted butter /15ml
- 1 tsp turmeric powder /5g
- 1½ tsp s sweet paprika /7.5g
- ½ tsp freshly ground black pepper /5g
- ½ tsp salt /5g

Directions:
1. Choose Sear/Sauté on the pot and set to Medium High. Choose Start/Stop to preheat the pot. Melt the butter and add the sausage. Cook until browned on both sides, about 3 minutes while stirring frequently. Remove the sausage to a plate and set aside.
2. Sauté the onion and garlic in the same fat for 3 minutes until fragrant and pour in the wine. Use a wooden spoon to scrape the bottom of the pot of any brown bits and cook for 2 minutes or until the wine reduces by half.
3. Stir in the rice and water. Season with the paprika, turmeric, black pepper, and salt. Seal the pressure lid, choose Pressure and set to High. Set the time to 5 minutes, then Choose Start/Stop. When done cooking, do a quick pressure release and carefully open the lid.
4. Choose Sear/Sauté, set to Medium High, and choose Start/Stop. Add the squid and shrimp to the pot and stir gently without mashing the rice.
5. Seal the pressure lid again and cook for 6 minutes, until the shrimp are pink and opaque. Return the sausage to the pot and mix in the bell pepper. Warm through for 2 minutes. Dish the paella and serve immediately.

Baked Cod Casserole

Servings: 6
Cooking Time: 20 Minutes
Ingredients:
- Nonstick cooking spray
- 1 lb. mushrooms, chopped
- 1 onion, chopped
- ½ cup fresh parsley, chopped
- ½ tsp salt, divided
- ½ tsp pepper, divided
- 6 cod fillets
- ¾ cup dry white wine
- ¾ cup plain bread crumbs
- 2 tbsp. butter, melted
- 1 cup Swiss cheese, grated

Directions:
1. Spray the cooking pot with cooking spray.
2. In a medium bowl, combine mushrooms, onion, parsley, ¼ teaspoon salt, and ¼ teaspoon pepper and mix well. Spread evenly on the bottom of the cooking pot.
3. Place the fish on top of the mushroom mixture and pour the wine over them.
4. In a separate medium bowl, combine remaining ingredients and mix well. Sprinkle over the fish.
5. Add the tender-crisp lid and set to bake on 450°F (230°C). Bake 15-20 minutes or until golden brown and fish flakes easily with a fork. Serve immediately.

Nutrition:
- InfoCalories 284,Total Fat 10g,Total Carbs 16g,Protein 27g,Sodium 693mg.

Pineapple Rice With Coconut-crusted Shrimp

Servings:4
Cooking Time: 45 Minutes
Ingredients:
- 2 tablespoons canola oil
- 1 (20-ounce / 567-g) can diced pineapple
- 1 yellow onion, diced
- 1 cup long-grain white rice
- 1½ cups chicken stock
- ½ cup freshly squeezed lime juice
- ¾ cup all-purpose flour
- 1 tablespoon kosher salt
- ½ teaspoon freshly ground black pepper
- 2 large eggs
- ½ cup coconut flakes
- ½ cup plain panko bread crumbs

- 10 ounces (283 g) deveined shrimp, tails removed
- Cooking spray

Directions:
1. Select SEAR/SAUTÉ and set temperature to HI. Select START/STOP to begin. Let preheat for 5 minutes.
2. Add the oil and heat for 1 minute. Add the pineapple and onion. Cook, stirring frequently, for about 8 minutes, or until the onion is translucent.
3. Add the rice, chicken stock, and lime juice. Assemble pressure lid, making sure the pressure release valve is in the SEAL position.
4. Select PRESSURE and set to HI. Set time to 2 minutes. Select START/STOP to begin.
5. When pressure cooking is complete, allow press to naturally release for 10 minutes. After 10 minutes, quick release remaining pressure by turning the pressure release valve to the VENT position. Carefully remove lid when unit has finished releasing pressure.
6. Transfer the rice mixture to a bowl and cover to keep warm. Clean the cooking pot and return to the unit.
7. Create a batter station with three medium bowls. In the first bowl, mix together the flour, salt and pepper. In the second bowl, whisk the eggs. In the third bowl, combine the coconut flakes and bread crumbs. Dip each shrimp into the flour mixture. Next dip it in the egg. Finally, coat in the coconut mixture, shaking off excess as needed. Once all the shrimp are battered, spray them with cooking spray.
8. Place Cook & Crisp Basket into pot. Place the shrimp in basket and close crisping lid.
9. Select AIR CRISP, set temperature to 390°F(200°C), and set time to 10 minutes. Select START/STOP to begin.
10. After 5 minutes, open lid, then lift basket and shake the shrimp. Lower basket back into the pot and close the lid to continue cooking until the shrimp reach your desired crispiness.
11. When cooking is complete, serve the shrimp on top of the rice.

Spiced Red Snapper

Servings: 6
Cooking Time: 20 Minutes
Ingredients:
- Nonstick cooking spray
- 1 onion, sliced
- 14 ½ oz. stewed tomatoes, undrained, chopped
- 1/3 cup dry white wine
- 3 tbsp. fresh lemon juice
- 1 tsp cumin
- 1/8 tsp cinnamon
- 6 red snapper fillets

Directions:
1. Spray the cooking pot with cooking spray.
2. Set to sauté on med-high heat and add the onion. Cook, stirring, 3-4 minutes or until onions are soft.
3. Add tomatoes, wine, lemon juice, cumin,, and cinnamon and cook about 5 minutes or until sauce has thickened slightly.
4. Add the fish and spoon sauce over the top. Add the lid and reduce heat to medium. Cook 8-10 minutes until fish flakes with a fork.
5. Transfer fish to serving plates and top with sauce. Serve immediately.

Nutrition:
- InfoCalories 155,Total Fat 2g,Total Carbs 8g,Protein 25g,Sodium 201mg.

Spanish Steamed Clams

Servings: 6
Cooking Time: 20 Minutes
Ingredients:
- 3 tbsp. olive oil
- 1 onion, chopped fine
- 3 oz. prosciutto, chopped
- ¼ cup dry sherry
- 36 littleneck clams

Directions:
1. Add the oil to the cooking pot and set to sauté on med-high heat.
2. Add the onion and cook, stirring, 1 minutes. Reduce heat to low, add the lid and cook 10-15 minutes until onion is soft.
3. Stir in remaining ingredients and increase heat to medium. Add the lid and cook 5 minutes, or until the clams open.
4. Discard any unopened clams and serve immediately.

Nutrition:
- InfoCalories 166,Total Fat 9g,Total Carbs 5g,Protein 15g,Sodium 657mg.

Pepper Smothered Cod

Servings: 4
Cooking Time: 20 Minutes
Ingredients:
- ¼ cup olive oil
- ½ cup red onion, chopped
- 2 tsp garlic, chopped
- ½ cup red bell pepper, chopped
- ½ cup green bell pepper, chopped
- Salt and pepper, to taste
- 4 tbsp. flour
- 2 cups chicken broth, low sodium
- ½ cup tomato, seeded & chopped
- 2 tsp fresh thyme, chopped
- 4 cod filets

Directions:
1. Set to sauté on med-high heat and add oil to the cooking pot.
2. Add the onion and garlic and cook, stirring, 1 minute.
3. Add the peppers, salt, and pepper and cook, stirring frequently about 2-3 minutes, or until peppers start to get tender.
4. Stir in the flour and cook until it turns a light brown.
5. Pour in the broth and cook, stirring, until smooth and the sauce starts to thicken. Stir in tomato and thyme.
6. Season the fish with salt and pepper. Place in the pot and add the lid. Cook 3-4 minutes, then turn the fish over and cook another 3-4 minute or until fish flakes easily with a fork. Transfer the fish to serving plates and top with sauce. Serve immediately.

Nutrition:
- InfoCalories 249,Total Fat 14g,Total Carbs 11g,Protein 19g,Sodium 1107mg.

Coconut Cilantro Shrimp

Servings: 4
Cooking Time: 4 ½ Hours
Ingredients:
- 3 ¾ cups coconut milk, unsweetened
- 1 ¾ cups water
- 2 tbsp. red curry paste
- 2 ½ tsp lemon garlic seasoning
- 1 lb. shrimp, peeled & deveined
- ¼ cup cilantro, chopped

Directions:
1. Place all ingredients, except shrimp and cilantro, in the cooking pot and stir to well to mix.
2. Add the lid and set to slow cook on low heat. Cook 4 hours, stirring occasionally.
3. Stir in shrimp and continue cooking another 15-30 minutes until shrimp turn pink and tender.
4. Transfer mixture to a serving plate and garnish with cilantro. Serve immediately.

Nutrition:
- InfoCalories 525,Total Fat 46g,Total Carbs 8g,Protein 28g,Sodium 168mg.

Salmon Chowder

Servings: 8
Cooking Time: 30 Minutes
Ingredients:
- 3 tbsp. butter
- ½ cup celery, chopped
- ½ cup onion, chopped
- ½ cup green bell pepper, chopped
- 1 clove garlic, chopped fine
- 14 ½ oz. chicken broth, low sodium
- 1 cup potatoes, peeled & cubed
- 1 cup carrots, chopped
- 1 tsp salt
- ½ tsp pepper
- 1 tsp fresh dill, chopped
- 1 can cream-style corn
- 2 cups half and half
- 2 cups salmon, cut in 1-inch pieces

Directions:
1. Add the butter to the cooking pot and set to sauté on med-high heat.
2. Add the celery, onion, green pepper, and garlic and cook, stirring frequently, until vegetables start to soften.
3. Add the broth, potatoes, carrots, salt, pepper and dill and stir to mix.
4. Add the lid and set to pressure cook on high. Set the timer for 10 minutes. When the timer goes off, release the pressure with quick release.
5. Set back to sauté on medium and add the corn, cream, and salmon. Bring to a simmer and cook 15 minutes, or until salmon is cooked through. Serve.

Nutrition:
- InfoCalories 244,Total Fat 10g,Total Carbs 21g,Protein 18g,Sodium 905mg.

Ranch Warm Fillets

Servings: 4
Cooking Time: 13 Minutes
Ingredients:
- ¼ cup panko
- ½ packet ranch dressing mix powder
- 1 and ¼ tablespoons vegetable oil
- 1 egg beaten
- 2 tilapia fillets
- A garnish of herbs and chilies

Directions:
1. Pre-heat your Ninja Foodi with the Crisping Basket inside at 350 degrees F
2. Take a bowl and mix in ranch dressing and panko
3. Beat eggs in a shallow bowl and keep it on the side
4. Dip fillets in the eggs, then in the panko mix
5. Place fillets in your Ninja Foodie's insert and transfer insert to Ninja Foodi
6. Lock Air Crisping Lid and Air Crisp for 13 minutes at 350 degrees F
7. Garnish with chilies and herbs. Enjoy!

Shrimp Scampi With Tomatoes

Servings: 2 To 4
Cooking Time: 3 Minutes
Ingredients:
- 2 tablespoons olive oil
- 1 clove garlic, minced
- 1 pound (454 g) shrimp, peeled and deveined
- 10 ounces (284 g) canned tomatoes, chopped
- ⅓ cup (83 mL) tomato paste
- ⅓ cup (83 mL) water
- 1 tablespoon parsley, finely chopped
- ¼ teaspoon dried oregano
- ½ teaspoon kosher salt
- ½ teaspoon ground black pepper, to taste
- 1 cup (250 mL) grated Parmesan Cheese

Directions:
1. Press the Sauté button and heat the oil.
2. Add the garlic and sauté for 1 minute until fragrant.
3. Stir in the shrimp, tomatoes, tomato paste, water, parsley, oregano, salt and pepper.
4. Assemble pressure lid, making sure the pressure release valve is in the Seal position. Select Pressure and set to high. Set time to 3 minutes. Press Start to begin.
5. When the timer beeps, do a quick pressure release. Carefully remove the lid.
6. Serve scattered with the Parmesan Cheese.

Salmon Paprika

Servings: 4
Cooking Time: 7 Minutes
Ingredients:
- 2 wild caught salmon fillets, 1 to 1 and ½ inches thick
- 2 teaspoons avocado oil
- 2 teaspoons paprika
- Salt and pepper to taste
- Green herbs to garnish

Directions:
1. Season salmon fillets with salt, pepper, paprika, and olive oil
2. Place Crisping basket in your Ninja Foodi, and pre-heat your Ninja Foodie at 390 degrees F
3. Place insert insider your Foodi and place the fillet in the insert, lock Air Crisping lid and cook for 7 minutes. Once done, serve the fish with herbs on top. Enjoy!

Panko Crusted Cod

Servings: 4
Cooking Time: 15 Minutes
Ingredients:
- 2 uncooked cod fillets
- 3 teaspoons kosher salt
- ¾ cup panko bread crumbs
- 2 tablespoons butter, melted
- 1/4 cup fresh parsley, minced
- 1 lemon. Zested and juiced

Directions:
1. Pre-heat your Ninja Foodi at 390 °F (200°C) and place the Air Crisper basket inside.
2. Season cod and salt.
3. Take a suitable and stir in bread crumbs, parsley, lemon juice, zest, butter, and mix well.
4. Coat fillets with the bread crumbs mixture and place fillets in your Air Crisping basket.
5. Lock Air Crisping lid and cook on Air Crisp mode for 15 minutes at 360 °F (180°C).
6. Serve and enjoy.

Nutrition:
- InfoCalories: 554; Fat: 24g; Carbohydrates: 5g; Protein: 37g

Spicy Shrimp Pasta With Vodka Sauce

Servings: 6
Cooking Time: 11 Minutes
Ingredients:
- 2 tablespoons extra-virgin olive oil
- 2 tablespoons minced garlic
- 1 teaspoon crushed red pepper flakes
- 1 small red onion, diced
- Kosher salt
- Freshly ground black pepper
- ¾ cup vodka
- 2¾ cups vegetable stock
- 1 can crushed tomatoes
- 1 box penne pasta
- 1 pound frozen shrimp, peeled and deveined
- 1 package cream cheese, cubed
- 4 cups shredded mozzarella cheese

Directions:
1. Select SEAR/SAUTÉ and set to MD:HI. Select START/STOP to begin. Let preheat for 5 minutes.
2. Add the olive oil, garlic, and crushed red pepper flakes. Cook until garlic is golden brown, about 1 minute. Add the onions and season with salt and pepper and cook until translucent, about 2 minutes.
3. Stir in the vodka, vegetable stock, crushed tomatoes, penne pasta, and frozen shrimp. Assemble pressure lid, making sure the pressure release valve is in the SEAL position.
4. Select PRESSURE and set temperature to HI. Set time to 6 minutes. Select START/STOP to begin.
5. When pressure cooking is complete, quick release the pressure by turning the pressure release valve to the VENT position. Carefully remove lid when unit has finished releasing pressure.
6. Stir in the cream cheese until it has melted. Layer the mozzarella on top of the pasta. Close crisping lid.
7. Select AIR CRISP, set temperature to 400°F (205°C), and set time to 5 minutes. Select START/STOP to begin.
8. When cooking is complete, open lid and serve.

Nutrition:
- InfoCalories: 789,Total Fat: 35g,Sodium: 1302mg,Carbohydrates: 63g,Protein: 47g.

Speedy Clams Pomodoro

Servings: 4
Cooking Time: 10 Minutes
Ingredients:
- 2 dozen clams
- 14 ½ oz. stewed tomatoes, chopped & undrained
- ¼ cup dry white wine
- 2 tbsp. fresh basil, chopped
- ¼ tsp pepper
- 1 lemon, cut in wedges

Directions:
1. Set cooker to sauté on med-high heat.
2. Add all the ingredients to the cooking pot and stir to mix.
3. Add the lid and bring mixture to a boil. Reduce heat to low and simmer 6-8 minutes or until the clams open.
4. Discard any unopened clams and serve immediately with lemon wedges.

Nutrition:
- InfoCalories 123,Total Fat 1g,Total Carbs 12g,Protein 14g,Sodium 715mg.

Shrimp Spaghetti With Parmesan

Servings: 4
Cooking Time: 10 Minutes
Ingredients:
- 6 tablespoons butter, divided
- 12 ounces (340 g) small shrimp, peeled and deveined
- ½ teaspoon salt
- 4 cups (1 L) chicken broth
- 1 pound (454 g) spaghetti
- 1 cup (250 mL) grated Parmesan cheese
- 1 cup (250 mL) heavy whipping cream
- 1 teaspoon lemon pepper

Directions:
1. Press the Sauté button and add 2 tablespoons of butter.
2. Add the shrimp and salt to the cooking pot and sauté for 4 minutes, or until the flesh is pink and opaque. Remove the shrimp and set aside.
3. Add the broth and scrape up any bits on the bottom of the pot.
4. Break the spaghetti in half and add to the pot. Place the remaining 4 tablespoons of butter on top.
5. Assemble pressure lid, making sure the pressure release valve is in the Seal position. Select Pressure and set to high. Set time to 5 minutes. Press Start to begin.
6. Once the timer goes off, use a quick pressure release. Carefully open the lid.
7. Fold in the cooked shrimp, Parmesan, cream, and lemon pepper. Stir until thoroughly combined.
8. Transfer to a serving plate and serve hot.

Salmon Florentine

Servings: 4
Cooking Time: 15 Minutes
Ingredients:
- 2 tbsp. olive oil, divided
- 4 salmon filets
- ½ tsp salt
- ¼ tsp pepper
- 4 cloves garlic, chopped fine
- 10 oz. fresh spinach
- ½ tbsp. lemon juice
- ¼ tsp basil

Directions:
1. Add 1 tablespoon oil to the cooking pot and set to sauté on medium heat.
2. Season salmon with salt and pepper and add to the pot. Cook 8-10 minutes or until fish flakes easily with a fork, turning over halfway through cooking time. Transfer to a plate.
3. Add remaining oil and let heat up. Add remaining ingredients and cook 2-3 minutes until spinach is wilted.
4. Place fish on serving plates and top with spinach mixture. Serve immediately.

Nutrition:
- InfoCalories 436,Total Fat 30g,Total Carbs 4g,Protein 37g,Sodium 448mg.

Favorite Salmon Stew

Servings:4
Cooking Time: 11 Minutes
Ingredients:
- 1 cup fish broth
- Salt and pepper to taste
- 1 medium onion, chopped
- 1-2 pounds salmon fillets, cubed
- 1 tablespoon butter

Directions:
1. Add the listed to a large-sized bowl and let the shrimp marinate for 30-60 minutes
2. Grease the inner pot of the Ninja Foodi with butter and transfer marinated shrimp to the pot
3. Lock the lid and select "Bake/Roast" mode and bake for 15 minutes at 355 degrees F
4. Once done, serve and enjoy!

White Wine Mussels With Saffron Threads

Servings:4
Cooking Time: 25 Minutes
Ingredients:
- 2 tablespoons vegetable oil
- 2 shallots, sliced
- 3 garlic cloves, minced
- 1 cup cherry tomatoes, halved
- 2 pounds (907 g) fresh mussels, washed with cold water, strained, scrubbed, and debearded, as needed
- 2 cups white wine (chardonnay or sauvignon blanc)
- 2 cups heavy cream
- 1½ teaspoons cayenne pepper
- 1½ teaspoons freshly ground black pepper
- ½ teaspoon saffron threads
- 1 loaf sourdough bread, cut into slices, for serving

Directions:
1. Select SEAR/SAUTÉ and set the temperature to HI. Select START/STOP to begin and allow to preheat for 5 minutes.
2. Add oil to the pot and allow to heat for 1 minute. Add the shallots, garlic, and cherry tomatoes. Stir to ensure the ingredients are coated and sauté for 5 minutes.
3. Add the mussels, wine, heavy cream, cayenne, black pepper, and saffron threads to the pot.
4. Assemble the pressure lid, making sure the pressure release valve is in the VENT position.
5. Select STEAM and set the temperature to HI. Set the time to 20 minutes. Select START/STOP to begin.
6. When cooking is complete, carefully remove the lid.
7. Transfer the mussels and broth to bowls or eat straight from the pot. Discard any mussels that have not opened.
8. Serve with the bread and enjoy!

Heartfelt Sesame Fish

Servings: 4
Cooking Time: 8 Minutes
Ingredients:
- 1 and ½ pound salmon fillet
- 1 teaspoon sesame seeds
- 1 teaspoon butter, melted
- ½ teaspoon salt
- 1 tablespoon apple cider vinegar
- ¼ teaspoon rosemary, dried

Directions:
1. Take apple cider vinegar and spray it to the salmon fillets
2. Then add dried rosemary, sesame seeds, butter and salt
3. Mix them well. Take butter sauce and brush the salmon properly
4. Place the salmon on the rack and lower the air fryer lid. Set the air fryer mode
5. Cook the fish for 8 minutes at 360 F.Serve hot and enjoy!

Buttery Lemon Cod Over Couscous

Servings: 4
Cooking Time: 27-29 Minutes
Ingredients:
- 1 tbsp. extra-virgin olive oil
- 2 cups tricolor Israeli or pearl couscous
- 1 red bell pepper, diced
- 1 yellow bell pepper, diced
- 2½ cups chicken broth
- 4 tbsps. (½ stick) unsalted butter, melted
- 1 cup panko bread crumbs
- Juice of 1 lemon
- 1 tsp. grated lemon zest
- ¼ cup minced fresh parsley
- 1 tsp. sea salt
- 4 (5- to 6-ounce, 142 to 170 g) cod fillets

Directions:

1. Preheat the pot by selecting Sear/Sauté. Select Start/Stop to begin. Preheat for 5 minutes.
2. In the preheated pot, add the oil, couscous and red and yellow bell peppers, cook for 1 minute. Stir in the chicken broth.
3. Assemble the Pressure Lid, set the pressure release valve to Seal. Select Pressure and set the time to 6 minutes, then select Start/Stop to begin.
4. While the couscous is pressure cooking, add the butter, panko bread crumbs, lemon juice, lemon zest, parsley, and salt in a small mixing bowl, stir them together. Press the panko mixture evenly on top of each cod fillet.
5. After pressure cooking the couscous is finish, move the pressure release valve to the Vent position to quick release the pressure. Remove the lid when the pressure has finished releasing carefully.
6. Put the Reversible Rack in the pot over the couscous, put the cod fillets on the rack.
7. Close the Crisping Lid. Select Air Crisp, set the temperature to 350°F (175°C), and set the time to 12 minutes. Select Start/Stop to begin. Check the cod and cook for up to another 2 minutes if needed. Cooking is finish when the internal temperature of the fillets reaches 145°F (60°C).

Delightful Salmon Fillets

Servings: 4
Cooking Time: 5 Minutes
Ingredients:
- 2 salmon fillets
- ¼ cup onion, chopped
- 2 stalks green onion stalks, chopped
- 1 whole egg
- Almond meal as needed
- Salt and pepper to taste
- 2 tablespoons olive oil

Directions:
1. Add a cup of water to your Ninja Foodi and place a steamer rack on top
2. Place the fish. Season the fish with salt and pepper and lock up the lid
3. Cook on HIGH pressure for 3 minutes. Once done, quick release the pressure
4. Remove the fish and allow it to cool
5. Break the fillets into a bowl and add egg, yellow and green onions
6. Add ½ a cup of almond meal and mix with your hand. Divide the mixture into patties
7. Take a large skillet and place it over medium heat. Add oil and cook the patties. Enjoy!

Garlic Sauce And Mussels

Servings: 4
Cooking Time: 1 Minute
Ingredients:
- 3 pounds mussels
- 1 tablespoon extra-virgin olive oil
- 4 garlic cloves, minced
- 1 large roasted bell pepper
- ¾ cup fish stock
- ½ cup white wine vinegar
- 1/8 teaspoon red pepper flakes
- 2 tablespoons cashew cream
- 3 tablespoons parsley, chopped

Directions:
1. Clean the mussels well and scrub them, debeard if needed. Make a steaming liquid
2. Set your Ninja Foodi to Saute mode and add olive oil, allow it to heat up
3. Add garlic and cook for 1 minute
4. Add roasted red pepper, vinegar, fish stock, red pepper flakes and stir
5. Add mussels to the Ninja Foodi and lock up the lid
6. Cook on HIGH pressure for 1 minute and quick release the pressure
7. Remove the lid and check the mussels, if they are open then enjoy
8. If not, lock up the lid and steam for 1 minute more. Garnish with a bit of parsley. Enjoy!

Seafood Minestrone

Servings: 14
Cooking Time: 20 Minutes
Ingredients:
- 3 14 oz. cans beef broth, low sodium
- 28 oz. tomatoes, crushed
- 19 oz. garbanzo beans, undrained
- 15 ¼ oz. red kidney beans, undrained
- 16 oz. pkg. frozen mixed vegetables, thawed
- 16 oz. frozen spinach, thawed, chopped & drained
- 1 onion, chopped
- 1 tsp garlic powder
- ½ tsp pepper
- ½ cup elbow macaroni, uncooked
- 1 lb. cod, cut in 1-inch pieces
- 1 lb. shrimp, peeled & deveined

Directions:
1. Set cooker to sauté on med-high. Add the broth, tomatoes, garbanzo beans, kidney beans, vegetables, spinach, onion, and seasonings to the cooking pot, stir to mix. Bring to a boil.
2. Stir in the macaroni and cook until tender, about 8 minutes.
3. Reduce the heat to med-low and add the fish and shrimp. Cook 5-7 minutes until shrimp turn pink and fish flakes easily. Serve immediately.

Nutrition:
- InfoCalories 292, Total Fat 3g, Total Carbs 42g, Protein 25g, Sodium 645mg.

Fish Finger Sandwich

Servings: 4
Cooking Time: 15 Minutes
Ingredients:
- 2 eggs
- 8 ounces ale
- 1 cup cornstarch
- 1 cup all-purpose flour
- ½ tablespoon chili powder
- 1 tablespoon ground cumin
- 1 teaspoon sea salt

- 1 teaspoon freshly ground black pepper
- 4 cod fillets, cut into 16 half-inch strips
- Cooking spray
- Tartar sauce, for garnish
- 8 slices sandwich bread

Directions:
1. Insert Cook & Crisp Basket in pot. Close crisping lid. Select AIR CRISP, set temperature to 375°F (190°C), and set time to 5 minutes. Select START/STOP to begin preheating.
2. In a shallow bowl, whisk together the eggs and beer. In a medium bowl, whisk together the cornstarch, flour, chili powder, cumin, salt, and pepper.
3. Dip each strip of cod fillet in the egg mixture, then dredge in the flour mixture, coating on all sides.
4. Once unit has preheated, spray the basket with the cooking spray. Place the fish strips in the basket and coat them with cooking spray. Close crisping lid.
5. Select AIR CRISP, set temperature to 375°F (190°C), and set time to 15 minutes. Select START/STOP to begin.
6. When cooking is complete, check the fish for your desired crispiness. Remove the fish from the basket.
7. Spread tartar sauce on four slices of bread. Place four fish strips on each slice and top the sandwiches with the four remaining slices. Serve.

Nutrition:
- InfoCalories: 565,Total Fat: 13g,Sodium: 1216mg,Carbohydrates: 74g,Protein: 36g.

Buttery Salmon With Green Beans And Rice

Servings: 4
Cooking Time: 19 Minutes
Ingredients:
- 1½ cups water
- 1 cup quinoa, rinsed
- 4 (4-ounce, 113 g) frozen skinless salmon fillets
- 1 tsp. sea salt, divided
- 1 tsp. freshly ground black pepper, divided
- 1 tbsp. extra-virgin olive oil
- 8 ounces (227 g) green beans
- ½ tbsp. brown sugar
- 4 tbsps. (½ stick) unsalted butter, melted
- 2 garlic cloves, minced
- ½ tbsp. freshly squeezed lemon juice
- ½ tsp. dried thyme
- ½ tsp. dried rosemary

Directions:
1. In the pot, add the water and quinoa and stir to combine. Place the Reversible Rack in the pot.
2. Put the salmon fillets on the rack. Assemble the Pressure Lid, set the pressure release valve to Seal.
3. Select Pressure. Set the time to 2 minutes, then select Start/Stop to begin.
4. Meanwhile, add ½ teaspoon of salt, ½ teaspoon of black pepper, the olive oil and green beans into a medium bowl, toss well. Add the remaining ½ teaspoon each of salt and black pepper, the brown sugar, butter, garlic, lemon juice, thyme, and rosemary in a small bowl mix them together.
5. After pressure cooking the rice and salmon is finish, move the pressure release valve to the Vent position to quick release the pressure. Remove the lid when the pressure has finished releasing carefully.
6. Use a paper towel to gently pat dry the salmon, then coat with the garlic butter sauce.
7. Arrange around the salmon with the green beans. Close the Crisping Lid. Select Broil and set the time to 7 minutes, then select Start/Stop to begin.
8. After cooking is finish, remove the salmon from the rack and serve with the rice and green beans.

Beef, Pork & Lamb

Rosemary Pork Roast

Servings: 6
Cooking Time: 8 Hours
Ingredients:
- 3 pounds pork shoulder roast
- 1 cup bone broth
- 6 sprigs fresh rosemary
- 4 sprigs basil leaves
- 1 tablespoon chives, chopped
- ¼ teaspoon ground black pepper

Directions:
1. Add listed to Ninja Foodi
2. Lock lid and cook on SLOW COOK Mode for 8-10 hours. Serve and enjoy!

Mississippi Pot Roast With Potatoes

Servings: 6
Cooking Time: 1 Hr 40 Min
Ingredients:
- 2 pounds chuck roast /900g
- 5 potatoes, peeled and sliced
- 10 pepperoncini
- 2 bay leaves
- 1 onion, finely chopped
- ½ cup pepperoncini juice /125ml
- 6 cups beef broth /1500ml
- ¼ cup butter /32.5g
- 1 tbsp canola oil /15ml
- ½ tsp dried thyme /2.5g
- ½ tsp dried parsley /2.5g
- 1 tsp onion powder /5g
- 1 tsp garlic powder /5g
- 2 tsp salt /10g
- ½ tsp black pepper /2.5g

Directions:
1. Warm oil on Sear/Sauté. Season chuck roast with pepper and salt, then sear in the hot oil for 2 to 4 minutes for each side until browned. Set aside.
2. Melt butter and cook onion for 3 minutes until fragrant. Sprinkle with dried parsley, onion powder, dried thyme, and garlic powder and stir for 30 seconds.
3. Into the pot, stir bay leaves, beef broth, pepperoncini juice, and pepperoncini. Nestle chuck roast down into the liquid. Seal the pressure lid, choose Pressure, set to High, and set the timer to 60 minutes. Press Start.
4. Release pressure naturally for about 10 minutes. Set the chuck roast to a cutting board and use two forks to shred. Serve immediately.

Rich Beef Rendang

Servings: 6
Cooking Time: 25 Minutes
Ingredients:
- 1 cup onion, chopped
- 1 tablespoon ginger, chopped
- 1 tablespoon garlic, minced
- 1 small jalapeno pepper
- 2 tablespoons olive oil
- 1 pack rendang curry paste
- 1 pound skirt steak, cut into 2 inch chunks
- ½ cup of water
- 1 cup coconut milk (full fat)
- 2 tablespoons coconut, shredded

Directions:
1. Mince the onion, garlic, and ginger. Set your Ninja Foodi to Saute mode and add oil
2. Allow the oil to heat up and add veggies and stir them well. Add rending paste and stir for 3-4 minutes. Add skirt steak and stir to coat with the spices for about 2 minutes
3. Pour ¼ cup of water and deglazed. Lock up the lid and cook on HIGH pressure for 25 minutes
4. Release the pressure naturally over 10 minutes. Add ½ a cup of coconut milk and stir
5. Garnish with shredded coconut and serve!

Italian Rigatoni, Sausage, And Meatball Potpie

Servings: 8
Cooking Time: 55 Minutes
Ingredients:
- 5 cups, plus 1 teaspoon water, divided
- 1 (16-ounce / 454-g) box rigatoni pasta
- 4 (4-ounce / 113-g) fresh Italian sausage links
- 1 (12-ounce / 340-g) bag frozen cooked meatballs
- 16 ounces (454 g) whole milk Ricotta cheese
- 1 (25½-ounce / 723-g) jar marinara sauce
- 2 cups shredded Mozzarella cheese
- 1 refrigerated store-bought pie crust, room temperature
- 1 large egg

Directions:
1. Pour 5 cups of water and the rigatoni in the pot. Assemble pressure lid, making sure the pressure release valve is in the SEAL position.
2. Select PRESSURE and set to LO. Set time to 0 minutes. Select START/STOP to begin.
3. When pressure cooking is complete, quick release the pressure by turning the pressure release valve to the VENT position. Carefully remove lid when unit has finished releasing pressure.
4. Drain the pasta and set it aside, keeping warm. Wipe out pot and return it to base. Insert Cook & Crisp Basket into pot. Close crisping lid.

Ninja Foodi Cookbook

5. Select AIR CRISP, set temperature to 390°F(200°C), and set time to 15 minutes. Select START/STOP to begin. Let preheat for 5 minutes.
6. Open lid and place the sausages in the basket. Close lid and cook for 10 minutes.
7. When cooking is complete, remove sausages to a cutting board. Add the meatballs to the basket. Close crisping lid.
8. Select AIR CRISP, set temperature to 390°F(200°C), and set time to 10 minutes. Select START/STOP to begin.
9. Slice sausages into very thin rounds.
10. When cooking is complete, transfer the meatballs to the cutting board and slice them in half.
11. In the pot, in this order, add a layer of Ricotta, marinara sauce, sausage, Mozzarella cheese, pasta, marinara sauce, meatballs, Mozzarella cheese, pasta, Ricotta, and marinara sauce. Place the pie crust on top of the filling.
12. In a small bowl, whisk together the egg and remaining 1 teaspoon of water. Brush this on top of the pie crust. With a knife, slice a couple of small holes in the middle of crust to vent it. Close crisping lid.
13. Select BAKE/ROAST, set temperature to 350°F(175°C), and set time to 30 minutes. Select START/STOP to begin.
14. When cooking is complete, open lid. Let sit for 10 minutes before serving.

One Pot Ham & Rice

Servings: 4
Cooking Time: 10 Minutes
Ingredients:
- 2 tbsp. water
- ¼ cup celery, chopped
- ¼ cup onion, chopped
- ¼ cup green bell pepper, chopped
- ¼ cup fresh parsley, chopped
- ½ tsp garlic powder
- ¼ tsp pepper
- Nonstick cooking spray
- 5 slices lean deli ham, chopped
- 2 cups brown rice, cooked
- 2 eggs, beaten
- 1 green onion, sliced

Directions:
1. Add water to the cooking pot and set to sauté on medium heat.
2. Add the celery, onion, peppers, parsley, garlic powder, and pepper and cook until water evaporates and vegetables are tender, about 4-5 minutes.
3. Spray the vegetables and pot with cooking spray. Add ham and cook 1-2 minutes until heated through.
4. Stir in rice and mix well. Pour in eggs and cook until they are completely set, stirring occasionally.
5. Sprinkle with green onions and serve immediately.

Nutrition:
- InfoCalories 184,Total Fat 4g,Total Carbs 25g,Protein 11g,Sodium 413mg.

Pork, Green Beans, And Corn

Servings: 4
Cooking Time: 35 Minutes
Ingredients:
- 2 pounds (907 g) pork shoulder, boneless and cubed
- 1 cup (250 mL) green beans, trimmed and halved
- 1 cup (250 mL) corn
- 1 cup (250 mL) beef stock
- 2 garlic cloves, minced
- 1 teaspoon ground cumin
- A pinch of salt and black pepper

Directions:
1. Combine all the ingredients in the cooking pot.
2. Assemble pressure lid, making sure the pressure release valve is in the Seal position. Select Pressure and set to high. Set time to 35 minutes. Press Start to begin.
3. Once cooking is complete, do a natural pressure release for 10 minutes, then release any remaining pressure. Carefully open the lid.
4. Divide the mix among four plates and serve.

Crispy Pork Chops

Servings: 4
Cooking Time: 20 Minutes
Ingredients:
- 3 oz. pork rinds, crushed
- 1 tsp salt
- 1 tsp smoked paprika
- ½ tsp garlic powder
- ½ tsp onion powder
- 2 eggs
- Nonstick cooking spray
- 4 pork chops, boneless

Directions:
1. In a shallow bowl, combine pork rinds and seasonings.
2. In a separate shallow bowl, add eggs and beat lightly.
3. Spray the fryer basket with cooking spray.
4. Dip the chops first in the egg then coat with pork rind mixture. Place in the basket.
5. Add the tender-crisp lid and set to air fry on 400°F (205°C). Cook 1-inch chops 12 minutes, and 2-inch thick chops 20 minutes, turning chops over halfway through cooking time. Serve immediately.

Nutrition:
- InfoCalories 277,Total Fat 15g,Total Carbs 1g,Protein 32g,Sodium 680mg.

Bacon Strips

Servings: 2
Cooking Time: 7 Minutes
Ingredients:
- 10 bacon strips
- 1/4 teaspoon chilli flakes
- 1/3 teaspoon salt
- 1/4 teaspoon basil, dried

Directions:
1. Rub the bacon strips with chilli flakes, dried basil, and salt.
2. Turn on your air fryer and place the bacon on the rack.
3. Lower the air fryer lid. Cook the bacon at 400 °F (205°C) for 5 minutes.
4. Cook for 3 minutes more if the bacon is not fully cooked. Serve and enjoy.

Nutrition:
- InfoCalories: 500; Fat: 46g; Carbohydrates: 0g; Protein: 21g

Paprika Pork And Brussels Sprouts

Servings: 4
Cooking Time: 30 Minutes
Ingredients:
- 2 tablespoons olive oil
- 2 pounds (907 g) pork shoulder, cubed
- 2 cups (500 mL) Brussels sprouts, trimmed and halved
- 1½ cups (375 mL) beef stock
- 1 tablespoon sweet paprika
- 1 tablespoon chopped parsley

Directions:
1. Press the Sauté button and heat the olive oil.
2. Add the pork and brown for 5 minutes. Stir in the remaining ingredients.
3. Assemble pressure lid, making sure the pressure release valve is in the Seal position. Select Pressure and set to high . Set time to 25 minutes. Press Start to begin.
4. Once cooking is complete, do a natural pressure release for 10 minutes, then release any remaining pressure. Carefully open the lid.
5. Divide the mix between plates and serve warm.

Pineapple Rack Ribs

Servings:4
Cooking Time: 29 Minutes
Ingredients:
- 1 (3-pound / 1.4-kg) rack St. Louis ribs, cut in thirds
- 1 teaspoon sea salt
- ½ teaspoon freshly ground black pepper
- ½ cup water
- ¼ cup apple cider vinegar
- ½ cup tomato ketchup
- 1 (8-ounce / 227-g) can crushed pineapple
- 3 tablespoons brown sugar
- 2 tablespoons cornstarch
- 1 tablespoon soy sauce

Directions:
1. Season the ribs with salt and pepper.
2. Pour the water into the pot. Place the ribs in the Cook & Crisp Basket and insert basket in pot. Assemble pressure lid, making sure the pressure release valve is in the SEAL position.
3. Select PRESSURE and set to HI. Set time to 19 minutes. Select START/STOP to begin.
4. Add the vinegar, ketchup, pineapple, brown sugar, cornstarch, and soy sauce to a blender and blend under high speed until well combined.
5. When pressure cooking is complete, quick release the pressure by turning the pressure release valve to the VENT position. Carefully remove pressure lid when unit has finished releasing pressure.
6. Liberally brush the ribs with the sauce. Close crisping lid.
7. Select AIR CRISP, set temperature to 400°F(205°C) , and set time to 20 minutes. Select START/STOP to begin.
8. After 10 minutes, open lid and liberally brush ribs with additional sauce. Flip the ribs and brush the other side. Close lid and continue cooking. Add additional time and basting as desired for crispier results.
9. When cooking is complete, the internal temperature of the meat should read at least 185°F(85°C) on a meat thermometer. Remove basket and ribs and serve.

Greek Lamb Gyros

Servings:4
Cooking Time: 25 Minutes
Ingredients:
- 8 garlic cloves
- 1 and ½ teaspoon salt
- 2 teaspoons dried oregano
- 1 and ½ cups of water
- 2 pounds lamb meat, ground
- 2 teaspoons rosemary
- ½ teaspoon pepper
- 1 small onion, chopped
- 2 teaspoons ground marjoram

Directions:
1. Add onion, garlic, marjoram, rosemary, salt and pepper to food processor and process
2. Add ground lamb meat and process again. Press meat mixture into pan
3. Transfer loaf to Ninja Foodi and "BAKE/ROAST" for 25 minutes at 375 degrees f
4. Serve and enjoy!

Beef Stew With Beer

Servings: 4
Cooking Time: 60 Min
Ingredients:
- 2 lb. beef stewed meat; cut into bite-size pieces /900g
- 1 packet dry onion soup mix
- 2 cloves garlic; minced
- 2 cups beef broth /500ml
- ¼ cup flour /32.5g
- 1 medium bottle beer
- 3 tbsp butter/45g
- 2 tbsp Worcestershire sauce /30ml
- 1 tbsp tomato paste /15g
- Salt and black pepper to taste

Directions:
1. In a zipper bag, add beef, salt, all-purpose flour, and pepper. Close the bag up and shake it to coat the meat well with the mixture. Select Sear/Sauté mode on the Foodi. Melt the butter, and brown the beef on both sides, for 5 minutes.
2. Pour the broth to deglaze the bottom of the pot. Stir in tomato paste, beer, Worcestershire sauce, and the onion soup mix.
3. Close the lid, secure the pressure valve, and select Pressure mode on High pressure for 25 minutes. Press Start/Stop to start cooking.
4. Once the timer is done, do a natural pressure release for 10 minutes, and then a quick pressure release to let out any remaining steam.
5. Open the pressure lid and close the crisping lid. Cook on Broil mode for 10 minutes. Spoon the beef stew into serving bowls and serve with over a bed of vegetable mash with steamed greens.

Beef Lasagna

Servings: 4
Cooking Time: 10-15 Minutes
Ingredients:
- 2 small onions
- 2 garlic cloves, minced
- 1-pound ground beef
- 1 large egg
- 1 and 1/2 cups ricotta cheese
- 1/2 cup parmesan cheese
- 1 jar 25 ounces0 marinara sauce
- 8 ounces mozzarella cheese, sliced

Directions:
1. Select "Sauté" mode on your Ninja Foodi and stir in beef, brown the beef.
2. Add onion and garlic.
3. Add parmesan, ricotta, egg in a small dish and keep it on the side.
4. Stir in sauce to browned meat, reserve half for later.
5. Sprinkle mozzarella and half of ricotta cheese into the browned meat.
6. Top with remaining meat sauce.
7. For the final layer, add more mozzarella cheese and the remaining ricotta.
8. Stir well.
9. Cover with a foil transfer to Ninja Foodi.
10. Lock and secure the Ninja Foodi's lid, then cook on "HIGH" pressure for 8-10 minutes.
11. Quick-release pressure.
12. Drizzle parmesan cheese on top.
13. Enjoy.

Nutrition:
- InfoCalories: 365; Fats: 25g; Carbohydrates: 6g; Protein: 25g

Cuban Flank Steak

Servings: 6
Cooking Time: 8 Hours
Ingredients:
- 15 oz. tomatoes, crushed
- 1 tbsp. apple cider vinegar
- 2 cloves garlic, chopped fine
- 1 tbsp. cumin
- 1 jalapeño, chopped fine
- 2 lbs. flank steak
- 2 red bell peppers, chopped
- 1 onion, chopped
- ½ tsp salt
- ¼ cup black olives, pitted & chopped
- 3 tbsp. green onions, sliced

Directions:
1. Add all ingredients, except the olives, to the cooking pot. Stir to coat.
2. Add the lid and set to slow cook on low. Cook 8 hours or until beef is tender.
3. Transfer beef to a large bowl and shred, using 2 forks. Return the beef to the pot.
4. Add the olives and stir to combine. Serve as is garnished with green onions, or over hot, cooked rice.

Nutrition:
- InfoCalories 348,Total Fat 13g,Total Carbs 11g,Protein 45g,Sodium 380mg.

Pork And Peanut Lettuce Wraps

Servings:6
Cooking Time: 30 Minutes
Ingredients:
- 3 pounds (1.4 kg) boneless pork shoulder, cut into 1- to 2-inch cubes
- 2 cups light beer
- 1 cup brown sugar
- 1 teaspoon chipotle chiles in adobo sauce
- 1 cup barbecue sauce
- 1 head iceberg lettuce, quartered and leaves separated
- 1 cup roasted peanuts, chopped or ground
- Cilantro leaves

Directions:
1. Place the pork, beer, brown sugar, chipotle, and barbecue sauce in the pot. Assemble pressure lid, making sure the pressure release valve is in the SEAL position.
2. Select PRESSURE and set to HI. Set the timer to 30 minutes. Select START/STOP to begin.
3. When pressure cooking is complete, quick release the pressure by turning the pressure release valve to the VENT position. Carefully remove lid when unit has finished releasing pressure.
4. Using a silicone-tipped utensil, shred the pork in the pot. Stir to mix the meat in with the sauce.
5. Place a small amount of pork in a piece of lettuce. Top with peanuts and cilantro to serve.

Lime And Ginger Low Carb Pork

Servings:4
Cooking Time:4-7 Hours
Ingredients:
- 1 tablespoon avocado oil
- 2 and ½ pounds pork loin
- Salt and pepper to taste
- 1 teaspoon stevia drops
- ¼ cup tamari
- 1 tablespoon Worcestershire sauce
- Juice of 1 lime
- 2 garlic cloves, minced
- 1 tablespoon fresh ginger
- Fresh cilantro

Directions:
1. Set your Ninja Foodi to Saute mode and add oil, let the oil heat up
2. Season pork with salt and pepper and add to the pot
3. Take a bowl and whisk in remaining except for cilantro and pour it over pork
4. Lock lid and cook on SLOW COOK mode. Cook for 4-7 hours on HIGH pressure
5. Naturally, release pressure over 10 minutes. Garnish with cilantro. Serve and enjoy!

The Chipotle Copycat Dish

Servings: 6
Cooking Time: 90 Minutes
Ingredients:
- 3 pounds grass-fed chuck roast, large chunks
- 1 large onion, peeled and sliced
- 6 garlic cloves
- 2 cans (14.5 ounces green chilies
- 1 tablespoon oregano
- 1 teaspoon salt and pepper
- 3 dried chipotle pepper, stems removed, broken into small pieces
- Juice of 3 limes
- 3 tablespoons coconut vinegar
- 1 tablespoon cumin
- ½ cup of water

Directions:
1. Add the listed to your Ninja Foodi
2. Stir and lock up the lid, cook on HIGH pressure for 60 minutes
3. Release the pressure naturally over 10 minutes. Remove the lid and shred using a fork
4. Set your pot to Saute mode and reduce for 30 minutes. Enjoy once ready!

Lamb Chops And Potato Mash

Servings: 8
Cooking Time: 40 Min
Ingredients:
- 5 potatoes, peeled and chopped
- 4 cilantro leaves, for garnish
- 8 lamb cutlets
- 1 green onion; chopped
- ⅓ cup milk /88ml
- 1 cup beef stock /250ml
- 3 sprigs rosemary leaves; chopped
- 3 tbsp butter, softened /45g
- 1 tbsp olive oil /15ml
- 1 tbsp tomato puree /15ml
- salt to taste

Directions:
1. Rub rosemary leaves and salt to the lamb chops. Warm oil and 2 tbsp or 30g of butter on Sear/Sauté. Add in the lamb chops and cook for 1 minute for each side until browned; set aside on a plate.
2. In the pot, mix tomato puree and green onion; cook for 2-3 minutes. Add beef stock into the pot to deglaze, scrape the bottom to get rid of any browned bits of food.
3. Return lamb cutlets alongside any accumulated juices to the pot. Set a reversible rack on lamb cutlets. Place steamer basket on the reversible rack. Arrange potatoes in the steamer basket.
4. Seal the pressure lid, choose Pressure, set to High, and set the timer to 4 minutes. Press Start.
5. When ready, release the pressure quickly. Remove trivet and steamer basket from pot. In a high speed blender, add potatoes, milk, salt, and remaining tbsp butter. Blend well until you obtain a smooth consistency.
6. Divide the potato mash between serving dishes. Lay lamb chops on the mash. Drizzle with cooking liquid obtained from pressure cooker; apply cilantro sprigs for garnish.

Tomato-basil Bread Pizza

Servings: 6
Cooking Time: 10 Minutes
Ingredients:
- 6 slices frozen garlic bread or Texas Toast
- ¾ cup tomato-basil sauce or your favorite tomato sauce
- 6 slices Mozzarella cheese

Directions:
1. Insert Cook & Crisp Basket in pot. Close crisping lid. Select AIR CRISP, set temperature to 390°F(200°C), and set time to 5 minutes. Select START/STOP to begin preheating.
2. Once unit has preheated, place three of the garlic bread slices in the basket, and top with half the sauce and 3 slices of cheese. Close crisping lid.
3. Select AIR CRISP, set temperature to 375°F(190°C), and set time to 5 minutes. Select START/STOP to begin.
4. When cooking is complete, remove the pizzas from the basket. Repeat steps 2 and 3 with the remaining slices of garlic bread, sauce, and cheese.

Cauliflower And Chickpea Green Salad

Servings: 6
Cooking Time: 15 Minutes
Ingredients:
- 1 head cauliflower, cut into florets
- 1 (14-ounce / 397-g) can chickpeas, rinsed and drained
- 3 tablespoons, plus ¼ cup extra-virgin olive oil
- 1 tablespoon chili powder
- 2 teaspoons paprika
- 3 garlic cloves, minced
- 4 cups mixed baby greens
- 1 cucumber, sliced
- 3 tablespoons chopped fresh parsley
- Juice of 1 lemon
- 2 tablespoons honey
- 2 tablespoons Dijon mustard
- 2 tablespoons apple cider vinegar
- ⅓ cup crumbled feta cheese
- Sea salt
- Freshly ground black pepper

Directions:
1. Insert Cook & Crisp Basket in pot. Close crisping lid. Select AIR CRISP, set temperature to 390°F(200°C), and set the time to 5 minutes. Select START/STOP to begin preheating.
2. In a large bowl combine the cauliflower florets, chickpeas, 3 tablespoons of olive oil, chili powder, paprika, and garlic.
3. Once unit has preheated, open lid and add the cauliflower and chickpeas to the basket. Close lid.
4. Select AIR CRISP, set temperature to 390°F(200°C), and set time to 15 minutes. Select START/STOP to begin.
5. In another large bowl, combine the mixed greens, cucumber, and parsley.
6. In a small bowl, whisk together the lemon juice, honey, mustard, and vinegar.

7. When cooking is complete, carefully remove basket with cauliflower and chickpeas. Add them to the bowl of greens and toss well to combine. Top with feta cheese and dressing, season with salt and pepper, and serve.

Calzones With Sausage And Mozzarella

Servings: 4
Cooking Time: 35 Min
Ingredients:
- 1 pound frozen bread dough /450g
- 1 small green bell pepper, seeded and chopped
- 2 or 3 Italian sausages
- ¼ cup tomato sauce /62.5ml
- 1 cup shredded mozzarella cheese /130g
- 2 tbsp olive oil/30ml

Directions:
1. On your Foodi, choose Sear/Sauté, and adjust to Medium-High to preheat the inner pot. Press Start to preheat the pot. Heat 1 tbsp of olive oil in the pot and sauté the bell pepper for 1 minute or until just starting to soften. Remove the pepper into a plate and set aside. Brown the sausages for 2 to 3 minutes on one side. Turn the sausages and brown the other side.
2. Add ¾ cup of water to the inner pot. Then, lock the pressure lid into place and set to seal. Choose Pressure; adjust the pressure to High and the cook time to 4 minutes. Press Start. After cooking, perform a quick pressure release and carefully open the pressure lid.
3. Remove the sausages from the pot onto a cutting board and cool for several minutes. Discard the water in the pot, wipe the pot dry with a clean napkin, and return the pot to the base. When the sausages have cooled, slice into ¼-inch rounds.
4. Cut four pieces of parchment paper about 8 inches and divide the dough into four equal pieces. One at a time and on a piece of parchment, use your hands to press each dough into a circle about 6 to 7 inches in diameter.
5. Close the crisping lid. Choose Bake/Roast and adjust the temperature to 400°F or 205°C. Press Start to preheat the pot for 5 minutes.
6. While the preheats, make the calzones. One after the other, spread 1 tbsp of tomato sauce over half a dough circle, leaving a ½-inch clear border. Arrange the sausage rounds in a single layer and sprinkle a quarter of the green peppers over the top.
7. Top with a quarter cup of cheese. Use the parchment to pull the other side of the dough over the filling and pinch the edges together to seal. Repeat the process with another dough.
8. Cut the parchment around each calzone, so it is about ½ inch larger than the calzone. Brush the calzones with some of the remaining olive oil. With a large spatula, transfer the two calzones to the reversible rack set in the lower position in the pot. Open the lid and place the rack in the pot.
9. Close the crisping lid and choose Bake/Roast; adjust the temperature to 400°F or 205°C and the cook time to 12 minutes. Press Start.
10. After 6 minutes, check the calzones, which will be a dark golden brown. Remove the rack and turn the calzones over. Remove the parchment paper and brush the tops with a little olive oil. Return the rack to the pot. Close the lid and continue cooking for the last 6 minutes.
11. While the first two calzones bake, assemble the remaining two. When the first set of calzones are done, transfer to a wire rack to cool and bake the second batch.

Beef Prime Roast

Servings: 4
Cooking Time: 45 Minutes
Ingredients:
- 2 pounds chuck roast
- 1 tablespoon olive oil
- 1 teaspoon salt
- 1 teaspoon black pepper
- 1 teaspoon onion powder
- 1 teaspoon garlic powder
- 4 cups beef stock

Directions:
1. Place roast in Ninja Food pot and season it well with black pepper and salt.
2. Stir in oil and set the pot to Sauté mode, sear each side of the roast for 3 minutes until slightly browned.
3. Add beef broth, onion powder, garlic powder, and stir.
4. Lock and secure the Ninja Foodi's lid, then cook on "HIGH" pressure for 40 minutes.
5. Once done, naturally release the pressure over 10 minutes.
6. Open the Ninja Foodi's lid and serve hot. Enjoy.

Nutrition:
- InfoCalories: 308; Fat: 22g; Carbohydrates: 2g; Protein: 24g

Farro, Fennel And Arugula Salad

Servings:6
Cooking Time: 10 Minutes
Ingredients:
- 1 cup farro
- 2 fennel bulbs, fronds separated and reserved (optional), bulbs halved, cored, and diced
- 1 tablespoon fennel seeds
- Zest and juice of 1 lemon
- 1 teaspoon kosher salt, plus more as needed
- 2 tablespoons extra-virgin olive oil
- 5 ounces (142 g) arugula leaves

Directions:
1. Place the farro, half the fennel, the fennel seeds, lemon zest, and salt into the Foodi's inner pot. Add 1¾ cups water, lock on the Pressure Lid, making sure the valve is set to Seal, and set to Pressure on High for 10 minutes. When the timer reaches 0, allow the pressure to naturally release for 5 minutes, then quick-release any remaining pressure and carefully remove the lid. Allow the farro to cool completely.
2. Chop the fennel fronds, if using, and add them to the cooled farro along with the remaining chopped fennel, the lemon juice, and the olive oil. Toss to coat. Add the arugula and toss once more. Season with salt and serve.

Maple Apples & Pork Chops

Servings: 4
Cooking Time: 40 Minutes
Ingredients:
- Nonstick cooking spray
- 2 Granny Smith apples, cored & sliced thin
- ¼ cup water
- ½ tsp cinnamon
- 1 tbsp. maple syrup, sugar free
- 4 pork chops, boneless

Directions:
1. Spray the cooking pot with cooking spray. Set to sauté on medium heat.
2. Add the apples and cook until browned on both sides, stirring occasionally.
3. Add water and cinnamon, cover, and simmer 10-15 minutes or until apples are tender.
4. Remove lid, increase heat and cook, stirring until water has evaporated. Transfer apples to a bowl and stir in the syrup. Keep warm.
5. Spray the rack with cooking spray and place it in the pot. Place the pork chops on the plate and add the tender-crisp lid. Set to broil. Broil chops about 10 minutes per side.
6. Transfer chops to serving plates and top with apple mixture. Serve immediately.

Nutrition:
- InfoCalories 292,Total Fat 13g,Total Carbs 13g,Protein 29g,Sodium 70mg.

Spanish White Quinoa

Servings:6
Cooking Time: 2 Minutes
Ingredients:
- 1 cup white quinoa, rinsed
- 1 (14-ounce / 397-g) can diced tomatoes with juice
- 2 garlic cloves, minced
- 1 teaspoon ground cumin
- ½ teaspoon chili powder
- ½ teaspoon kosher salt
- 1 tablespoon unsalted butter

Directions:
1. Place the quinoa, tomatoes and juice, garlic, cumin, chili powder, salt, butter, and ½ cup water into the Foodi's inner pot and stir to combine. Lock on the Pressure Lid, set the valve to Seal, and set the Foodi to Pressure on High for 2 minutes. When the timer reaches 0, allow the pressure to naturally release for 10 minutes, then quick-release any remaining pressure and carefully remove the lid.
2. Fluff with a silicone spatula and serve.

Simple Beef & Shallot Curry

Servings: 4
Cooking Time: 40 Minutes
Ingredients:
- 1 lb. beef stew meat
- ¼ tsp salt
- 1/8 tsp turmeric
- 2 tbsp. olive oil
- 2 tbsp. shallots, sliced
- 1 tbsp. fresh ginger, grated
- 1 tbsp. garlic, chopped fine
- 3 cups water
- 2 tsp fish sauce
- 8 shallots, peeled & left whole
- ½ tsp chili powder

Directions:
1. In a large bowl, combine beef, salt, and turmeric, use your fingers to massage the seasonings into the meat. Cover and refrigerate 1 hour.
2. Add the oil to the cooking pot and set to sauté on med-high.
3. Add the sliced shallot and cook until golden brown, 6-8 minutes. Transfer to a bowl.
4. Add the garlic and ginger to the pot and cook 1 minute or until fragrant.
5. Add the beef and cook until no pink shows, about 5-6 minutes. Stir in the water and fish sauce until combined.
6. Add the lid and set to pressure cook on high. Set the timer for 20 minutes. When the timer goes off, use manual release to remove the pressure.
7. Set back to sauté on med-high and add the fried shallots, whole shallots, and chili powder. Cook, stirring frequently, until shallots are soft and sauce has thickened, about 10 minutes. Serve.

Nutrition:
- InfoCalories 70,Total Fat 9g,Total Carbs 4g,Protein 7g,Sodium 130mg.

Generous Shepherd's Pie

Servings: 4
Cooking Time: 10-15 Minutes
Ingredients:
- 2 cups of water
- 4 tablespoons butter
- 4 ounces cream cheese
- 1 cup mozzarella
- 1 whole egg
- Salt and pepper to taste
- 1 tablespoon garlic powder
- 2-3 pounds ground beef
- 1 cup frozen carrots
- 8 ounces mushrooms, sliced
- 1 cup beef broth

Directions:
1. Add water to Ninja Foodi, arrange cauliflower on top, lock lid and cook for 5 minutes on HIGH pressure
2. Quick release and transfer to a blender, add cream cheese, butter, mozzarella cheese, egg, pepper, and salt. Blend well. Drain water from Ninja Foodi and add beef
3. Add carrots, garlic powder, broth and pepper, and salt
4. Add in cauliflower mix and lock lid, cook for 10 minutes on HIGH pressure
5. Release pressure naturally over 10 minutes. Serve and enjoy!

Cajun Red Beans And Rice

Servings: 4
Cooking Time: 47 Minutes
Ingredients:
- For the Rice:
- 2 cups short-grain white rice, rinsed well
- ½ teaspoon kosher salt
- For the Beans:
- 3 tablespoons peanut oil or vegetable oil
- 3 celery stalks, chopped
- 1 medium yellow onion, diced
- 1 green bell pepper, seeded, ribbed, and diced
- 3 garlic cloves, minced
- 5 sprigs fresh thyme
- 2 dried bay leaves, or 1 fresh
- 3 tablespoons Cajun seasoning
- 1 smoked ham hock
- 1 pound (454 g) dried red kidney beans
- 1 teaspoon kosher salt
- Fresh thyme leaves, for garnish
- Black pepper, for garnish

Directions:
1. Make the Rice
2. Add the rice, 2 cups water, and the salt to the Foodi's inner pot. Lock on the Pressure Lid, making sure the valve is set to Seal, and set to Pressure on High for 3 minutes. When the timer reaches 0, allow the pressure to naturally release for 11 minutes, then quick-release any remaining pressure and carefully remove the lid. Transfer the rice to a large bowl. Wash and dry the inner pot.
3. Make the Beans
4. Add the oil to the inner pot, set the Foodi to Sear/Saute on High, and heat the oil for 5 minutes. Add the celery, onion, and bell pepper and cook until beginning to soften, about 6 minutes, stirring often.
5. Add the garlic, thyme, bay leaves, and Cajun seasoning and cook until aromatic, about 3 minutes, stirring occasionally.
6. Add the ham hock, kidney beans, and 4 cups water and stir. Lock on the Pressure Lid, making sure the valve is set to Seal, and set the Foodi to Pressure on High for 30 minutes. When the timer reaches 0, allow the pressure to naturally release for 15 minutes, then quick-release any remaining pressure and carefully remove the lid. Stir in the salt. Add a ladleful of beans and broth to a bowl, top with a small scoop of rice, and serve with extra thyme and pepper.

Crispy Korean-style Ribs

Servings: 4
Cooking Time: 25 Minutes
Ingredients:
- ½ cup soy sauce
- 2 tablespoons rice vinegar
- 2 tablespoons sesame oil
- 1 tablespoon cayenne pepper
- 8 garlic cloves, minced
- 1 tablespoon grated fresh ginger
- 1 small onion, minced
- 1 rack baby back ribs, cut into quarters
- ½ cup water
- ¼ cup honey
- Sesame seeds, for garnish

Directions:
1. In a mixing bowl, combine the soy sauce, rice vinegar, sesame oil, cayenne pepper, garlic, ginger, and onion. Pour the mixture over the ribs, cover, and let marinate in the refrigerator for 30 minutes.
2. Place the ribs in the Cook & Crisp Basket, reserving the remaining marinade. Pour the water in the pot and place basket in pot. Assemble pressure lid, making sure the pressure release valve is in the SEAL position.
3. Select PRESURE and set to HI. Set time to 10 minutes. Select START/STOP to begin.
4. When pressure cooking is complete, quick release the pressure by turning the pressure release valve to the VENT position. Carefully remove lid when pressure has finished releasing.
5. Pour the remaining marinade over the ribs. Close lid.
6. Select AIR CRISP, set temperature to 400°F (205°C), and set time to 15 minutes. Select START/STOP to begin.
7. After 10 minutes, open lid and liberally brush the ribs with the honey. Close lid and continue cooking.
8. When cooking is complete, open lid and remove the ribs. Cut them into individual ribs. Sprinkle with the sesame seeds and serve.

Nutrition:
- InfoCalories: 1133, Total Fat: 88g, Sodium: 2055mg, Carbohydrates: 25g, Protein: 57g.

Zinfandel Braised Beef

Servings: 6
Cooking Time: 2 Hours
Ingredients:
- 3 ½ lb. chuck roast, boneless
- 1 ½ tsp salt, divided
- 2 tsp water
- 4 oz. pancetta, cut in ¼-inch cubes
- 2 onions, chopped
- 2 carrots, chopped
- 2 stalks celery
- 1 tbsp. tomato paste
- 3 cloves garlic, chopped fine
- 14 ½ oz. tomatoes, diced & drained
- 1 tbsp. fresh oregano, chopped
- 1 tsp fresh rosemary, chopped
- 1 bottle Zinfandel wine

Directions:
1. Season the roast with salt and let sit.
2. Add 2 teaspoons water to the cooking pot and set to sauté on medium heat. When water starts to simmer, add pancetta, reduce heat to med-low and cook until pancetta is brown and crisp. Use a slotted spoon to transfer to a paper towel lined plate.
3. Increase the heat to medium and brown the roast on all sides. Transfer it to a bowl.
4. Add the onions, carrot, celery, and remaining salt to the pot. Cook, stirring frequently, 2-3 minutes.
5. Stir in the tomato paste and cook 1-2 minutes. Add the garlic and cook 1 minute more.

6. Add the tomatoes, pancetta, herbs, and wine and stir to mix. Return the roast to the pot. Add the lid and set to pressure cook on high. Set the timer for 90 minutes. When the timer goes off, use manual release to remove the pressure.
7. Beef should be tender, transfer to a bowl and tent with foil to keep warm. Use an immersion blender and blend the vegetables remaining in the pot.
8. Set the cooker back to sauté on med-high heat. Bring to a boil and cook until sauce reduces by half. Season with salt and pepper to taste.
9. Slice the meat and place on serving plate, top with sauce and serve.

Nutrition:
- InfoCalories 131,Total Fat 5g,Total Carbs 2g,Protein 14g,Sodium 128mg.

Philippine Pork Chops

Servings: 6
Cooking Time: 2 Hours 20 Min
Ingredients:
- 2 lb. pork chops /900g
- 5 garlic cloves, coarsely chopped
- 2 bay leaves
- 1 tbsp peanut oil /15ml
- 2 tbsp soy sauce /30ml
- 1 tbsp peppercorns /15g
- 1 tsp salt /5g

Directions:
1. Combine the bay leaves, soy sauce, garlic, salt, peppercorns, and oil, in a bowl. Rub the mixture onto meat. Wrap the pork with a plastic foil and refrigerate for 2h.
2. Place the pork in the Foodi, close the crisping lid and cook for 10 minutes on Air Crisp mode at 350 °F or 175°C. Increase the temperature to 370 °F or 185°C, flip the chops, and cook for another 10 minutes. Discard bay leaves before serving.

Beef Short Rib & Ale Stew

Servings: 8
Cooking Time: 3 Hours 30 Minutes
Ingredients:
- 4 slices bacon, thick cut
- ½ cup flour
- 2 tbsp. hot paprika
- 2 tsp smoked paprika
- 1 ½ tsp salt, divided
- 1 teaspoon pepper
- 4 lbs. beef short ribs, bone in & trimmed
- 1 onion, chopped
- 4 cloves garlic, chopped fine
- 12 oz. malty brown ale
- 14 ½ oz. whole peeled tomatoes, chopped & juices reserved
- 2 lbs. Yukon Gold potatoes, peel & cut in 1-inch pieces
- 2 large carrots, peel & cut in 1-inch pieces
- 1 lb. turnips, peel & cut in 1-inch pieces

Directions:
1. Add the bacon to the cooking pot and set to sauté on med-high heat. Cook until most of the fat has been rendered, about 5 minutes. Transfer bacon to a paper towel lined plate. Drain off all but 1 tablespoon of the fat.
2. In a large bowl, combine flour, both paprika, 1 teaspoon salt, and pepper, until well mixed. Coat the ribs on all sides.
3. Add the ribs to the pot, working in batches if needed, and brown on all sides, about 3-5 minutes per side. Transfer to a bowl.
4. Add the onions to the pot and season with ½ teaspoon salt. Cook, stirring occasionally, until translucent, about 4 minutes. Add the garlic and cook 1 minute more.
5. Stir in ale, scraping up brown bits from the bottom of the pot. Add tomatoes and crumble the bacon in the pot. Increase heat to high and bring to a boil.
6. Return the ribs to the pot. Add the lid and set to pressure cook on high. Set timer for 1 hour. When timer goes off, use quick release to remove the pressure.
7. Add the potatoes, turnips, and carrots, stir to combine. Replace the lid and pressure cook on high 20 minutes. When the timer goes off, use quick release again.
8. Remove the bones before ladling into bowls and serving.

Nutrition:
- InfoCalories 114,Total Fat 5g,Total Carbs 7g,Protein 9g,Sodium 119mg.

Ham, Bean & Butternut Soup

Servings: 6
Cooking Time: 4 ½ Hours
Ingredients:
- 2 tbsp. extra virgin olive oil
- 2 cups onion, chopped
- 3 bay leaves
- 2 stalks celery, chopped
- 4 cloves garlic, chopped fine
- 3 ½ cups sugar pumpkin, cut in 1-inch pieces
- ½ lb. ham hock
- 8 cups chicken broth, low sodium
- 1 tomato, chopped
- ½ tsp thyme
- 30 oz. cannellini beans, drained & rinsed
- ¼ tsp pepper
- 4 Swiss chard leaves, rib removed & chopped

Directions:
1. Add the oil to the cooking pot and set to sauté on med-high heat.
2. Add the onion and bay leaves and cook, stirring frequently, until onion starts to soften, about 2-3 minutes.
3. Add celery and cook 3 minutes. Add garlic and cook 1 minute more.
4. Add pumpkin, broth, tomatoes, thyme, and ham hock, stir to mix. Add the lid and set to slow cook on high. Cook 4 hours or until ham if falling off the bone.
5. Transfer ham hock to a plate to cool slightly. Stir the beans, pepper, and chard into the soup. Recover and let cook until chard is wilted.
6. Remove the ham from the bone and chop it. Return it to the pot and continue cooking until heated through. Discard bay leaves before serving.

Nutrition:
- InfoCalories 51,Total Fat 2g,Total Carbs 7g,Protein 3g,Sodium 224mg.

The Calabacita Squash Meal

Servings: 4
Cooking Time: 90 Minutes
Ingredients:
- 1 pork tenderloin
- 1 tablespoon of chili powder
- 1 tablespoon of ground cumin
- 1 tablespoon of garlic powder
- 1 and a ½ teaspoon of salt
- 1 tablespoon of butter/ghee
- 14 ounce of tomatoes, diced
- 6 Calabacita squash, deseeded
- For the chipotle cream sauce
- 1/3 cup of canola-oil free mayo
- 3 tablespoon of fresh lime juice
- 1 and a ½ a teaspoon of chipotle/ chili powder

Directions:
1. Prepare the tenderloin by dusting it with half of the chili powder, garlic, cumin and salt
2. Set your Ninja Foodi to Saute mode and add butter, allow the butter to melt
3. Add seasoned pork and sear all sides for 3-4 minutes until browned
4. Add 4-6 cups of water and lock up the lid
5. Cook on MEAT mode at default settings and release the pressure naturally over 10 minutes
6. Transfer the pork to a large mixing bowl and shred it into small pieces
7. Add canned tomatoes and remaining spice to the bowl. Stir well
8. Spread the deseeded squash into a large rimmed baking sheet with the cut side facing up
9. Stuff the squash with the pork mixture and bake for 45 minutes at 350 degrees Fahrenheit
10. Prepare the sauce by mixing the sauce
11. Pour the sauce on top of the pork and garnish with cilantro. Serve and enjoy!

Maple Glazed Pork Chops

Servings: 4
Cooking Time: 12 Minutes
Ingredients:
- 2 tablespoons choc zero maple syrup
- 4 tablespoons mustard
- 2 tablespoons garlic, minced
- Black pepper and salt to taste
- 4 pork chops
- Cooking spray

Directions:
1. Mix the choc zero maple syrup, mustard, garlic, black pepper and salt in a suitable.
2. Marinate the choc zero maple syruped pork chops in the mixture for 20 minutes.
3. Place the pork chops on the Ninja Foodi basket.
4. Put the basket inside the pot. Seal with the crisping lid.
5. Set it to air crisp. Cook at 350 °F (175°C) for about 12 minutes, flipping halfway through.

Nutrition:
- InfoCalories: 348; Fat: 23.3g; Carbohydrate: 14g; Protein: 21.1g

Short Ribs With Mushroom And Asparagus Sauce

Servings: 6
Cooking Time: 1 Hr 15 Min
Ingredients:
- 3½ pounds boneless beef short ribs; cut into pieces /1575g
- 10 ounces mushrooms, quartered /300g
- 2 carrots, peeled and chopped
- 2 garlic cloves; minced
- 5 sprigs parsley; chopped
- 2 sprigs rosemary; chopped
- 3 sprigs oregano; chopped
- 1 onion; diced
- 4 cups beef stock /1000ml
- 1 cup dry red wine /250ml
- 1 cup asparagus, trimmed and roughly chopped /250g
- ¼ cup cold water /62.5ml
- 1 tbsp cornstarch /15g
- 3 tbsp olive oil /45ml
- 1 tbsp tomato puree /15ml
- 2 tsp salt /10g
- 1 tsp ground black pepper 5g

Directions:
1. Apply a seasoning of black pepper and salt to the ribs. Warm oil on Sear/Sauté. In batches, add the short ribs to the oil and cook for 3 to 5 minutes each side until browned. Set aside on a bowl. Add onions to the hot oil and cook for 3 to 5 minutes until soft.
2. Add tomato puree and red wine into the pot to deglaze, scrape the bottom to get rid of any browned beef bits. Cook for 2 minutes until wine reduces slightly. Return the ribs to pot and top with carrots, oregano, rosemary, and garlic. Add in beef broth.
3. Seal the pressure lid, choose Pressure, set to High, and set the timer to 35 minutes. Press Start. Release pressure naturally for 10 minutes. Transfer ribs to a plate. Strain and get rid of herbs and vegetables, and return cooking broth to inner pot. Add mushrooms and asparagus to the broth.
4. Press Sear/Sauté and cook for 2 to 4 minutes until vegetables are soft. In a bowl, mix water and cornstarch until cornstarch dissolves completely. Add the cornstarch mixture into the broth as you stir for 1 to 3 minutes until broth thickens slightly. Season the sauce with black pepper and salt. Pour the sauce over ribs, add chopped parsley for garnish before serving.

Sausage & Roasted Red Pepper Linguine

Servings: 4
Cooking Time: 15 Minutes
Ingredients:
- 1 tbsp. extra virgin olive oil
- ¾ lb. Italian sausage
- 3 cloves garlic, chopped fine
- 1 cup roasted red bell peppers, chopped
- 1 tbsp. capers
- ½ cup black olives, pitted & halved
- 3 tomatoes, seeded & chopped

- ¼ cup fresh basil, chopped
- 1 lb. linguine, cooked & drained

Directions:
1. Add the oil to the cooking pot and set to sauté on medium heat.
2. Add sausage and break it up while it's cooking. When it starts to brown add the garlic and cook 1 minute more.
3. Stir in the peppers, capers, and olives and cook stirring 2 minutes.
4. Increase heat to high and add tomatoes and basil, cook 2 minutes more.
5. Add the pasta to the sausage mixture and toss to combine. Serve.

Nutrition:
- InfoCalories 203,Total Fat 9g,Total Carbs 23g,Protein 7g,Sodium 200mg.

Spicy "faux" Pork Belly

Servings: 4
Cooking Time: 15 Minutes

Ingredients:
- 1 pound of pork belly, chopped
- 4 cups cauliflower, riced
- ½ a cup of bone broth
- ½ red onion, sliced
- ½ a cup of cilantro
- 2 green onion, sliced
- 1 tablespoon of lime juice
- 3 cloves garlic cloves, sliced
- 1 teaspoon turmeric
- 1 tablespoon oregano
- 1 tablespoon cumin
- ½ a teaspoon salt

Directions:
1. Add all of the to your Instant Pot except ¼ cup of cilantro
2. Lock up the lid and cook on HIGH pressure for 15 minutes
3. Release the pressure naturally over 10 minutes
4. Open the lid and serve with sprinkled cilantro leaves
5. Enjoy!

Chipotle Burgers

Servings: 6
Cooking Time: 20 Minutes

Ingredients:
- Nonstick cooking spray
- 2 poblano chilies
- 1 tsp. olive oil
- 1 ¼ tsp salt, divided
- 1 ½ lbs. lean ground beef
- 1/3 cup onion, grated
- 3 chipotle peppers in adobo sauce, chopped fine
- 1 tbsp. adobo sauce
- 1 tsp cumin
- 1 tsp pepper
- 6 slices jack cheese
- 6 hamburger buns
- 2 avocados, sliced
- 1/3 cup cilantro, chopped
- Hot sauce, to taste

Directions:
1. Spray the fryer basket with cooking spray and add to the cooking pot.
2. Place the whole poblano chilies in the basket. Add the tender-crisp lid and set to air fry on 400°F (205°C). Cook chilies until charred on all sides. Transfer chilies to Ziploc bag, seal, and let rest 15 minutes.
3. Remove the skins and seeds from the chilies. Slice them into ribbons and place in a medium bowl. Drizzle with oil and season with ¼ teaspoon salt, toss to coat. Cover until ready to use.
4. In a large bowl, combine ground beef, onion, chipotles, adobo sauce, remaining salt, cumin, and pepper. Mix until everything is combined. Form into 6 patties.
5. Spray the rack with cooking spray and place it in the cooking pot. Place the patties on the rack.
6. Add the tender-crisp lid and set to broil. Cook patties 6-7 minutes per side, or until patties reach desired doneness. Top each patty with cheese and broil until cheese is melted.
7. To serve, place patty on bottom bun, top with avocado and some of the roasted chilies, cilantro and hot sauce. Serve immediately.

Nutrition:
- InfoCalories 168,Total Fat 8g,Total Carbs 11g,Protein 13g,Sodium 498mg.

Premium Mexican Beef Dish

Servings:4
Cooking Time: 12 Minutes

Ingredients:
- 2 and ½ pounds boneless beef short ribs
- 1 tablespoon chili powder
- 1 and ½ teaspoons salt
- 1 tablespoon fat
- 1 medium onion, thinly sliced
- 1 tablespoon tomato sauce
- 6 garlic cloves, peeled and smashed
- ½ cup roasted tomato salsa
- ½ cup bone broth
- Fresh ground black pepper
- ½ cup cilantro, minced
- 2 radishes, sliced

Directions:
1. Take a large sized bowl and add the cubed beef, salt, and chili powder, give it a nice mix
2. Set your Ninja Foodi to Saute mode and add butter, allow it to melt
3. Add garlic and tomato paste and Saute for 30 seconds. Add seasoned beef, stock and fish sauce
4. Lock up the lid and cook on HIGH pressure for 35 minutes on MEAT/STEW mode
5. Release the pressure naturally over 10 minutes . Season with some salt and pepper and enjoy!

Baby Back Ribs With Barbeque Sauce

Servings: 4
Cooking Time: 45 Min
Ingredients:
- 2 pounds baby back pork ribs /900g
- Juice from 1 lemon
- 4 cups orange juice /1000ml
- For BBQ sauce:
- ½ cup ketchup /125ml
- Juice from ½ lemon
- 1 tbsp Worcestershire sauce /15ml
- 2 tbsp honey /30ml
- 2 tsp paprika /10g
- ½ tsp cayenne pepper /2.5g
- 1tsp mustard /5g
- Salt to taste

Directions:
1. Mix all the BBQ sauce ingredients in a bowl until well incorporated. Set aside. Place ribs in your Foodi pot; add in lemon juice and orange juice.
2. Seal the pressure lid, choose Pressure, set to High, and set the timer to 20 minutes. Press Start. Release pressure naturally for 15 minutes. Meanwhile, preheat oven to 400° °F or 205°C. Line the sheet pan with aluminum foil.
3. Transfer the ribs to the prepared sheet. Do away with the cooking liquid. Onto both sides of ribs, brush barbecue sauce. Bake ribs in the oven for 10 minutes until sauce is browned and caramelized; set the ribs aside and cut into individual bones to serve.

Balsamic Pot Roast Of Beef

Servings:4
Cooking Time: 55 Minutes
Ingredients:
- 1 teaspoon of each pepper and garlic powder
- 1 tablespoon kosher salt
- 1 (3 pounds boneless chuck roast
- ¼ cup balsamic vinegar
- ½ cup onion, chopped
- 2 cups of water
- ¼ teaspoon xanthan game
- For garnish, chopped parsley

Directions:
1. Slice roast in half and season with garlic powder, salt, and pepper
2. Set your Ninja Foodi to Saute mode and add meat, brown the meat
3. Add onion and pour water and vinegar. Lock lid and cook on HIGH pressure for 35 minutes
4. Release pressure naturally over 10 minutes. Transfer meat to a container and break it apart, discard fat. Set your pot to Saute mode and simmer the cooking liquid
5. Whisk in xanthan gum to the Pot and transfer back the chicken. Stir
6. Cancel Saute mode. Garnish and enjoy!

Beef And Turnip Chili

Servings: 6
Cooking Time: 30 Min
Ingredients:
- 1 pound turnips, peeled and cubed /450g
- 1 pound ground beef meat /450g
- 1 can whole tomatoes /840g
- 1 bell pepper; chopped
- 1 yellow onion; chopped
- 4 garlic cloves; minced
- 2 cups beef stock /500ml
- 2 tomatoes; chopped
- 1 tbsp chili powder /15g
- 1 tbsp olive oil /15ml
- 2 tbsp tomato puree /30ml
- ½ tsp ground turmeric /2.5g
- 2 tsp ground cumin /10g
- 1 tsp dried oregano /5g
- 1 pinch cayenne pepper
- salt to taste

Directions:
1. Warm oil on Sear/Sauté. Add in onion with a pinch of salt and cook for 3 to 5 minutes until softened. Stir in garlic, chili powder, turmeric, cumin, tomato puree, oregano, and cayenne pepper; cook for 2 to 3 minutes as you stir until very soft and sticks to the pot's bottom; add beef and cook for 5 minutes until completely browned. Mix in tomatoes, turnips, bell pepper, and beef stock.
2. Seal the pressure lid, choose Pressure, set to High, and set the timer to 15 minutes; press Start. When ready, release the pressure quickly.

Italian Pot Roast

Servings: 8
Cooking Time: 8 Hours
Ingredients:
- 1 tsp salt
- ½ tsp pepper
- 1 tsp garlic powder
- 1 tsp onion powder
- 2 tsp Italian seasoning
- 6 oz. tomato paste
- 2 lb. beef sirloin roast
- 1 onion, sliced thin
- 1 green bell pepper, sliced thin
- 1 banana pepper, sliced thin
- ½ cup beef broth, low sodium

Directions:
1. In a small bowl, combine salt, pepper, garlic powder, onion powder, Italian seasoning, and tomato paste, mix well.
2. Coat the roast, on all sides, with spice mixture and place in the cooking pot. Place the onions and peppers on top of the roast and pour in the broth.
3. Add the lid and set to slow cook on low. Cook 7-8 hours or until beef is tender.
4. You can slice the beef and serve topped with the onions and peppers. Or, you can shred the beef and use it to make sandwiches.

Nutrition:
- InfoCalories 270,Total Fat 16g,Total Carbs 6g,Protein 24g,Sodium 392mg.

Sesame Beef Ribs

Servings: 6
Cooking Time: 60 Minutes
Ingredients:
- 1 tablespoon sesame oil
- 2 garlic cloves, peeled and smashed
- Knob fresh ginger, peeled and finely chopped
- 1 pinch red pepper flakes
- ¼ cup white wine vinegar
- 2/3 cup coconut aminos
- 2/3 cup beef stock
- 4 pounds beef ribs, chopped in half
- 2 tablespoons arrowroot
- 1-2 tablespoons water

Directions:
1. Set your Ninja Foodi to Saute mode and add sesame oil, garlic, ginger, red pepper flakes and Saute for 1 minute. Deglaze pot with vinegar and mix in coconut aminos and beef stock
2. Add ribs to the pot and coat them well. Lock lid and cook on HIGH pressure for 60 minutes
3. Release pressure naturally over 10 minutes. Remove the ribs and keep them on the side
4. Take a small bowl and mix in arrowroot and water, stir and mix in the liquid into the pot, set the pot to Saute mode and cook until the liquid reaches your desired consistency
5. Put the ribs under a broiler to brown them slightly. Serve ribs with the cooking liquid. Enjoy!

Asian-glazed Pork Shoulder

Servings: 4
Cooking Time: 1 Hour, 5 Minutes
Ingredients:
- 1 boneless pork shoulder, between 2½ and 3 pounds
- 2½ cups garlic-hoisin sauce, divided, plus additional for glazing
- ¾ cups water
- 1 head broccoli, cut into 2-inch florets
- 1 tablespoon canola oil
- Kosher salt
- Freshly ground black pepper

Directions:
1. Place the pork shoulder and 1½ cups of hoisin sauce in large, resealable plastic bag. Move contents to ensure that all pork has been coated with the sauce and seal bag. Refrigerate and let marinate for at least 10 minutes and up to 4 hours.
2. Place Cook & Crisp Basket in pot. Place the water in the pot. Place the pork in the basket. Assemble pressure lid, making sure the pressure release valve is in the SEAL position.
3. Select PRESSURE and set to HI. Set time to 45 minutes. Select START/STOP to begin.
4. Combine the broccoli, oil, ½ cup of hoisin sauce, and salt and pepper in a large bowl. Mix well to coat broccoli with sauce and seasonings.
5. When pressure cooking is complete, quick release the pressure by moving the pressure release valve to the VENT position. Carefully remove lid when unit has finished releasing pressure.
6. Move the pork to one side of the basket and place broccoli in the other side. Brush the remaining ½ cup of hoisin sauce over the pork. Close crisping lid.
7. Select AIR CRISP, set temperature to 390°F (200°C), and set time to 20 minutes. Select START/STOP to begin.
8. Every 5 minutes or so, open lid and glaze pork with additional hoisin sauce. Close lid and continue cooking. Begin checking pork for desired crispiness after 15 minutes, cooking for up to an additional 5 minutes if desired.
9. When cooking is complete, remove pork and broccoli and serve in a family-style dish. If desired, pour some of the cooking liquid over the top of pork and broccoli for even more flavor.

Nutrition:
- InfoCalories: 1139,Total Fat: 67g,Sodium: 2802mg,Carbohydrates: 77g,Protein: 55g.

Cranberry Pork Bbq Dish

Servings: 4
Cooking Time: 45 Minutes
Ingredients:
- 3-4 pounds pork shoulder, boneless, fat trimmed
- For Sauce
- 3 tablespoons of liquid smoke
- 2 tablespoons tomato paste
- 2 cups fresh cranberries
- ¼ cup hot sauce (Keto-Friendly)
- 1/3 cup blackstrap molasses
- ½ cup of water
- ½ cup apple cider vinegar
- 1 teaspoon salt
- 1 tablespoon adobo sauce (Keto Friendly and Sugar-Free)
- 1 cup tomato puree (Keto-Friendly and Sugar-Free)
- 1 chipotle pepper in adobo sauce, diced

Directions:
1. Cut pork against halves/thirds and keep it on the side
2. Set your Ninja Foodi to "SAUTE" mode and let it heat up. Add cranberries and water to the pot
3. Let them simmer for 4-5 minutes until cranberries start to pop, add rest of the sauce and simmer for 5 minutes more. Add pork to the pot and lock lid
4. Cook on HIGH pressure for 40 minutes. Quick release pressure
5. Use a fork to shred the pork and serve on your favorite greens

Chicken And Crispy Dumplings

Servings: 6
Cooking Time: 30 Minutes
Ingredients:
- 1 tablespoon extra-virgin olive oil
- 1 yellow onion, chopped
- 2 celery stalks, diced
- 2 carrots, diced
- 1 pound boneless, skinless chicken breasts, cut in 1-inch pieces
- 2 cups chicken broth
- 1 teaspoon fresh thyme

- ½ teaspoon sea salt
- ½ cup heavy (whipping) cream
- 1 package refrigerated biscuits, at room temperature

Directions:
1. Select Sear/Sauté and set to Medium High. Select Start/Stop to begin. Allow the pot to preheat for 5 minutes.
2. Put the oil and onion in the preheated pot and sauté until the onion is softened, about 3 minutes.
3. Add the celery, carrots, chicken, and broth to the pot. Season with the thyme and salt. Assemble the Pressure Lid, making sure the pressure release valve is in the Seal position.
4. Select Pressure and set to High. Set the time to 2 minutes, then select Start/Stop to begin.
5. When pressure cooking is complete, quick release the pressure by moving the pressure release valve to the Vent position. Carefully remove the lid when the pressure has finished releasing.
6. Stir the cream into the soup. Arrange the biscuits in a single layer on top of the soup.
7. Close the Crisping Lid. Select Broil and set the time to 15 minutes. Select Start/Stop to begin.
8. When cooking is complete, remove the pot from the Ninja Foodi™ and place it on a heat-resistant surface. Let rest for 10 minutes before serving.

Beer Braised Bacon & Cabbage

Servings: 4
Cooking Time: 15 Minutes

Ingredients:
- 1 tbsp. butter
- 1 onion, sliced in strips
- 3 ½ oz. bacon, chopped
- 1 savoy cabbage, sliced in strips
- 1 cup blonde beer

Directions:
1. Add the butter to the cooking pot and set to sauté on medium heat.
2. Once butter has melted, add onion and bacon and cook, stirring occasionally, until onions is soft, about 5 minutes.
3. Add the cabbage and beer, stir to mix.
4. Add the lid and set to pressure cook on high. Set the timer for 3 minutes. When the timer goes off, use manual release to remove the pressure.
5. Stir and serve immediately.

Nutrition:
- InfoCalories 267,Total Fat 18g,Total Carbs 15g,Protein 9g,Sodium 257mg.

Orange Chicken And Broccoli

Servings: 2
Cooking Time: 27 Minutes

Ingredients:
- 1 cup long-grain white rice
- 1 cup plus 2 tablespoons water
- 1 head broccoli, trimmed into florets
- 2 tablespoons extra-virgin olive oil, divided
- ¼ teaspoon sea salt
- ¼ teaspoon freshly ground black pepper
- Nonstick cooking spray
- 4 boneless, skinless chicken tenders
- ¼ cup barbecue sauce
- ¼ cup sweet orange marmalade
- ½ tablespoon soy sauce
- 1 tablespoon sesame seeds, for garnish
- 2 tablespoons sliced scallions, for garnish

Directions:
1. Put the rice and water in the pot and stir to combine. Assemble the Pressure Lid, making sure the pressure release valve is in the Seal position. Select Pressure and set to High. Set the time to 2 minutes, then select Start/Stop to begin.
2. Meanwhile, in a medium mixing bowl, toss the broccoli with 1 tablespoon of olive oil. Season with the salt and black pepper.
3. When pressure cooking is complete, quick release the pressure by moving the pressure release valve to the Vent position. Carefully remove the lid when the pressure has finished releasing.
4. Place the Reversible Rack inside the pot over the rice, making sure the rack is in the higher position. Spray the rack with nonstick cooking spray. Place the chicken tenders on the rack and brush them with the remaining 1 tablespoon of olive oil. Arrange the broccoli around the chicken tenders.
5. Close the Crisping Lid. Select Air Crisp, set the temperature to 400°F (205°C), and set the time to 10 minutes. Press Start/Stop to begin.
6. Meanwhile, in a medium mixing bowl, stir together the barbecue sauce, orange marmalade, and soy sauce until well combined.
7. When Air Crisping is complete, coat the chicken with the orange sauce. Use tongs to flip the chicken and coat the other side. Close the Crisping Lid. Select Broil and set the time to 5 minutes. Select Start/Stop to begin.
8. After cooking is complete, check for your desired crispiness and remove the rack from the pot. The chicken is cooked when its internal temperature reaches 165°F (75°C) on a meat thermometer.
9. Garnish with the sesame seeds and scallions and serve.

Pesto Pork Chops & Asparagus

Servings: 4
Cooking Time: 20 Minutes

Ingredients:
- Nonstick cooking spray
- 4 pork chops, bone-in, 1-inch thick
- 1 tsp salt, divided
- 1 tsp pepper, divided
- 1 bunch asparagus, trimmed
- 1 cup cherry tomatoes
- 3 tbsp. extra-virgin olive oil, divided
- ¼ cup pesto
- ¼ cup fresh basil, chopped

Directions:
1. Spray the rack with cooking spray and place it in the cooking pot.
2. Rub chops with 2 tablespoons oil and sprinkle with ½ teaspoon salt and pepper on both sides. Cover and let sit 20 minutes.

3. Place chops on the rack and add the tender-crisp lid. Set to broil. Cook chops 6-8 minutes per side or until they reach desired doneness. Remove to serving plate.
4. Place the asparagus and tomatoes in a large bowl and add remaining oil, salt, and pepper, toss to coat. Place the vegetables on the rack and broil 6-8 minutes until asparagus is tender-crisp and tomatoes start to char, turning vegetables every couple of minutes.
5. Place pork chops and vegetables on serving plates, drizzle with pesto and sprinkle with basil. Serve immediately.

Nutrition:
- InfoCalories 332,Total Fat 24g,Total Carbs 4g,Protein 25g,Sodium 647mg.

Baked Ziti With Rich Meat Sauce

Servings: 4
Cooking Time: 32 Minutes
Ingredients:
- 1 tbsp. extra-virgin olive oil
- 2 pounds (907 g) ground beef
- 1 (16-ounce, 455 g) box ziti
- 1 cup dry red wine
- 2 (24-ounce, 672 g) jars marinara sauce
- 1 cup water
- ½ tsp. garlic powder
- ½ tsp. sea salt
- 1 cup ricotta cheese
- 1 cup shredded mozzarella cheese
- ½ cup chopped fresh parsley

Directions:
1. Preheat the pot by selecting Sear/Sauté. Select Start/Stop to begin. Preheat for 5 minutes.
2. In the preheated pot, add the oil, then stir in the ground beef and cook until browned and cooked through, about 5 to 8 minutes.
3. Stir in the ziti, wine, marinara sauce and water, combine well. Use garlic powder and salt to season.
4. Assemble the Pressure Lid, set the steamer valve to Seal. Select Pressure. Set the time to 2 minutes, then select Start/Stop to begin.
5. After pressure cooking is complete, naturally release the pressure for 10 minutes, then move the pressure release valve to the Vent position to quick release any remaining pressure. Remove the lid when the pressure has finished releasing carefully.
6. Add the ricotta and stir well, then evenly place the mozzarella cheese over the top of the pasta.
7. Close the Crisping Lid. Select Broil, and set the time to 3 minutes. Select Start/Stop to begin. Cook until the cheese is melted, bubbly, and slightly browned, about 3 minutes.
8. Top with the parsley and serve immediately.

Chinese Bbq Ribs

Servings: 6
Cooking Time: 8 Hours
Ingredients:
- 4 tbsp. hoisin sauce
- 4 tbsp. oyster sauce
- 2 tbsp. soy sauce, low sodium
- 2 tbsp. rice wine
- 2 lbs. pork ribs, cut in 6 pieces
- Nonstick cooking spray
- 2-inch piece fresh ginger, grated
- 3 green onions, sliced
- 2 tbsp. honey

Directions:
1. In a large bowl, whisk together hoisin sauce, oyster sauce, soy sauce, and rice wine. Add the ribs and turn to coat. Cover and refrigerate overnight.
2. Spray the cooking pot with cooking spray.
3. Add the ribs and marinade. Top with ginger and green onions. Add the lid and set to slow cook on low. Cook 6-8 hours or until ribs are tender.
4. Transfer ribs to a serving plate. Spray the rack with the cooking spray and place in the pot. Lay the ribs, in a single layer, on the rack and brush with honey.
5. Add the tender-crisp lid and set to broil. Cook 3-4 minutes to caramelize the ribs. Serve.

Nutrition:
- InfoCalories 135,Total Fat 4g,Total Carbs 6g,Protein 17g,Sodium 419mg.

Quinoa, Nut, And Chickpea Stuffed Butternut Squash

Servings:4
Cooking Time: 13 Minutes
Ingredients:
- 2 tablespoons extra-virgin olive oil
- 1 tablespoon minced garlic
- 1 small shallot, minced
- Kosher salt
- Freshly ground black pepper
- ½ cup dried cranberries
- 1 cup tri-colored quinoa
- 2¾ cups water, divided
- 2 cups roughly chopped kale
- 1 small butternut squash, top trimmed, halved lengthwise
- 1 tablespoon freshly squeezed orange juice
- Zest of 1 orange
- 1 (2-ounce / 57-g) jar pine nuts
- 1 (15-ounce / 425-g) can chickpeas, rinsed and drained

Directions:
1. Select SEAR/SAUTÉ and set to HI. Select START/STOP to begin. Let preheat for 5 minutes.
2. Add the olive oil, garlic, shallot, salt, and pepper. Cook until garlic and shallot have softened and turned golden brown, about 2 minutes.
3. Stir in the cranberries, quinoa, and 1¼ cups of water. Assemble pressure lid, making sure the pressure release valve is in the SEAL position.
4. Select PRESSURE and set to HI. Set time to 2 minutes. Select START/STOP to begin.
5. When pressure cooking is complete, allow pressure to naturally release for 10 minutes. After 10 minutes, quick release remaining pressure by turning the pressure release valve to the VENT position. Carefully remove lid when the unit has finished releasing pressure.

6. Place the quinoa in a large bowl. Stir in the kale. Cover the bowl with aluminum foil and set aside.
7. Pour the remaining 1½ cups of water into the pot. Place the butternut squash cut-side up on the Reversible Rack, then lower it into the pot. Assemble pressure lid, making sure the pressure release valve is in the SEAL position.
8. Select PRESSURE and set to HI. Set the time to 8 minutes. Select START/STOP to begin.
9. Mix the orange juice, orange zest, pine nuts, and chickpeas into the quinoa mixture.
10. When pressure cooking is complete, quick release the pressure by turning the pressure release valve to the VENT position. Carefully remove lid when unit has finished releasing pressure.
11. Carefully remove rack from pot. Using a spoon slightly hollow out the squash. Spoon the quinoa mixture into the squash. Cut in half and serve.

All-tim Favorite Beef Chili

Servings: 4
Cooking Time: 40 Minutes
Ingredients:
- 1 and ½ pounds ground beef
- 1 sweet onion, peeled and chopped
- Salt and pepper to taste
- 28 ounces canned tomatoes, diced
- 17 ounces beef stock
- 6 garlic clove, peeled and chopped
- 7 jalapeno peppers, diced
- 2 tablespoons olive oil
- 4 carrots, peeled and chopped
- 3 tablespoons chili powder
- 1 bay leaf
- 1 teaspoon chili powder

Directions:
1. Set your Ninja Foodi to "Saute" mode and add half of the oil, let it heat up
2. Add beef and stir brown for 8 minutes, transfer to a bowl
3. Add remaining oil to the pot and let it heat up, add carrots, onion, jalapenos, garlic and stir Saute for 4 minutes. Add tomatoes and stir
4. Add bay leaf, stock, chili powder, chili powder, salt, pepper, and beef, stir and lock lid
5. Cook on HIGH pressure for 25 minutes . Release pressure naturally over 10 minutes
6. Stir the chili and serve. Enjoy!

Parmesan Broccoli Florets

Servings: 4
Cooking Time: 8 Minutes
Ingredients:
- 12 ounces (340 g) fresh broccoli florets
- 1 tablespoon peanut oil or vegetable oil
- ¼ teaspoon kosher salt
- Pinch of freshly ground black pepper
- ½ cup freshly shredded Parmesan cheese

Directions:
1. Place the broccoli florets in the crisping basket and set the basket into the Foodi's inner pot along with ½ cup water. Lock on the Pressure Lid, making sure the valve is set to Seal, and set to Pressure on High for 0 minutes. When the timer reaches 0, quick-release the pressure and carefully remove the lid. Transfer the broccoli to a medium bowl. Drain the liquid from the inner pot, wash, and dry it.
2. Add the oil, salt, pepper, and Parmesan to the broccoli in the bowl. Stir to combine. Place the crisping basket back into the inner pot and transfer the broccoli mixture to the basket, scraping any cheese left in the bowl on top of the broccoli. Drop the Crisping Lid and set the Foodi to Air Crisp at 390°F(200°C) for 8 minutes, or until the broccoli is crisped and the cheese is browned. Lift the lid and serve hot.

Beef Congee

Servings: 6
Cooking Time: 1 Hr
Ingredients:
- 2 pounds ground beef /900g
- 1 piece fresh ginger; minced
- 2 cloves garlic; minced
- 6 cups beef stock /1500ml
- 1 cup jasmine rice /130g
- 1 cup kale, roughly chopped /130g
- 1 cups water /250ml
- salt and ground black pepper to taste
- Fresh cilantro; chopped

Directions:
1. Run cold water and rinse rice. Add garlic, rice, and ginger into the Foodi. Pour water and stock into the pot and spread the beef on top of rice.
2. Seal the pressure lid, choose Pressure, set to High, and set the timer to 30 minutes. Press Start. Once ready, release pressure naturally for 10 minutes.
3. Stir in kale to obtain the desired consistency. Add pepper and salt for seasoning. Divide into serving plates and top with cilantro.

Mushroom And Cheddar Poutine

Servings: 4
Cooking Time: 46 Minutes
Ingredients:
- 2 tablespoons unsalted butter
- 1 small yellow onion, diced
- 1 garlic clove, minced
- 8 ounces (227 g) cremini mushrooms, sliced
- ¼ cup red wine
- 3 cups vegetable stock
- ¼ cup all-purpose flour
- Kosher salt
- Freshly ground black pepper
- 1 pound (454 g) frozen French fries
- 8 ounces (227 g) Cheddar cheese, cubed

Directions:
1. Select SEAR/SAUTÉ and set to MED. Select START/STOP to begin. Let preheat for 3 minutes.
2. Add the butter, onion, and garlic. Cook, stirring occasionally, for 5 minutes. Add the mushrooms and sauté for 5 minutes. Add the wine and let it simmer and reduce for 3 minutes.

3. In large bowl, slowly whisk together the stock and flour. Whisk this mixture into the vegetables in the pot. Cook the gravy for 10 minutes. Season with salt and pepper. Transfer the gravy to a medium bowl and set aside. Clean out the pot and return to unit.
4. Insert Cook & Crisp Basket and add the French fries. Close crisping lid.
5. Select AIR CRISP, set temperature to 360ºF(180ºC), and set time to 18 minutes. Select START/STOP to begin.
6. Every 5 minutes, open lid and remove and shake basket to ensure even cooking.
7. Once cooking is complete, remove fries from basket and place in the pot. Add the cheese and stir. Cover with the gravy. Close crisping lid.
8. Select AIR CRISP, set temperature to 375ºF(190ºC), and set time 5 minutes. Select START/STOP to begin.
9. When cooking is complete, serve immediately.

Lone Star Chili

Servings: 8
Cooking Time: 8 Hours
Ingredients:
- 2 tbsp. flour
- 2 lbs. lean beef chuck, cubed
- 1 tbsp. olive oil
- 1 onion, chopped fine
- 2 jalapeño peppers, chopped
- 4 cloves garlic, chopped fine
- 1 tbsp. cumin
- 4 oz. green chilies, drained & chopped
- 3 tbsp. Ancho chili powder
- 1 tsp crushed red pepper flakes
- 1 tsp oregano
- 3 cups beef broth, fat-free & low-sodium
- 28 oz. tomatoes, diced, undrained
- ¼ cup Greek yogurt, fat free
- 3 tbsp. green onions, chopped

Directions:
1. Place the flour in a large Ziploc bag. Add the beef and toss to coat.
2. Add the oil to the cooking pot and set to sauté on med-high.
3. Add the beef and cook, stirring occasionally, until browned on all sides. Add the onions and jalapenos and cook until soft. Stir in the garlic and cook 1 minute more.
4.
5. Stir in remaining ingredients, except yogurt and green onions, mix well. Add the lid and set to slow cook on low. Cook 7-8 hours until chili is thick and beef is tender.
6. Ladle into bowls and top with a dollop of yogurt and green onions. Serve.

Nutrition:
- InfoCalories 267, Total Fat 9g, Total Carbs 8g, Protein 36g, Sodium 317mg.

Super Cheesy Pepperoni Calzones

Servings: 4
Cooking Time: 18 Minutes
Ingredients:
- All-purpose flour, for dusting
- 16 ounces (454 g) store-bought pizza dough
- 1 egg, beaten
- 2 cups shredded Mozzarella cheese
- 1 cup Ricotta cheese
- ½ cup grated Parmesan cheese
- ½ cup sliced pepperoni
- Cooking spray
- Pizza sauce, for dipping

Directions:
1. Dust a clean work surface with the flour. Divide the pizza dough into four equal pieces. Place the dough on the floured surface and roll each piece into an 8-inch round of even thickness. Dust your rolling pin and work surface with additional flour, as needed, to ensure the dough does not stick. Brush egg wash around the edges of each round.
2. Place Cook & Crisp Basket in pot. Close crisping lid. Select AIR CRISP, set temperature to 390ºF(200ºC), and set time to 5 minutes. Select START/STOP to begin preheating.
3. In a medium bowl, combine the Mozzarella, Ricotta, and Parmesan cheese. Fold in the pepperoni.
4. Spoon one-quarter of the cheese mixture onto one side of each dough round. Fold the other half over the filling and press firmly to seal the edges together. Brush each calzone all over with the egg wash.
5. Once unit is preheated, open lid and coat the basket with cooking spray. Place two calzones in the basket in a single layer. Close crisping lid.
6. Select AIR CRISP, set temperature to 390ºF(200ºC), and set time to 9 minutes. Select START/STOP to begin.
7. After 7 minutes, open lid to check for doneness. If desired, cook for up to 2 minutes more, until golden brown.
8. When cooking is complete, remove calzone from basket. Repeat steps 5 and 6 with the remaining calzones. Serve warm.

Poultry

Awesome Ligurian Chicken

Servings: 4
Cooking Time: 15 Minutes
Ingredients:
- 2 garlic cloves, chopped
- 3 sprigs fresh rosemary
- 2 sprigs fresh sage
- ½ bunch parsley
- 3 lemon, juiced
- 4 tablespoons extra virgin olive oil
- 1 teaspoon salt
- ¼ teaspoon pepper
- 1 and ½ cup of water
- 1 whole chicken, cut into parts
- 3 and ½ ounces black gourmet salt-cured olives
- 1 fresh lemon

Directions:
1. Take a bowl and add chopped up garlic, parsley, sage, and rosemary
2. Pour lemon juice, olive oil to a bowl and season with salt and pepper
3. Remove the chicken skin and from the chicken pieces and carefully transfer them to a dish
4. Pour the marinade on top of the chicken pieces and allow them to chill for 2-4 hours
5. Set your Ninja Foodi to Saute mode and add olive oil, allow it to heat up. Add chicken and browned on all sides
6. Measure out the marinade and add to the pot . Lock up the lid and cook on HIGH pressure for 10 minutes
7. Release the pressure naturally. The chicken out and transfer to a platter
8. Cover with a foil and allow them to coolSet your pot in Saute mode and reduce the liquid to ¼
9. Add the chicken pieces again to the pot and allow them to warm
10. Sprinkle a bit of olive, lemon slices, and rosemary. Enjoy!

Barbeque Chicken Drumettes

Servings: 4
Cooking Time: 30 Min
Ingredients:
- 2 lb. chicken drumettes, bone in and skin in /900g
- 1 stick butter; sliced in 5 pieces
- ½ cup chicken broth /125ml
- BBQ sauce to taste
- ½ tbsp cumin powder /7.5g
- ½ tsp onion powder /2.5g
- ¼ tsp Cayenne powder/1.25g
- ½ tsp dry mustard /2.5g
- ½ tsp sweet paprika /2.5g
- Salt and pepper, to taste
- Cooking spray

Directions:
1. Pour the chicken broth into the inner pot of Foodi P and insert the reversible rack. In a zipper bag, pour in dry mustard, cumin powder, onion powder, cayenne powder, salt, and pepper.
2. Add the chicken, close the bag and shake to coat the chicken well with the spices. You can toss the chicken in the spices in batches too.
3. Then, remove the chicken from the bag and place on the rack. Spread the butter slices on the drumsticks. Close the lid, secure the pressure valve, and select Pressure mode on High pressure for 10 minutes. Press Start/Stop.
4. Once the timer has ended, do a quick pressure release, and open the lid. Remove the chicken onto a clean flat surface like a cutting board and brush them with the barbecue sauce using the brush. Return to the rack and close the crisping lid. Cook for 10 minutes at 400 °F or 205°C on Air Crisp mode.

Greek Style Turkey Meatballs

Servings: 6
Cooking Time: 30 Min
Ingredients:
- 1 pound ground turkey /450g
- 1 carrot; minced
- ½ celery stalk; minced
- 1 onion; minced and divided
- 1 egg, lightly beaten
- 3 cups tomato puree /750ml
- 2 cups water /500ml
- ½ cup plain bread crumbs /65g
- ⅓ cup feta cheese, crumbled /44g
- 1 tbsp olive oil /15ml
- 2 tsp salt; divided /10g
- ½ tsp dried oregano /2.5g
- ¼ tsp ground black pepper /1.25g

Directions:
1. In a mixing bowl, thoroughly combine half the onion, oregano, ground turkey, salt, bread crumbs, pepper, and egg and stir until everything is well incorporated.
2. Heat oil on Sear/Sauté, and cook celery, remaining onion, and carrot for 5 minutes until soft. Pour in water, and tomato puree. Adjust the seasonings as necessary.
3. Roll the mixture into meatballs, and drop into the sauce. Seal the pressure lid, choose Pressure, set to High, and set the timer to 5 minutes. Press Start. Allow the cooker to cool and release pressure naturally for 20 minutes. Serve topped with feta cheese.

Cabbage And Chicken Meatballs

Servings: 4
Cooking Time: 4-6 Minutes
Ingredients:
- 1 pound ground chicken
- ¼ cup heavy whip cream
- 2 teaspoons salt
- ½ teaspoon ground caraway seeds
- 1 and ½ teaspoons fresh ground black pepper, divided
- 1/4 teaspoon ground allspice
- 4-6 cups green cabbage, thickly chopped
- ½ cup almond milk
- 2 tablespoons unsalted butter

Directions:
1. Transfer meat to a bowl and add cream, 1 teaspoon salt, caraway, ½ teaspoon pepper, allspice and mix it well. Let the mixture chill for 30 minutes
2. Once the mixture is ready, use your hands to scoop the mixture into meatballs
3. Add half of your balls to Ninja Foodi pot and cover with half of the cabbage
4. Add remaining balls and cover with rest of the cabbage
5. Add milk, pats of butter, season with salt and pepper
6. Lock lid and cook on HIGH pressure for 4 minutes. Quick release pressure
7. Unlock lid and serve. Enjoy!

Fluffy Whole Chicken Dish

Servings: 4
Cooking Time: 8 Hours
Ingredients:
- 1 cup mozzarella cheese
- 4 whole garlic cloves, peeled
- 1 whole chicken (2 pounds, cleaned and pat dried
- Salt and pepper to taste
- 2 tablespoons fresh lemon juice

Directions:
1. Stuff chicken cavity with garlic cloves and mozzarella cheese
2. Season chicken generously with salt and pepper
3. Transfer chicken to Ninja Foodi and drizzle lemon juice
4. Lock lid and set to Slow Cooker mode, let it cook on LOW for 8 hours
5. Once done, serve and enjoy!

Shredded Chicken & Black Beans

Servings: 4
Cooking Time: 4 Hours
Ingredients:
- 16 oz. fresh salsa
- 15 oz. black beans, rinsed & drained
- 1 lb. chicken thighs, boneless & skinless
- 1/3 cup cheddar cheese, reduced fat, grated
- 1 tsp cumin
- ½ tsp chili powder
- 1/8 tsp salt
- 1/8 tsp pepper

Directions:
1. Place the salsa, beans, and chicken in the cooking pot. Add the lid and set to slow cook on high. Cook 3 ½ hours or until chicken is tender.
2. Transfer chicken to a cutting board and use 2 forks to shred. Return to the pot.
3. Stir in remaining ingredients and mix well. Cook another 15 minutes or until cheese is melted. Serve immediately.

Nutrition:
- InfoCalories 283,Total Fat 6g,Total Carbs 25g,Protein 33g,Sodium 1474mg.

Taiwanese Chicken Delight

Servings: 4
Cooking Time: 10 Minutes
Ingredients:
- 6 dried red chilis
- ¼ cup sesame oil
- 2 tablespoons ginger
- ¼ cup garlic, minced
- ¼ cup red wine vinegar
- ¼ cup coconut aminos
- Salt as needed
- 1.2 teaspoon xanthan gum (for the finish)
- ¼ cup Thai basil, chopped

Directions:
1. Set your Ninja Foodi to Saute mode and add ginger, chilis, garlic and Saute for 2 minutes
2. Add remaining . Lock lid and cook on HIGH pressure for 10 minutes
3. Quick release pressure. Serve and enjoy!

Spicy Chicken Tortilla Soup

Servings: 8
Cooking Time: 20 Minutes
Ingredients:
- 1 pound (455 g) boneless, skinless chicken breasts
- 1 (15-ounce (425 g)) can black beans, rinsed and drained
- 2 cups frozen corn
- 6 cups chicken broth
- 1 tbsp. extra-virgin olive oil
- 1 onion, chopped
- 1 (12-ounce (340 g)) jar salsa
- 4 ounces (113 g) tomato paste
- 1 tbsp. chili powder
- 2 tsps. cumin
- ½ tsp. freshly ground black pepper
- 1 pinch of cayenne pepper
- ½ tsp. sea salt
- Tortilla strips, for garnish

Directions:
1. Select the Saute mode to preheat for 5 minutes.
2. Combine the olive oil and onions in the pot. Cook 5 minutes, stirring occasionally.
3. Add chicken breast, chicken broth, salsa, tomato paste, chili powder, cumin, salt, pepper, and cayenne pepper to the pot. Assemble pressure lid, set the steamer valve to Seal.
4. Select Pressure, set time 10 minutes.

Ninja Foodi Cookbook

5. After cooking is complete, move pressure release valve to VENT to quickly release the pressure. Carefully remove lid.
6. Take chicken breasts out from pot and use two forks to shred them.
7. Add the black beans and corn. Select SEAR/SAUTÉ. Cook 5 minutes.
8. Add shredded chicken back to the pot. Decorate with tortilla strips before serving.

Cheesy Chicken & Zucchini Rolls

Servings: 4
Cooking Time: 15 Minutes
Ingredients:
- Nonstick cooking spray
- 2 chicken breasts, boneless & skinless
- ½ tsp salt
- ¼ tsp pepper
- 2 zucchini, sliced very thin
- 4 slices provolone cheese, fat free
- ½ cup bread crumbs

Directions:
1. Spray the fryer basket with cooking spray.
2. Cut the chicken in half horizontally. Place pieces between 2 sheets of plastic wrap and pound out to ¼-inch thick.
3. Lay the chicken pieces, one at a time, on a plate and season with salt and pepper.
4. Place slices of zucchini and cheese on the chicken. Roll up and secure with a toothpick.
5. Place the bread crumbs in a shallow dish. Coat chicken rolls with bread crumbs and place in the basket.
6. Add the tender-crisp lid and set to air fry on 375°F (190°C). Cook 15 minutes until golden brown on the outsides and cooked through on the inside, turning over halfway through cooking time. Serve immediately.

Nutrition:
- InfoCalories 166, Total Fat 2g, Total Carbs 12g, Protein 23g, Sodium 472mg.

Italian Chicken Muffins

Servings: 4
Cooking Time: 25 Minutes
Ingredients:
- Nonstick cooking spray
- 4 chicken breast halves, boneless & skinless
- ½ tsp salt, divided
- ½ tsp pepper, divided
- 1/3 cup part-skim ricotta cheese
- ¼ cup mozzarella cheese, grated
- 2 tbsp. parmesan cheese
- ½ tsp Italian seasoning
- ½ tsp garlic powder
- 2 tbsp. whole-wheat panko bread crumbs
- 1 tbsp. light butter, melted
- Paprika for sprinkling

Directions:
1. Place the rack in the cooking pot. Spray 4 cups of a 6-cup muffin tin.
2. Lay chicken between 2 sheets of plastic wrap and pound to ¼-inch thick. Season with ¼ teaspoon of salt and pepper.
3. In a medium bowl, combine ricotta, mozzarella, parmesan, Italian seasoning, garlic powder, and remaining salt and pepper, mix well. Spoon evenly onto centers of chicken. Wrap chicken around filling and place, seam side down, in prepared muffin cups.
4. In a small bowl, stir together bread crumbs and butter, sprinkle over the chicken then top with paprika.
5. Place muffin tin on rack and add the tender-crisp lid. Set to bake on 350°F (175°C). Cook chicken 25-30 minutes or until chicken is cooked through. Serve immediately.

Nutrition:
- InfoCalories 224, Total Fat 8g, Total Carbs 4g, Protein 31g, Sodium 485mg.

Chicken With Black Beans

Servings: 4
Cooking Time: 25 Min
Ingredients:
- 4 boneless; skinless chicken drumsticks
- 2 green onions, thinly sliced
- 3 garlic cloves, grated
- 2 cups canned black beans /260g
- ½ cup soy sauce /125ml
- ½ cup chicken broth /125ml
- 1 piece fresh ginger, grated
- 1 tbsp sriracha /15g
- 1 tbsp sesame oil /15ml
- 1 tbsp cornstarch /15g
- 1 tbsp water /15ml
- 2 tbsp toasted sesame seeds; divided /30g
- 3 tbsp honey /45ml
- 2 tbsp tomato paste /30ml

Directions:
1. In your Foodi, mix the soy sauce, honey, ginger, tomato paste, chicken broth, sriracha, and garlic. Stir well until smooth; toss in the chicken to coat.
2. Seal the pressure lid, choose Pressure, set to High, and set the timer to 3 minutes. Press Start. Release the pressure immediately.
3. Open the lid and Press Sear/Sauté. In a small bowl, mix water and cornstarch until no lumps remain; stir into the sauce and cook for 5 minutes until thickened.
4. Stir sesame oil and 1½ tbsp or 22.5g sesame seeds through the chicken mixture; garnish with extra sesame seeds and green onions. Serve with black beans.

Chicken With Bacon And Beans

Servings: 4
Cooking Time: 45 Min
Ingredients:
- 4 boneless; skinless chicken thighs
- 4 garlic cloves; minced
- 15 ounces red kidney beans, drained and rinsed /450g
- 4 slices bacon, crumbled
- 1 can whole tomatoes /435g
- 1 red bell pepper; chopped
- 1 onion; diced

- 1 cup shredded Monterey Jack cheese /130g
- 1 cup sliced red onion /130g
- ¼ cup chopped cilantro /32.5g
- 1 cup chicken broth /250ml
- 1 tbsp tomato paste /15ml
- 1 tbsp olive oil /15ml
- 1 tbsp oregano /15g
- 1 tbsp ground cumin/15g
- 1 tsp chili powder /5g
- ½ tsp cayenne pepper /2.5g
- 1 tsp salt /5g
- 1 cup cooked corn /130g

Directions:
1. Warm oil on Sear/Sauté. Sear the chicken for 3 minutes for each side until browned. Set the chicken on a plate. In the same oil, fry bacon until crispy, about 5 minutes and set aside.
2. Add in onions and cook for 2 to 3 minutes until fragrant. Stir in garlic, oregano, cayenne pepper, cumin, tomato paste, bell pepper, and chili powder and cook for 30 more seconds. Pour the chicken broth, salt, and tomatoes and bring to a boil. Press Start/Stop.
3. Take back the chicken and bacon to the pot and ensure it is submerged in the braising liquid. Seal the pressure lid, choose Pressure, set to High, and set the timer to 15 minutes. Press Start. When ready, release the pressure quickly.
4. Pour the kidney beans in the cooker, press Sear/Sauté and bring the liquid to a boil; cook for 10 minutes. Serve topped with shredded cheese and chopped cilantro.

Chicken With Rice And Peas

Servings: 4
Cooking Time: 30 Min
Ingredients:
- 4 boneless; skinless chicken breasts; sliced
- 1 onion; chopped
- 1 celery stalk; diced
- 1 garlic clove; minced
- 2 cups chicken broth; divided /500ml
- 1 cup long grain rice /130g
- 1 cup frozen green peas /130g
- 1 tbsp oil olive /15ml
- 1 tbsp tomato puree /15ml
- ½ tsp paprika /2.5g
- ¼ tsp dried oregano/1.25g
- ¼ tsp dried thyme /1.25g
- ⅛ tsp cayenne pepper /0.625g
- ⅛ tsp ground white pepper /0.625g
- Salt to taste

Directions:
1. Season chicken with garlic powder, oregano, white pepper, thyme, paprika, cayenne pepper, and salt. Warm the oil on Sear/Sauté. Add in onion and cook for 4 minutes until fragrant. Mix in tomato puree to coat.
2. Add ¼ cup or 65ml chicken stock into the Foodi to deglaze the pan, scrape the pan's bottom to get rid of browned bits of food. Mix in celery, rice, and the seasoned chicken. Add in the remaining broth to the chicken mixture.
3. Seal the pressure lid, choose Pressure, set to High, and set the timer to 8 minutes. Press Start. Once ready, do a quick release. Mix in green peas, cover with the lid and let sit for 5 minutes. Serve warm.

Ginger Orange Chicken Tenders

Servings: 4
Cooking Time: 25 Minutes
Ingredients:
- Nonstick cooking spray
- 1 ½ lbs. chicken tenders
- 1 cup orange juice
- 2 tsp tamari, low sodium
- ½ tsp ginger
- 11 oz. mandarin oranges, drained

Directions:
1. Spray the fryer basket with cooking spray.
2. Place chicken in a single layer in the basket, these may need to be cooked in batches.
3. Add the tender-crisp lid and set to air fry on 350°F (175°C). Cook 10 minutes, turning over halfway through cooking time.
4. Add all the tenders to the cooking pot.
5. In a small bowl, whisk together orange juice, soy sauce, and ginger. Pour over chicken and stir to coat all the pieces.
6. Set to sauté on medium heat. Cover and cook chicken, stirring occasionally, about 10 minutes.
7. Add the orange slices and cook another 5 minutes. Serve.

Nutrition:
- InfoCalories 259,Total Fat 5g,Total Carbs 17g,Protein 36g,Sodium 210mg.

Crunchy Chicken Schnitzels

Servings: 4
Cooking Time: 25 Min
Ingredients:
- 4 chicken breasts, boneless
- 2 eggs, beaten
- 4 slices cold butter
- 4 slices lemon
- 1 cup flour /130g
- 1 cup breadcrumbs /130g
- 2 tbsp fresh parsley; chopped 30g
- Cooking spray
- Salt and pepper to taste

Directions:
1. Combine the breadcrumbs with the parsley in a dish and set aside. Season the chicken with salt and pepper. Coat in flour; shake off any excess. Dip the coated chicken into the beaten egg followed by breadcrumbs. Spray the schnitzels with cooking spray.
2. Put them into the Foodi basket, close the crisping lid and cook for 10 minutes at 380 °F or 195°C. After 5 minutes, turn the schnitzels over. Arrange the schnitzels on a serving platter and place the butter and lemon slices over to serve.

Apricot Bbq Duck Legs

Servings: 6
Cooking Time: 8 Hours
Ingredients:
- Nonstick cooking spray
- 2 cups spicy BBQ sauce
- 1 cup apricot preserves
- 1 tsp ginger
- 1 tbsp. garlic powder
- 2 tbsp. Worcestershire sauce
- 4 lbs. duck legs

Directions:
1. Spray the cooking pot with cooking spray.
2. In a medium bowl, whisk together BBQ sauce, preserves, ginger, garlic powder, and Worcestershire until combined. Reserve ½ cup of the sauce.
3. Add the duck to the cooking pot and pour the sauce over. Stir to coat the duck.
4. Add the lid and select slow cook on low. Cook 6-8 hours or until duck is tender.
5. Add the tender-crisp lid and set to broil. Cook another 2-3 minutes to caramelize the duck legs. Turn the legs over and repeat. Serve.

Nutrition:
- InfoCalories 651,Total Fat 26g,Total Carbs 44g,Protein 61g,Sodium 1027mg.

Chicken Gumbo

Servings: 6
Cooking Time: 30 Minutes
Ingredients:
- 3 chicken breasts, boneless & skinless
- 8 oz. turkey sausage rope, sliced ¼-inch thick
- 1 onion, chopped
- 1 green bell pepper, chopped
- 2 stalks celery, chopped
- 3 cloves garlic, chopped fine
- 4 cups chicken broth, low sodium
- 1 ½ cups okra, sliced
- 2 tsp pepper
- 1 tsp cayenne pepper
- 1 tsp thyme
- ½ tsp salt
- ½ cup green onion, chopped
- 3 cups brown rice, cooked

Directions:
1. Place all the ingredients, except the green onions and rice, in the cooking pot and stir to mix.
2. Add the lid and set to pressure cook on high. Set the timer for 30 minutes. When the timer goes off use natural release to remove the lid.
3. Transfer the chicken to a cutting board and shred. Return chicken to the pot and stir to combine.
4. Divide rice evenly among 6 bowls. With a slotted spoon, ladle gumbo over rice and top with green onion. Serve.

Nutrition:
- InfoCalories 416,Total Fat 10g,Total Carbs 35g,Protein 45g,Sodium 686mg.

Garlic And Butter Chicken Dish

Servings: 4
Cooking Time: 35 Minutes
Ingredients:
- 4 pieces of chicken breasts, chopped up
- ¼ cup of turmeric ghee/ normal ghee
- 1 teaspoon of salt
- 10 cloves of garlic, peeled and diced up

Directions:
1. Add chicken breast to the Ninja Foodi
2. Add ghee, salt, diced garlic and lock up the lid
3. Cook on HIGH pressure for 35 minutes
4. Release the pressure naturally and open the lid
5. Serve with extra ghee

Korean Barbecued Satay

Servings: 4
Cooking Time: 4h 15 Min
Ingredients:
- 1 lb. boneless; skinless chicken tenders /450g
- ½ cup pineapple juice /125ml
- ½ cup soy sauce /125ml
- ⅓ cup sesame oil /84ml
- 4 scallions; chopped
- 1 pinch black pepper
- 4 cloves garlic; chopped
- 2 tsp sesame seeds, toasted /10g
- 1 tsp fresh ginger, grated /5g

Directions:
1. Skew each tender and trim any excess fat. Mix the other ingredients in one large bowl. Add the skewered chicken and place in the fridge for 4 to 24 hours.
2. Preheat the Foodi to 370 For 188°C. Using a paper towel, pat the chicken dry. Fry for 10 minutes on Air Crisp mode.

Chicken & Black Bean Chowder

Servings: 6
Cooking Time: 6 Hours
Ingredients:
- 15 oz. black beans, rinsed & drained
- 3 chicken breasts, boneless & skinless
- 1 cup corn, frozen
- 16 oz. salsa
- 4 cups chicken broth, low sodium
- 4 oz. green chilies, diced
- ¼ cup cilantro, chopped
- 1 lime, cut in wedges

Directions:
1. Place all ingredients, except cilantro and limes, in the cooking pot, stir to mix well.
2. Add the lid and set to slow cook on low. Cook 5-6 hours until chicken is tender.
3. Transfer chicken to a cutting board and shred. Return to the pot and increase temperature to high. Cook 30 minutes.
4. Ladle into bowls and serve garnished with cilantro and a lime wedge.

Nutrition:
- InfoCalories 350,Total Fat 8g,Total Carbs 29g,Protein 42g,Sodium 749mg.

Cheesy Chicken And Broccoli Casserole

Servings: 6
Cooking Time: 30 Minutes
Ingredients:
- 4 boneless, skinless chicken breasts
- 2 cups chicken stock
- 1 cup whole milk
- 1 cans condensed Cheddar cheese soup
- 1 teaspoon paprika
- 2 cups shredded Cheddar cheese
- Kosher salt
- Freshly ground black pepper
- 2 cups crushed buttered crackers

Directions:
1. Place the chicken and stock in the pot. Assemble pressure lid, making sure the pressure release valve is in the SEAL position.
2. Select PRESSURE and set to HI. Set timer to 20 minutes. Select START/STOP to begin.
3. When pressure cooking is complete, quick release the pressure by turning the pressure release valve to the VENT position. Carefully remove lid when unit has finished releasing pressure.
4. Using silicone-tipped utensils, shred the chicken inside the pot.
5. Add the milk, condensed soup, paprika, and cheese. Stir to combine with the chicken. Season with salt and pepper. Top with the crushed crackers. Close crisping lid.
6. Select AIR CRISP, set temperature to 360°F (180°C), and set time to 10 minutes. Select START/STOP to begin.
7. When cooking is complete, open lid and let cool before serving.

Nutrition:
- InfoCalories: 449,Total Fat: 23g,Sodium: 925mg,Carbohydrates: 18g,Protein: 42g.

Turkey Rellenos

Servings: 4
Cooking Time: 20 Minutes
Ingredients:
- Nonstick cooking spray
- 4 poblano chilies
- ½ lb. hot Italian turkey sausage, casings removed
- 1 cup cottage cheese, reduced fat, drained
- ½ cup mozzarella cheese, grated

Directions:
1. Lightly spray fryer basket with cooking spray and place in the cooking pot.
2. Split the chilies with a knife and remove the seeds, do not remove the stems. Place in the basket.
3. Add the tender-crisp lid and set to broil. Cook chilies until skin chars on all sides. Transfer to a large Ziploc bag and seal. When the chilies have cooled, carefully remove the skin.
4. Remove the fryer basket and set to cooker to sauté on med-high heat. Cook sausage until no longer pink. Transfer to a medium bowl.
5. Add the cottage cheese to the sausage and mix well.
6. Spoon the sausage mixture into the chilies and lay them in the basket, spit side up. Sprinkle the mozzarella cheese over.
7. Add the basket back to the pot and set to bake on 350°F (175°C). Bake 15 minutes until the cheese is melted and bubbly. Serve immediately.

Nutrition:
- InfoCalories 179,Total Fat 7g,Total Carbs 9g,Protein 20g,Sodium 977mg.

Poached Chicken With Coconut Lime Cream Sauce

Servings: 4
Cooking Time: 10 Minutes
Ingredients:
- 1-ounce shallot, minced
- 1 ounces ginger, sliced
- 2 medium banana peppers,
- 1 cup of coconut milk
- 1 cup chicken stock
- Juice of 1 lime, and zest
- 2 tablespoons fish sauce
- 3 pieces of 1/3 pounds each chicken breasts, meat

Directions:
1. Add listed to your Ninja Foodi
2. Stir well and lock lid, cook on HIGH pressure for 10 minutes
3. Quick release pressure. Top with fresh cilantro. Serve and enjoy!

Honey Garlic Chicken

Servings: 4
Cooking Time: 30 Min
Ingredients:
- 4 boneless; skinless chicken breast; cut into chunks
- 4 garlic cloves, smashed
- 1 onion; diced
- ½ cup honey /125ml
- 1 tbsp cornstarch /15g
- 1 tbsp water /15ml
- 2 tbsp lime juice /30ml
- 3 tbsp soy sauce /45ml
- 2 tsp sesame oil /10ml
- 1 tsp rice vinegar /5ml
- Salt and black pepper to taste

Directions:
1. Mix garlic, onion and chicken in your Foodi. In a bowl, combine honey, sesame oil, lime juice, soy sauce, and rice vinegar; pour over the chicken mixture.
2. Seal the pressure lid, choose Pressure, set to High, and set the timer to 15 minutes. Press Start. When ready, release the pressure quickly.
3. Mix water and cornstarch until well dissolved; stir into the sauce. Press Sear/Sauté. Simmer the sauce and cook for 2 to 3 minutes as you stir until thickened.

Garlic-herb Roasted Chicken

Servings: 4
Cooking Time: 40 Minutes
Ingredients:
- 1 whole chicken
- 1 head garlic
- 2 fresh whole sprigs rosemary
- 2 fresh whole sprigs parsley
- 1 lemon, halved
- ¼ cup hot water
- ¼ cup white wine
- Juice of 2 lemons
- ¼ cup unsalted butter, melted
- 3 tablespoons extra-virgin olive oil
- 5 garlic cloves, minced
- 2 teaspoons minced fresh parsley
- 2 teaspoons minced fresh rosemary
- ½ teaspoon sea salt
- ¼ teaspoon freshly ground black pepper

Directions:
1. Discard the neck from inside the chicken cavity and remove any excess fat and leftover feathers. Rinse the chicken inside and out under running cold water. Stuff the garlic head into the chicken cavity along with the rosemary and parsley sprigs and lemon halves. Tie the legs together with cooking twine.
2. Add the water, wine, and lemon juice. Place the chicken into the Cook & Crisp Basket and insert the basket in the pot. Assemble pressure lid, making sure the pressure release valve is in the SEAL position.
3. Select PRESSURE and set to HI. Set time to 15 minutes. Select START/STOP to begin.
4. When pressure cooking is complete, quick release the pressure by moving the pressure release valve to the VENT position. Carefully remove lid when the unit has finished releasing pressure.
5. In a small bowl, combine the butter, olive oil, minced garlic, minced parsley, minced rosemary, salt, and pepper. Brush the mixture over the chicken. Close crisping lid.
6. Select AIR CRISP, set temperature to 400°F (205°C), and set time to 20 minutes. Select START/STOP to begin.
7. Cooking is complete when the internal temperature of the chicken reaches 165°F (75°C) on a meat thermometer inserted into the thickest part of the meat (it should not touch the bone). Carefully remove the chicken from the basket using 2 large serving forks.
8. Let the chicken rest for 10 minutes before carving and serving.

Nutrition:
- InfoCalories: 693, Total Fat: 50g, Sodium: 323mg, Carbohydrates: 12g, Protein: 48g.

Your's Truly Lime Chicken Chili

Servings: 6
Cooking Time: 23 Minutes
Ingredients:
- ¼ cup cooking wine (Keto-Friendly)
- ½ cup organic chicken broth
- 1 onion, diced
- 1 teaspoon salt
- ½ teaspoon paprika
- 5 garlic cloves, minced
- 1 tablespoon lime juice
- ¼ cup butter
- 2 pounds chicken thighs
- 1 teaspoon dried parsley
- 3 green chilies, chopped

Directions:
1. Set your Ninja-Foodi to Sauté mode and add onion and garlic
2. Sauté for 3 minutes, add remaining
3. Lock lid and cook on Medium-HIGH pressure for 20 minutes
4. Release pressure naturally over 10 minutes. Serve and enjoy!

Mexican Style Green Chili Chicken

Servings: 4
Cooking Time: 40 Min
Ingredients:
- 1½ pounds boneless skinless chicken breasts /675g
- 12 ounces, baby plum tomatoes, halved /360g
- 2 jalapeño peppers, seeded and chopped
- 2 large serrano pepper seeded and cut into chunks
- 2 large garlic cloves; minced
- ½ lime, juiced
- Tortilla chips
- 1 small onion; sliced
- ¼ cup minced fresh cilantro /32.5g
- ¾ cup chicken stock /188ml
- ½ cup shredded Cheddar Cheese /65g
- 1 tbsp olive oil /15ml
- ½ tsp salt /2.5g
- ½ tsp ground cumin /2.5g
- 1 tsp Mexican seasoning mix /5g
- Cooking spray

Directions:
1. Choose Sear/Sauté on your Foodi and adjust to High. Press Start to preheat the inner pot. Heat the olive oil add the plum tomatoes; cook without turning, for 3 to 4 minutes.
2. Add the chicken stock while scraping the bottom of the pot to dissolve any browned bits. Stir in the cumin, Mexican seasoning, and salt. Add the chicken, jalapeños, serrano pepper, garlic, onion, and half the cilantro.
3. Seal the pressure lid, choose pressure; adjust the pressure to High and the cook time to 10 minutes. Press Start.
4. Meanwhile, grease the reversible rack with cooking spray and fix the rack in the upper position of the pot. Cut out a circle of aluminum foil to fit the rack and place on the rack.
5. Lay on a single layer of tortilla chips, sprinkle with half of the Cheddar cheese and repeat with another layer of chips and cheese. Set aside.
6. After cooking, perform a natural pressure release for 5 minutes. Take out the chicken from the pot and set aside. Then, with an immersion blender, purée the vegetables into the sauce.

7. Shred the chicken with two forks and return the pieces to the sauce. Add the remaining cilantro and the lime juice. Taste and adjust the seasoning and carefully transfer the rack of chips to the pot.
8. Close the crisping lid and Choose Air Crisp; adjust the temperature to 375°F or 190°C and the time to 5 minutes; press Start. When done cooking, open the lid. Carefully take out the rack and pour the chips into a platter. Serve the chili in bowls with the chips on the side.

The Borderline Crack Chicken

Servings: 4
Cooking Time: 25 Minutes
Ingredients:
- 4 ounces cheddar cheese
- 3 tablespoons arrowroot
- 1 cup of water
- 8 ounces cream cheese
- 1 pack ranch seasoning
- 2 pounds boneless chicken breast
- 6-8 cooked bacon

Directions:
1. Add chicken to your Ninja Foodi. Add cream cheese
2. Sprinkle ranch seasoning over chicken add water
3. Lock lid and cook for 25 minutes on HIGH pressure. Quick release pressure
4. Take the chicken out and shred into pieces
5. Set your pot to SAUTE mode and add a mixture of arrowroot and water
6. Add cheese and shredded chicken. Stir and bacon. Enjoy!

Chicken With Bbq Sauce

Servings: 6
Cooking Time: 20 Min
Ingredients:
- 2 pounds boneless skinless chicken breasts /900g
- 1 small onion; minced
- 4 garlic cloves
- 1 cup carrots, thinly sliced /130g
- 1½ cups barbecue sauce /375ml
- 1 tsp salt /5g

Directions:
1. Apply a seasoning of salt to the chicken and place in the inner pot of the Foodi; add onion, carrots, garlic and barbeque sauce. Toss the chicken to coat.
2. Seal the pressure lid, choose Pressure, set to High, and set the timer to 15 minutes. Press Start. Once ready, do a quick release. Use two forks to shred chicken and stir into the sauce.

Chicken And Broccoli Stir-fry

Servings: 4
Cooking Time: 20 Minutes
Ingredients:
- 1 cup long-grain white rice
- 1 cup chicken stock
- 2 tablespoons canola oil
- 3 boneless, skinless chicken breasts, cut into 1-inch cubes
- 1 medium head broccoli, cut into 1-inch florets
- 2 teaspoons kosher salt
- ½ teaspoon freshly ground black pepper
- 1 tablespoon ground ginger
- ¼ cup teriyaki sauce
- Sesame seeds, for garnish

Directions:
1. Place the rice and chicken stock into the pot. Assemble pressure lid, making sure the pressure release valve is in the SEAL position.
2. Select PRESSURE and set to HI. Set time to 2 minutes. Select START/STOP to begin.
3. When pressure cooking is complete, allow pressure to naturally release for 10 minutes. After 10 minutes, quick release remaining pressure by turning the pressure release valve to the VENT position. Carefully remove lid when unit has finished releasing pressure.
4. Transfer the rice to a bowl and cover to keep warm. Clean the cooking pot and return to unit.
5. Select SEAR/SAUTÉ and set to HI. Select START/STOP to begin. Let preheat for 5 minutes.
6. Add the oil and heat for 1 minute. Add the chicken and cook, stirring frequently, for about 6 minutes.
7. Stir in the broccoli, salt, pepper, and ginger. Cook for 5 minutes, stirring frequently. Stir in the teriyaki sauce and cook, stirring frequently, until the chicken has reached internal temperature of 165°F (75°C) on a food thermometer.
8. Serve the chicken and broccoli mixture over the rice. Garnish with sesame seeds if desired.

Nutrition:
- InfoCalories: 425,Total Fat: 10g,Sodium: 1176mg,Carbohydrates: 49g,Protein: 35g.

Saucy Chicken Breasts

Servings: 4
Cooking Time: 45 Min
Ingredients:
- 4 chicken breasts, boneless and skinless
- ½ cup chicken broth /125ml
- ½ cup chives; sliced /130g
- 1 tbsp cornstarch /15g
- 1 tbsp water /15ml
- 2 tbsp olive oil /30ml
- 2 tbsp soy sauce /30ml
- 2 tbsp tomato paste /30ml
- 2 tbsp honey /30ml
- 2 tbsp minced garlic/30g
- salt and ground black pepper to taste

Directions:
1. Season the chicken with pepper and salt. Warm oil on Sear/Sauté. Add in chicken and cook for 5 minutes until lightly browned.
2. In a small bowl, mix garlic, soy sauce, honey, and tomato paste; pour the mixture over the chicken. Stir in ½ cup or 125ml broth. Seal the pressure lid, choose Pressure, set to High, and set the timer to 12 minutes. Press Start.
3. When ready, release the pressure quickly. Set the chicken to a bowl. Mix water and cornstarch to create a slurry; briskly stir the mixture into the sauce that is remaining in the pan for 2 minutes until thickened. Serve the chicken with the sauce and chives.

Ninja Foodi Cookbook

Crispy Chicken With Carrots And Potatoes

Servings: 4
Cooking Time: 35 Min
Ingredients:
- 4 bone-in skin-on chicken thighs
- 1 pound potatoes, quartered /450g
- 2 carrots; sliced into rounds
- 2 dashes hot sauce
- ¼ cup chicken stock /62.5ml
- 2 tbsp melted butter /30ml
- 1 tbsp olive oil /15ml
- 1 tsp dried oregano /5g
- ½ tsp dry mustard /2.5g
- ½ tsp garlic powder /2.5g
- ¼ tsp sweet paprika /1.25g
- ½ tsp salt /2.5g
- 2 tsp Worcestershire sauce /10ml
- 2 tsp turmeric powder /10g

Directions:
1. Season the chicken on both sides with salt. In a small bowl, mix the melted butter, Worcestershire sauce, turmeric, oregano, dry mustard, garlic powder, sweet paprika, and hot sauce to be properly combined and stir in the chicken stock.
2. On your Foodi, choose Sear/Sauté and adjust to Medium-High. Press Start to preheat the inner pot. Heat olive oil and add the chicken thighs and fry for 4 to 5 minutes or until browned. Turn and briefly sear the other side, about 1 minute. Remove from the pot.
3. Add the potatoes and carrots to the pot and stir to coat with the fat. Pour in about half of the spicy sauce and mix to coat. Put the chicken thighs on top and drizzle with the remaining sauce.
4. Seal the pressure lid, choose pressure; adjust the pressure to High and the cook time to 3 minutes; press Start. After cooking, do a quick pressure release, and carefully open the lid.
5. Transfer the chicken to the reversible rack. Use a spoon to gently move the potatoes and carrots aside and fetch some of the sauce over the chicken. Mix the potatoes and carrots back into the sauce and carefully set the rack in the pot.
6. Close the crisping lid and Choose Bake/Roast; adjust the temperature to 375°F or 190°C and the cook time to 16 minutes. Press Start to begin crisping the chicken. When done cooking, open the lid and transfer the potatoes, carrots and chicken to a serving platter, drizzling with any remaining sauce.

Hawaiian Pinna Colada Chicken Meal

Servings: 4
Cooking Time: 15 Minutes
Ingredients:
- 2 pounds organic chicken thigh
- 1 cup fresh pineapple chunks
- ½ cup coconut cream
- 1 teaspoon cinnamon
- 1/8 teaspoon salt
- 2 tablespoons coconut aminos
- ½ cup green onion, chopped
- Arrowroot flour

Directions:
1. Add all of the to your Ninja Foodi except green onion
2. Lock up the lid and cook for 15 minutes at HIGH pressure
3. Once done, allow the pressure to release naturally. Open up the lid and stir well
4. Take a bowl and mix arrowroot flour and a tablespoon of water to make a slurry
5. Add the slurry to your pot and mix well to make a thick mixture
6. Set your pot to Saute mode and wait until the sauce is just thick enough
7. Garnish with some green onion and enjoy!

Turkey & Pasta With Lemon Pesto

Servings: 4
Cooking Time: 15 Minutes
Ingredients:
- 2 eggs
- 1 tbsp. lemon zest
- ½ cup basil pesto
- 1 tbsp. olive oil
- 1 cup onion, chopped
- 1 clove garlic, chopped fine
- 2 cups turkey, cooked & chopped
- ½ lb. bow tie pasta, cooked & drained
- Freshly ground black pepper

Directions:
1. In a medium bowl, whisk together eggs, zest, and pesto until combined.
2. Add the oil to the cooking pot and set to sauté on medium heat.
3. Add the onions and cook 3-5 minutes until translucent. Add the garlic and turkey and cook until heated through.
4. Reduce heat to low. Add the pasta and toss to mix. Pour egg mixture over top and quickly stir to combine, cook 1 minute but be careful not to let the eggs scramble. Sprinkle with pepper and serve immediately.

Nutrition:
- InfoCalories 234,Total Fat 8g,Total Carbs 24g,Protein 15g,Sodium 193mg.

Stir-fried Chicken And Broccoli Rice Bowl

Servings: 4
Cooking Time: 20 Minutes
Ingredients:
- 1 cup long-grain white rice
- 1 cup chicken stock
- 2 tablespoons canola oil
- 3 boneless, skinless chicken breasts, cut into 1-inch cubes
- 1 medium head broccoli, cut into 1-inch florets
- 2 teaspoons kosher salt
- ½ teaspoon freshly ground black pepper
- 1 tablespoon ground ginger
- ¼ cup teriyaki sauce

- Sesame seeds, for garnish

Directions:
1. Place the rice and chicken stock into the pot. Assemble pressure lid, making sure the pressure release valve is in the SEAL position.
2. Select PRESSURE and set to HI. Set time to 2 minutes. Select START/STOP to begin.
3. When pressure cooking is complete, allow pressure to naturally release for 10 minutes. After 10 minutes, quick release remaining pressure by turning the pressure release valve to the VENT position. Carefully remove lid when unit has finished releasing pressure.
4. Transfer the rice to a bowl and cover to keep warm. Clean the cooking pot and return to unit.
5. Select SEAR/SAUTÉ and set to HI. Select START/STOP to begin. Let preheat for 5 minutes.
6. Add the oil and heat for 1 minute. Add the chicken and cook, stirring frequently, for about 6 minutes.
7. Stir in the broccoli, salt, pepper, and ginger. Cook for 5 minutes, stirring frequently. Stir in the teriyaki sauce and cook, stirring frequently, until the chicken has reached internal temperature of 165°F(75°C) on a food thermometer.
8. Serve the chicken and broccoli mixture over the rice. Garnish with sesame seeds if desired.

Lime And Cilantro Chicken Meal

Servings: 4
Cooking Time: 2 Hours 45 Minutes
Ingredients:
- 2 small limes
- ¼ cup cilantro, chopped
- ½ tablespoon fresh garlic, minced
- 1 teaspoon salt
- ½ teaspoon pepper
- 4 pounds chicken drumsticks

Directions:
1. Juice the lime and add them to your Ninja Foodi
2. Add ¼ cup of chopped cilantro, 1 teaspoon of salt, ½ a tablespoon of freshly minced garlic
3. Add the chicken drumsticks to the Ninja Foodi and coat them well
4. Cover and cook on SLOW COOK MODE for 2 and a ½ hour
5. Pre-heat your oven to a temperature of 500 degrees F. Line up a cookie sheet with foil
6. Transfer the cooker drumstick from the cooker to the foil using tongs
7. Bake for 10 minutes until they are nicely browned, making sure to turn them halfway through
8. Serve with the cooking juices. Enjoy!

Lemon Chicken

Servings: 4
Cooking Time: 18 Minutes
Ingredients:
- 4 bone-in, skin-on chicken thighs
- Black pepper and salt to taste
- 2 tablespoons butter
- 2 teaspoons garlic, minced
- ½ cup herbed chicken stock
- ½ cup heavy whip cream
- ½ a lemon, juiced

Directions:
1. Season the four chicken thighs generously with black pepper and salt.
2. Set your Ninja Foodi to sauté mode and add oil, let it heat up.
3. Add thigh, Sauté on both sides for 6 minutes.
4. Remove thigh to a platter and keep it on the side.
5. Add garlic, cook for 2 minutes.
6. Whisk in chicken stock, heavy cream, lemon juice and gently stir.
7. Bring the mix to a simmer and reintroduce chicken.
8. Lock and secure the Ninja Foodi's lid and cook for 10 minutes on "HIGH" pressure.
9. Release pressure over 10 minutes.
10. Serve and enjoy.

Nutrition:
- InfoCalories: 294; Fat: 26g; Carbohydrates: 4g; Protein: 12g

Salsa Verde Chicken With Salsa Verde

Servings: 4
Cooking Time: 50 Min
Ingredients:
- Salsa Verde:
- 1 jalapeño pepper, deveined and sliced
- ¼ cup extra virgin olive oil /62.5ml
- ¼ cup parsley /32.5g
- ½ cup capers /65g
- 1 lime, juiced
- 1 tsp salt /5g
- Chicken:
- 4 boneless skinless chicken breasts
- 1 cup quinoa, rinsed /130g
- 2 cups water /500ml

Directions:
1. In a blender, mix olive oil, salt, lime juice, jalapeño pepper, capers, and parsley and blend until smooth. Arrange chicken breasts in the bottom of the Foodi pot. Over the chicken, add salsa verde mixture.
2. In a bowl that can fit in the cooker, mix quinoa and water. Set a reversible rack onto chicken and sauce. Set the bowl onto the reversible rack. Seal the pressure lid, choose Pressure, set to High, and set the timer to 20 minutes. Press Start.
3. When ready, release the pressure quickly. Remove the quinoa bowl and reversible rack. Using two forks, shred chicken into the sauce; stir to coat. Divide the quinoa, between plates. Top with chicken and salsa verde before serving.

Authentic Belizean Stewed Chicken

Servings: 8
Cooking Time: 20 Minutes
Ingredients:
- 1 tablespoon coconut oil
- 3 cloves garlic, minced

Ninja Foodi Cookbook

- 1 onion, sliced
- 4 whole chicken legs
- 2 cups (500 mL) chicken stock
- 3 tablespoons Worcestershire sauce
- 2 tablespoons white vinegar
- 2 tablespoons achiote seasoning
- 1 tablespoon granulated sugar
- 1 teaspoon dried oregano
- 1 teaspoon ground cumin
- Salt and pepper, to taste

Directions:
1. Press the Sauté button and melt the coconut oil.
2. Add the garlic, onion, and chicken legs and keep stirring until the chicken legs are golden brown.
3. Add the remaining ingredients to the cooking pot and stir to combine.
4. Assemble pressure lid, making sure the pressure release valve is in the Seal position. Select Pressure and set to high. Set time to 15 minutes. Press Start to begin.
5. Once cooking is complete, do a quick pressure release. Carefully open the lid.
6. Divide the chicken legs among plates and serve.

Coq Au Vin

Servings: 4
Cooking Time: 60 Min
Ingredients:
- 4 chicken leg quarters, skin on
- 4 serrano ham slices; cut into thirds
- 1¼ cups dry red wine /312.5ml
- ⅓ cup chicken stock /84ml
- ½ cup sautéed mushrooms /65g
- ¾ cup shallots; sliced /98g
- ¼ cup brown onion slices /32.5g
- 1 tbsp olive oil /15ml
- 1½ tsp tomato puree/7.5ml
- ½ tsp brown sugar /2.5g
- 1½ tsp salt /7.5g
- Black pepper to taste

Directions:
1. Season the chicken on both sides with 1 tsp of salt and set aside on a wire rack. On the Foodi, choose Sear/Sauté and adjust to Medium. Press Start to preheat the inner pot.
2. Heat the olive oil and place the ham in the pot in a single layer and cook for 3 to 4 minutes or until browned. Remove the ham to a plate and set aside.
3. Add the chicken quarters to the pot. Cook for 5 minutes or until the skin is golden brown. Turn the chicken over and cook further for 2 minutes; remove to a plate.
4. Carefully pour out almost all the fat leaving about a tbsp to cover the bottom of the pot. Then, stir in the sliced onion and cook until the onion begins to brown.
5. Add ½ cup of red wine, stir, and scrape the bottom of the pan to let off any browned bits. Then, boil the mixture until the wine reduces by about 1/3, about 2 minutes.
6. Pour the remaining red wine, chicken stock, tomato puree, brown sugar, and a few grinds of black pepper into the pot. Boil the sauce for 1 minute, stirring to make sure the tomato paste is properly mixed. Add the chicken pieces with skin- side up, to the pot.
7. Put the pressure lid in place and lock to seal. Choose Pressure; adjust the pressure to High and the cook time to 12 minutes. Press Start to continue cooking.
8. After cooking, perform a natural pressure release for 10 minutes. Remove the chicken from the pot. Pour the sauce into a bowl and allow sitting until the fat rises to the top and starts firming up. Use a spoon to fetch off the fat on top of the sauce.
9. Pour the sauce back into the pot and stir in the mushrooms and pearl onions. Place the chicken on the sauce with skin side up. Close the crisping lid and select Broil. Adjust the cook time to 7 minutes; press Start.
10. When done cooking, open the lid and transfer the chicken to a serving platter. Spoon the sauce with mushrooms and pearl onions all around the chicken and crumble the reserved ham on top.

Chicken Posole

Servings: 4
Cooking Time: 30 Minutes
Ingredients:
- 1 tbsp. olive oil
- 3 chicken breasts, boneless & skinless
- 1 tsp salt
- ½ tsp pepper
- 1 onion, chopped
- 4 cloves garlic, chopped fine
- 1 jalapeno pepper, seeded & chopped fine
- 1 tsp oregano
- 1 tsp cumin
- 1 ½ cups corn
- 4 cups chicken broth, low sodium
- 6 tomatillos, husks removed, rinsed & chopped
- 1 tbsp. lime juice
- ¼ cup cilantro, chopped
- ½ cup avocado, cubed

Directions:
1. Add the oil to the cooking pot and set to sauté on med-high.
2. Season the chicken with salt and pepper and add to the pot. Sear on both sides until golden brown, about 4 minutes per side. Transfer chicken to a plate.
3. Add the onion and cook, stirring occasionally, until onions are translucent.
4. Add the garlic, jalapeno, oregano, and cumin and cook 1 minute.
5. Stir in the corn, broth and tomatillos and mix. Return the chicken to the pot.
6. Add the lid and set to pressure cook on high. Set the timer for 20 minutes. When the timer goes off use manual release to remove the lid.
7. Transfer the chicken to a cutting board and shred. Return it back to the pot and add the lime juice. Stir well. Ladle into bowls and top with cilantro and avocado. Serve.

Nutrition:
- InfoCalories 385,Total Fat 13g,Total Carbs 26g,Protein 42g,Sodium 617mg.

Turkey Cutlets

Servings: 4
Cooking Time: 15 Minutes

Ingredients:
- 1 teaspoon Greek seasoning
- 1-pound turkey cutlets
- 2 tablespoons olive oil
- 1 teaspoon turmeric powder
- ½ cup almond flour

Directions:
1. Take a suitable and stir in turmeric powder, Greek seasoning, almond flour and mix well.
2. Dredge turkey cutlets in the bowl and let it sit for 30 minutes.
3. Select "Sauté" mode on your Ninja Foodi and stir in oil, heat up.
4. Add cutlets and Sauté for 2 minutes.
5. Lock and secure the Ninja Foodi's lid and cook on Low-Medium Pressure for 20 minutes.
6. Release pressure naturally over 10 minutes.
7. Take the dish out, serve and enjoy.

Nutrition:
- InfoCalories: 340; Fat: 19g; Carbohydrates: 3.7g; Protein: 36g

Chicken Pasta With Pesto Sauce

Servings: 8
Cooking Time: 30 Min

Ingredients:
- 4 chicken breast, boneless, skinless; cubed
- 8 oz. macaroni pasta /240g
- 1 garlic clove; minced
- 1/4 cup Asiago cheese, grated /32.5g
- 2 cups fresh collard greens, trimmed /260g
- ¼ cup cream cheese, at room temperature /32.5g
- 1 cup cherry tomatoes, halved /130g
- ½ cup basil pesto sauce /125ml
- 3½ cups water /875ml
- 1 tbsp butter /15g
- 1 tbsp salt; divided /15g
- 1 tsp freshly ground black pepper to taste /5g
- Freshly chopped basil for garnish

Directions:
1. To the inner steel pot of the Foodi, add water, chicken, 2 tsp salt, butter, and macaroni, and stir well to mix and be submerged in water.
2. Seal the pressure lid, choose Pressure, set to High, and set the timer to 2 minutes. Press Start. When ready, release the pressure quickly. Press Start/Stop, open the lid, get rid of ¼ cup water from the pot.
3. Set on Sear/Sauté. Into the pot, mix in collard greens, pesto sauce, garlic, remaining 1 tsp o 5g salt, cream cheese, tomatoes, and black pepper. Cook, for 1 to 2 minutes as you stir, until sauce is creamy.
4. Place the pasta into serving plates; top with asiago cheese and basil before serving.

Chicken With Cilantro Rice

Servings: 4
Cooking Time: 70 Min

Ingredients:
- 1 pound bone-in, skin-on chicken thighs /450g
- 1 cup basmati rice /130g
- ¾ cup chicken broth /188ml
- ½ cup tomato sauce /125ml
- 1 red onion; diced
- 1 yellow bell pepper; diced
- 2 tbsp ghee divided /30g
- 1 tbsp cayenne powder /15g
- 1 tsp ground cumin /5g
- 1 tsp Italian herb mix /5g
- ½ tsp salt /2.5g
- Chopped fresh cilantro, for garnish
- Lime wedges; for serving

Directions:
1. Choose Sear/Sauté on the pot and set to Medium High. Choose Start/Stop to preheat the pot. Melt half of the ghee in the pot, and cook the onion for 3 minutes, stirring occasionally, until softened.
2. Include the yellow bell pepper, cayenne pepper, cumin, herb mix, and salt, and cook for 2 minutes more with frequent stirring.
3. Pour the rice, broth, and tomato sauce into the pot. Place the reversible rack in the higher position of the pot, which is over the rice. Put the chicken on the rack.
4. Seal the pressure lid, choose pressure, set to High, and set the time to 30 minutes. Choose Start/Stop to begin cooking the rice. When the time is over, perform a quick pressure release and carefully open the lid.
5. Brush the chicken thighs with the remaining 1 tbsp or 15g of ghee. Close the crisping lid. Choose Broil and set the time to 5 minutes. Press Start/Stop.
6. When ready, check for your desired crispiness and remove the rack from the pot. Plate the chicken, garnish with cilantro, and serve with lime wedges.

Sticky Drumsticks

Servings: 4
Cooking Time: 50 Min

Ingredients:
- 1 lb. drumsticks /450g
- 2 tbsp honey /30ml
- 2 tsp dijon mustard /10g
- Cooking spray
- Salt and pepper to taste

Directions:
1. Combine the honey, mustard, salt, and pepper in a large bowl. Add in the chicken and toss to coat. Cover and put in the fridge for 30 minutes.
2. Preheat your Foodi to 380 °F or 195°C. Grease the Foodi basket with cooking spray. Arrange the drumsticks on the basket. Cook for 20 minutes on Air Crisp mode. After 10 minutes, shake the drumsticks.

Lemon Turkey Risotto

Servings: 4
Cooking Time: 40 Min

Ingredients:
- 2 boneless turkey breasts; cut into strips
- 2 cups chicken broth /500ml
- 1 cup Arborio rice, rinsed /130g
- ¼ cup chopped fresh parsley, or to taste /32.5g

Ninja Foodi Cookbook

- 2 lemons, zested and juiced
- 1 onion; diced
- 8 lemon slices
- 2 garlic cloves; minced
- 1 tbsp dried oregano /15g
- 1½ tbsp olive oil /22.5ml
- ½ tsp sea salt /2.5g
- salt and freshly ground black pepper to taste

Directions:
1. In a ziplock back, mix turkey, oregano, sea salt, garlic, juice and zest of two lemons. Marinate for 10 minutes.
2. Warm oil on Sear/Sauté. Add onion and cook for 3 minutes until fragrant; add rice and chicken broth and season with pepper and salt.
3. Empty the ziplock having the chicken and marinade into the pot. Seal the pressure lid, choose Pressure, set to High, and set the timer to 12 minutes. Press Start. When ready, release the pressure quickly.
4. Divide the rice and turkey between 4 serving bowls; garnish with lemon slices and parsley.

Chicken Burgers With Avocado

Servings: 8
Cooking Time: 15 Min
Ingredients:
- 1 lb. ground chicken /450g
- 1 tomato; sliced
- 1 red onion; chopped
- 1 Avocado; sliced
- ½ cup mayonnaise /125ml
- 1 egg, beaten
- 4 buns, halved
- 1 small red potato, shredded
- A pinch of ground chili
- A pinch of ground cumin
- Fresh cilantro; chopped
- Salt and pepper to taste
- Cooking spray

Directions:
1. Mix the chicken, onion, egg, potato, cumin, chili, cilantro, salt, and pepper in a large bowl with your hands until you have an even burger mixture.
2. Shape the mixture into 8 patties. Grease your Foodi basket with cooking spray.
3. Arrange the burgers onto the basket. Close the crisping lid and cook for 10 minutes, at 360 °F or 180°C. After 5 minutes, shake the patties.
4. To assemble your burgers, spread mayonnaise on the bottom of each half of the buns, top with a chicken patty, then put over a tomato slice. Cover with the other half of the buns and arrange on a serving platter to serve.

Sesame Chicken Wings(2)

Servings: 4
Cooking Time: 25 Minutes
Ingredients:
- 24 chicken wing segments
- 2 tablespoons toasted sesame oil
- 2 tablespoons Asian-Chile-Garlic sauce
- 2 tablespoons stevia
- 2 garlic cloves, minced
- 1 tablespoon toasted sesame seeds

Directions:
1. Add 1 cup water to Foodi's inner pot, place reversible rack in the pot in lower portions, place chicken wings in the rack.
2. Place lid into place and seal the pressure valve.
3. Select pressure mode to HIGH and cook for 10 minutes.
4. Make the glaze by taking a large bowl and whisking in sesame oil, Chile-Garlic sauce, choc zero maple syrup and garlic.
5. Once the chicken is done, quick release the pressure and remove the pressure lid.
6. Remove rack from the pot and empty it.
7. Return inner pot to the base.
8. Cover with crisping lid and select Air Crisp mode, adjust the temperature to 375 °F (190°C), pre-heat for 3 minutes.
9. While the Foodi pre-heats, add wings to the sauce and toss well to coat it.
10. Transfer wings to the basket, leaving any excess sauce in the bowl.
11. Place the basket in Foodi and close with Crisping mode, select Air Crisp mode and let it cook for 8 minutes, gently toss the wings and let it cook for 8 minutes more.
12. Once done, drizzle any sauce and sprinkle sesame seeds.
13. Enjoy.

Nutrition:
- InfoCalories: 440; Fat: 32g; Carbohydrates: 12g; Protein: 28g

Spinach And Chicken Curry

Servings: 4
Cooking Time: 12 Minutes
Ingredients:
- 10 ounce of Spinach
- 1 pound of chicken thigh cut up into 2-3 pieces
- 1 tablespoon of oil
- ½ a teaspoon of cumin seeds
- 1-inch ginger chopped up
- 6 pieces of cloves
- 2 medium onions cut up into pieces
- Spices
- ¼ teaspoon of turmeric
- ½ a teaspoon of red chili powder
- 2 teaspoon of coriander
- 1 teaspoon of salt

Directions:
1. Set your Ninja Foodi to Saute mode and add oil, allow the oil to heat up
2. Add cumin seeds, garlic, and ginger and cook for 30 seconds
3. Stir in garlic and the cut onions and Saute them for 1 minute more
4. Add spices and give it a nice stir. Add spinach with the chicken pieces on top of the spinach
5. Lock up the lid and allow them to cook at HIGH pressure for 8 minutes

6. Once done, do a quick release and open up the lid. Remove the chicken pieces from the pot and keep them on the side
7. Take an immersion blender and blend the whole mixture until you have a creamy texture
8. Cut up your chicken in small portions and add them back to the curry
9. Set the pot to Saute mode once more and give the whole curry a quick boil .Enjoy!

Bacon & Cranberry Stuffed Turkey Breast

Servings: 4
Cooking Time: 1 Hour
Ingredients:
- ¼ oz. porcini mushrooms, dried
- 1 slice bacon, thick cut, chopped
- ¼ cup shallot, chopped fine
- 2 tbsp. cranberries, dried, chopped
- 1 tsp fresh sage, chopped fine
- ½ cup bread crumbs
- 1 tbsp. fresh parsley, chopped
- 3 tbsp. chicken broth, low sodium
- 2 lb. turkey breast, boneless
- 2 tbsp. butter, soft
- ½ tsp salt

Directions:
1. In a small bowl, add the mushrooms and enough hot water to cover them. Let sit 15 minutes, then drain and chop them.
2. Set the cooker to sauté on medium heat. Add the bacon and cook until crisp. Transfer to a paper-towel lined plate.
3. Add the shallots and cook until they start to brown, about 3-5 minutes. Add the cranberries, sage, and mushrooms and cook, stirring frequently, 2-3 minutes.
4. Stir in bread crumbs, parsley, bacon, and broth and mix well. Transfer to a bowl to cool.
5. Remove the skin from the turkey, in one piece, do not discard. Butterfly the turkey breast and place between 2 sheets of plastic wrap. Pound out to ¼-inch thick.
6. Spread the stuffing over the turkey, leaving a ¾-inch border. Start with a short end and roll up the turkey. Wrap the skin back around the roll.
7. Use butcher string to tie the turkey. Place in the cooking pot and rub with butter. Sprinkle with salt.
8. Add the tender-crisp lid and set to roast on 400°F (205°C). Cook 20 minutes, then decrease the heat to 325°F (160°C). Cook another 10-15 minutes or until juices run clear. Let rest 10 minutes before slicing and serving.

Nutrition:
- InfoCalories 159,Total Fat 7g,Total Carbs 3g,Protein 19g,Sodium 120mg.

Desserts

Blackberry Crisp

Servings: 6
Cooking Time: 45 Minutes
Ingredients:
- 6 cups blackberries
- 2 tbsp. sugar, divided
- 1 tbsp. cornstarch
- 1 cup oats
- ½ cup almond flour
- ½ cup almonds, chopped
- 1 tsp cinnamon
- ¼ tsp salt
- ¼ cup coconut oil, melted

Directions:
1. Add the rack to the cooking pot. Spray an 8-inch baking dish with cooking spray.
2. In a large bowl, add the blackberries, 1 tablespoon sugar, and cornstarch, toss to coat. Pour into prepared dish.
3. In the same bowl, combine oats, flour, nuts, cinnamon, salt, coconut oil, and remaining sugar, mix well. Pour over berries.
4. Place the dish on the rack. Add the tender-crisp lid and set to bake on 350°F (175°C). Bake 30-35 minutes or until top is golden brown. Transfer to wire rack to cool before serving.

Nutrition:
- InfoCalories 282,Total Fat 13g,Total Carbs 38g,Protein 6g,Sodium 100mg.

Egg And Ham Pockets

Servings: 4
Cooking Time: 29 Minutes
Ingredients:
- 5 large eggs, divided
- 1 tablespoon extra-virgin olive oil
- Sea salt
- Freshly ground black pepper
- 1 (8-ounce / 227-g) tube refrigerated crescent rolls
- 4 ounces (113 g) thinly sliced ham
- 1 cup shredded Cheddar cheese
- Cooking spray

Directions:
1. Select SEAR/SAUTÉ and set to MD:HI. Select START/STOP and let preheat for 5 minutes.
2. Lightly whisk 4 eggs in a medium bowl.
3. Once unit has preheated, add the oil and beaten eggs. Season with salt and pepper. Whisk the eggs until they just begin to set, cooking until soft and translucent, 3 to 5 minutes. Remove the eggs from the pot and set aside.
4. In a small bowl, whisk the remaining egg.
5. Remove the crescent rolls from the tube and divide them into 4 rectangles. Gently roll out each rectangle until it is 6-by-4 inches. Top one half of each rectangle with ham, cheese, and scrambled eggs, leaving about a ½-inch border.
6. Brush the edges of the filled dough with water. Fold over the rectangle and press firmly to seal. Brush the top of each pocket with the egg.
7. Place Cook & Crisp Basket in pot. Coat 2 pastries well on both sides with cooking spray and arrange them in the basket in a single layer. Close crisping lid.
8. Select AIR CRISP, set temperature to 375°F(190°C), and set time to 12 minutes. Select START/STOP to begin.
9. After 6 minutes, open lid, remove basket, and use silicone-tipped tongs to flip the breakfast pockets. Lower basket back into pot and close lid to continue cooking, until golden brown.
10. When cooking is complete, check for your desired crispiness. Place the pockets on a wire rack to cool. Repeat steps 7, 8, and 9 with the remaining 2 pastries.

Sweet And Salty Bars

Servings:12
Cooking Time: 10 Minutes
Ingredients:
- 1 cup light corn syrup
- 1 cup granulated sugar
- 1 teaspoon vanilla extract
- 1 bag mini marshmallows
- 1 cup crunchy peanut butter
- 1 bag potato chips with ridges, slightly crushed
- 1 cup pretzels, slightly crushed
- 1 bag hard-shelled candy-coated chocolates

Directions:
1. Select SEAR/SAUTÉ and set temperature to MD:HI. Select START/STOP to begin. Let preheat for 5 minutes.
2. Add the corn syrup, sugar, and vanilla and stir until the sugar is melted.
3. Add the marshmallows and peanut butter and stir until the marshmallows are melted.
4. Add the potato chips and pretzels and stir until everything is evenly coated in the marshmallow mixture.
5. Pour the mixture into a 9-by-13-inch pan and place the chocolate candies on top, slightly pressing them in. Let cool, then cut into squares and serve.

Nutrition:
- InfoCalories: 585,Total Fat: 21g,Sodium: 403mg,Carbohydrates: 96g,Protein: 9g.

Classic Cheesecake

Servings: 4
Cooking Time: 40 Minutes
Ingredients:
- 2 cups (500 mL) graham crackers, crushed
- 3 tablespoons brown sugar
- ¼ cup (63 mL) butter, melted
- 2 (8 ounce / 227-g) cream cheese, softened
- ½ cup (125 mL) granulated sugar

- 2 tablespoons all-purpose flour
- 1 teaspoon vanilla extract
- 3 eggs
- 1 cup (250 mL) water
- 1 cup (250 mL) caramel sauce

Directions:
1. Make the crust: Mix the crushed crackers with brown sugar and butter. Spread the mixture at the bottom of a springform pan and use a spoon to press to fit. Freeze in refrigerator for 10 minutes.
2. In a bowl, whisk the cream cheese and sugar until smooth. Mix in the flour and vanilla. Whisk in the eggs. Remove the pan from refrigerator and pour mixture over crust. Cover the pan with foil.
3. Pour the water in cooking pot, place the reversible rack in pot and place the pan on top.
4. Assemble pressure lid, making sure the pressure release valve is in the Seal position. Select Pressure and set to high. Set time to 40 minutes. Press Start to begin.
5. When cooking is complete, allow a natural pressure release for 10 minutes, then release any remaining pressure. Open the lid.
6. Carefully remove the cake pan and take off the foil. Let cool for 10 minutes. Pour the caramel sauce over and refrigerate for 3 hours.
7. Remove the pan from the refrigerator and invert the cheesecake on a plate. Slice and serve.

Coconut Lime Snack Cake

Servings: 8
Cooking Time: 20 Minutes
Ingredients:
- Butter flavored cooking spray
- 2 eggs
- ½ cup coconut milk
- 3 tbsp. honey
- 1 tsp vanilla
- ¼ cup + 1 tbsp. fresh lime juice, divided
- 1 tbsp. + 1 tsp lime zest, divided
- 2 ¼ cup almond flour, sifted
- 1 tsp baking soda
- ½ cup coconut, unsweetened & shredded
- ½ cup powdered Stevia

Directions:
1. Place the rack in the cooking pot. Spray an 8-inch baking pan with cooking spray.
2. In a large bowl, beat eggs, milk, honey, vanilla, ¼ cup lime juice and tablespoon zest until thick and frothy, about 6-8 minutes.
3. Fold in flour, baking soda, and coconut just until combined. Pour into prepared pan.
4. Place the cake on the rack and add the tender-crisp lid. Set to bake on 350°F (175°C). Bake 15-20 minutes or until cake passes the toothpick test.
5. Let cool in the pan for 10 minutes, then invert onto a serving plate.
6. In a small bowl, whisk together powdered sugar, remaining tablespoon lime juice, and remaining teaspoon lime zest. Drizzle over the top of cooled cake. Serve.

Nutrition:
- InfoCalories 183, Total Fat 13g, Total Carbs 28g, Protein 5g, Sodium 35mg.

Chocolate Mousse

Servings: 12
Cooking Time: 25 Minutes
Ingredients:
- Nonstick cooking spray
- 8 oz. semisweet chocolate chips
- 8 eggs, separated
- 1 teaspoon vanilla
- ¼ cup + 2 tbsp. powdered' sugar

Directions:
1. Spray an 8-inch springform pan with cooking spray. Line the bottom with parchment paper.
2. Melt the chocolate in a microwave safe bowl in 30 second intervals.
3. Beat the egg yolks until thick and pale. Slowly beat in the melted chocolate until combined. Fold in the vanilla.
4. Beat the egg whites with ¼ cup of sugar until soft peaks form. Fold ¼ of the egg whites into the chocolate mixture just until combined. Gently fold in remaining egg whites. Pour into the prepared pan.
5. Place the rack in the cooking pot and place the mousse on it. Add the tender-crisp lid and set to bake on 350°F (175°C). Bake 20-25 minutes until almost set, the mousse will still be a little jiggly in the middle.
6. Transfer mousse to a wire rack and let cool completely. Cover and refrigerate at least 4 hours. Dust with remaining sugar before serving.

Nutrition:
- InfoCalories 154, Total Fat 8g, Total Carbs 15g, Protein 5g, Sodium 48mg.

Butterscotch Almond Brownies

Servings: 12
Cooking Time: 30 Minutes
Ingredients:
- Butter flavored cooking spray
- ½ cup butter, soft
- 1 ½ cups Stevia brown sugar
- 4 eggs
- 1 ½ tbsp. vanilla
- ¾ cup flour
- 1 ½ tsp baking powder
- ¾ cup almonds, chopped

Directions:
1. Place the rack in the cooking pot. Spray an 8x8-inch baking pan with cooking spray.
2. In a large bowl, beat butter and Stevia together until smooth.
3. Add eggs and vanilla and mix well. Stir in remaining ingredients and spread in prepared pan.
4. Place the pan on the rack and add the tender-crisp lid. Set to bake on 350°F (175°C). Bake 25-30 minutes or until brownies pass the toothpick test.
5. Transfer to wire rack to cool before serving.

Nutrition:
- InfoCalories 147, Total Fat 11g, Total Carbs 36g, Protein 3g, Sodium 74mg.

Rhubarb, Raspberry, And Peach Cobbler

Servings: 6
Cooking Time: 40 Minutes
Ingredients:
- 1 cup all-purpose flour, divided
- ¾ cup granulated sugar
- ½ teaspoon kosher salt, divided
- 2½ cups diced fresh rhubarb
- 2½ cups fresh raspberries
- 2½ cups fresh peaches, peeled and sliced into ¾-inch pieces
- Cooking spray
- ¾ cup brown sugar
- ½ cup oat flakes (oatmeal)
- 1 teaspoon cinnamon
- Pinch ground nutmeg
- 6 tablespoons unsalted butter, sliced, at room temperature
- ½ cup chopped pecans or walnuts

Directions:
1. Select BAKE/ROAST, set temperature to 400°F (205°C), and set time to 30 minutes. Select START/STOP to begin. Let preheat for 5 minutes.
2. In a large bowl, whisk together ¼ cup of flour, granulated sugar, and ¼ teaspoon of salt. Add the rhubarb, raspberries, and peach and mix until evenly coated.
3. Grease a Ninja Multi-Purpose Pan or a 1½-quart round ceramic baking dish with cooking spray. Add the fruit mixture to the pan.
4. Place pan on Reversible Rack, making sure the rack is in the lower position. Cover pan with aluminum foil.
5. Once unit has preheated, place rack in pot. Close crisping lid and adjust temperature to 375°F (190°C). Cook for 25 minutes.
6. In a medium bowl, combine the remaining ¾ cup of flour, brown sugar, oat flakes, cinnamon, remaining ¼ teaspoon of salt, nutmeg, butter, and pecans. Mix well.
7. When cooking is complete, open lid. Remove the foil and stir the fruit. Spread the topping evenly over the fruit. Close crisping lid.
8. Select BAKE/ROAST, set temperature to 400°F (205°C), and set time to 15 minutes. Select START/STOP to begin. Cook until the topping is browned and the fruit is bubbling.
9. When cooking is complete, remove rack with pan from pot and serve.

Nutrition:
- InfoCalories: 476,Total Fat: 19g,Sodium: 204mg,Carbohydrates: 76g,Protein: 6g.

Pineapple Cake

Servings: 4
Cooking Time: 50 Min
Ingredients:
- 2 oz. dark chocolate, grated /60g
- 4 oz. butter /120g
- 7 oz. pineapple chunks /210g
- 8 oz. self-rising flour /240g
- ½ cup sugar /65g
- 1 egg
- ½ cup pineapple juice /125ml
- 2 tbsp milk /30ml

Directions:
1. Preheat the Foodi to 390 °F or 200°C. Place the butter and flour into a bowl and rub the mixture with your fingers until crumbed. Stir in the pineapple, sugar, chocolate, and juice. Beat the eggs and milk separately, and then add them to the batter.
2. Transfer the batter to a previously prepared (greased or lined) cake pan, and cook for 40 minutes on Roast mode. Let cool for at least 10 minutes before serving.

Steamed Lemon Pudding

Servings: 6
Cooking Time: 90 Minutes
Ingredients:
- Nonstick cooking spray
- ¾ cup butter, unsalted, soft
- 1 cup caster sugar
- 2 eggs
- 2 cups flour
- 1 tsp baking powder
- Zest & juice from 2 lemons

Directions:
1. Lightly spray a 1 liter oven-safe bowl with cooking spray.
2. Add the butter and sugar to the bowl and beat until light and fluffy.
3. Add the eggs, one at a time, beating well after each addition.
4. Stir in the flour and baking powder until combined.
5. Fold in the lemon zest and juice and mix until smooth. Cover lightly with foil.
6. Pour 1 ½ cups water into the cooking pot and add steamer rack.
7. Place the bowl on the rack, secure the lid. Set to steam on 212°F (100°C). Cook 90 minutes, or until pudding is cooked through.
8. Remove the pudding from the cooker and let sit 5 minutes before inverting onto serving plate.

Nutrition:
- InfoCalories 446,Total Fat 17g,Total Carbs 66g,Protein 7g,Sodium 33mg.

Pecan And Cherry Stuffed Apples

Servings: 4
Cooking Time: 20 Minutes
Ingredients:
- 4 apples (about 1¼ pounds / 567 g)
- ¼ cup (63 mL) chopped pecans
- ⅓ cup (83 mL) dried tart cherries
- 1 tablespoon melted butter
- 3 tablespoons brown sugar
- ¼ teaspoon allspice
- Pinch salt
- Ice cream, for serving

Directions:

1. Cut off top ½ inch from each apple; reserve tops. With a melon baller, core through stem ends without breaking through the bottom.
2. Preheat the Ninja Foodi Deluxe Pressure Cooker to 350°F(175°C). Combine pecans, cherries, butter, brown sugar, allspice, and a pinch of salt. Stuff mixture into the hollow centers of the apples. Cover with apple tops. Put in the cooking pot, using tongs. Close crisping lid. Select Bake and set time to 20 to 25 minutes. Press Start to begin.
3. Serve warm with ice cream.

Moon Milk

Servings: 2
Cooking Time: 10 Min
Ingredients:
- 1/4 cup hemp hearts /32.5g
- 1 cup milk /250ml
- 1 pinch ground nutmeg
- 1 pinch ground ginger
- 1 pinch freshly ground black pepper
- ½ tsp maca powder /2.5g
- 1/8 tsp ground cardamom/0.625g
- ½ tsp ground cinnamon, plus more for garnish /2.5g
- 1 tsp coconut oil /5ml
- ½ tsp ground turmeric /2.5g
- 1 tsp honey /5ml

Directions:
1. To the Foodi, add milk. Press Sear/Sauté and heat the milk for 3-4 minutes until the point of starting to bubble; stir in coconut oil, turmeric, nutmeg, pepper, ginger, hemp hearts, maca powder, cinnamon, and cardamom.
2. Press Start/Stop and allow mixture to cool for about a minute; whisk in honey. Transfer the mixture into a mug. Add more cinnamon for garnishing!

Dark Chocolate Brownies

Servings: 6
Cooking Time: 40 Min
Ingredients:
- 1 cup water /250ml
- 2 eggs
- ¼ cup olive oil /62.5ml
- ⅓ cup flour /44g
- ⅓ cup cocoa powder /44g
- ⅓ cup dark chocolate chips /44g
- ⅓ cup chopped Walnuts /44g
- ⅓ cup granulated sugar /44g
- 1 tbsp vanilla extract /15ml
- 1 tbsp milk/15ml
- ½ tsp baking powder /2.5g
- A pinch salt

Directions:
1. In the Foodi, add water and set in the reversible rack. Line a parchment paper on. a springform pan. In a bowl, beat eggs and sugar to mix until smooth; stir in olive oil, cocoa powder, milk, salt baking powder, chocolate chips, flour, walnuts, vanilla, and sea salt.
2. Transfer the batter to the prepared springform pan and place the pan in the pot on the rack. Close the crisping lid and select Bake/Roast; adjust the temperature to 250°F or 120°C and the cook time to 20 minutes. Press Start.
3. When the time is up, open the lid and. and allow the brownie to cool for 10 minutes before cutting. Use powdered sugar to dust the brownies before serving lightly.

Banana Rum Pudding

Servings: 4
Cooking Time: 15 Minutes
Ingredients:
- 1 banana
- 2 egg yolks
- 1 egg
- 3 tbsp. sugar
- ½ cup half and half
- ¼ cup sweetened condensed milk
- ¼ cup sour cream
- ¼ tsp dark rum
- ½ tsp vanilla
- 2 cups water

Directions:
1. Place the banana in a food processor and pulse until pureed.
2. Add egg yolks, egg, and sugar and pulse until smooth.
3. Add the half and half, milk, sour cream, rum, and vanilla and pulse until combined. Strain through a fine mesh sieve.
4. Pour the water into the cooking pot and add the steamer rack.
5. Pour the pudding into 6 ramekins and cover with foil. Place on the rack.
6. Secure the lid and set to pressure cooking on low. Set timer for 12 minutes.
7. When timer goes off, use quick release to remove the lid. Transfer ramekins to wire rack, uncover and let cool. Once cooled, cover with plastic wrap and refrigerate until ready to serve.

Nutrition:
- InfoCalories 216,Total Fat 8g,Total Carbs 30g,Protein 6g,Sodium 82mg.

Hearty Crème Brulee

Servings: 4
Cooking Time: 10 Minutes
Ingredients:
- 2 cups (500 mL) graham crackers, crushed
- 3 tablespoons brown sugar
- ¼ cup (63 mL) butter, melted
- Salt, to taste
- 2 (8-ounce / 227-g) cream cheese, softened
- ½ cup (125 mL) granulated sugar
- 2 large eggs
- 2 teaspoons vanilla extract
- ½ cup (125 mL) sour cream
- 2 tablespoons cornstarch
- 1 cup (250 mL) water
- 4 teaspoons white sugar

Directions:
1. Make the crust: Mix the crushed graham crackers with brown sugar, butter, and salt in a medium bowl. Spoon the

mixture into 4 medium ramekins. Place in refrigerator for 15 minutes to harden.
2. In a bowl, stir the cream cheese and sugar until smooth. Whisk in eggs and vanilla until smooth. Fold in sour cream and cornstarch.
3. Remove ramekins from the refrigerator, then pour in the cream cheese mixture, and cover with foil.
4. Pour the water in the cooking pot, then place the reversible rack in pot, and place ramekins on top.
5. Assemble pressure lid, making sure the pressure release valve is in the Seal position. Select Pressure and set to high. Set time to 10 minutes. Press Start to begin.
6. When cooking is complete, allow a natural pressure release for 10 minutes, then release any remaining pressure.
7. Unlock the lid, carefully remove the ramekins and take off the foil. Allow to cool for 10 minutes and then chill further for 2 hours in the refrigerator.
8. Remove the ramekins from the refrigerator and sprinkle 1 teaspoon of sugar on each ramekin. Use a torch to caramelize the sugar until browned in color. Serve immediately.

Fried Oreos

Servings: 9
Cooking Time: 8 Minutes
Ingredients:
- ½ cup complete pancake mix
- ⅓ cup water
- Cooking spray
- 9 Oreo cookies
- 1 tablespoon confectioners' sugar

Directions:
1. Close crisping lid. Select AIR CRISP, set temperature to 400°F (205°C), and set time to 5 minutes. Select START/STOP to begin preheating.
2. In a medium bowl, combine the pancake mix and water until combined.
3. Spray the Cook & Crisp Basket with cooking spray.
4. Dip each cookie into the pancake batter and then arrange them in the basket in a single layer so they are not touching each other. Cook in batches if needed.
5. When unit has preheated, open lid and insert basket into pot. Close crisping lid.
6. Select AIR CRISP, set temperature to 400°F (205°C), and set time to 8 minutes. Select START/STOP to begin.
7. After 4 minutes, open lid and flip the cookies. Close lid and continue cooking.
8. When cooking is complete, check for desired crispness. Remove basket and sprinkle the cookies with confectioners' sugar. Serve.

Nutrition:
- InfoCalories: 83, Total Fat: 2g, Sodium: 158mg, Carbohydrates: 14g, Protein: 1g.

Coffee Cake

Servings: 8
Cooking Time: 30 Minutes
Ingredients:
- Cooking spray
- 1 box yellow cake mix
- 1 cup water
- ⅓ cup vegetable oil
- 3 large eggs
- 4 cups all-purpose flour
- 1 cup granulated sugar
- 3 tablespoons cinnamon
- 2 cups unsalted butter, melted
- Confectioners' sugar, for garnish

Directions:
1. Grease a Ninja Tube Pan or a 7-inch Bundt pan with cooking spray.
2. Close crisping lid. Select BAKE/ROAST, set temperature to 325°F (160°C), and set time to 5 minutes. Select START/STOP to begin preheating.
3. In a large bowl, mix together the cake mix, water, oil, and eggs until combined. Pour the batter into the prepared pan.
4. When unit has preheated, place pan on Reversible Rack, making sure the rack is in the lower position. Open lid and place rack with pan in pot. Close crisping lid.
5. Select BAKE/ROAST, set temperature to 325°F (160°C), and set time to 30 minutes. Select START/STOP to begin.
6. In another large bowl, combine the flour, sugar, and cinnamon. Add the butter and mix until well combined and the mixture is a crumble.
7. After 25 minutes, open lid and check for doneness. If a toothpick inserted into the cake comes out clean, the cake is done. If necessary, close lid and continue baking.
8. Open lid and spread the crumble topping on top of the cakes. Close lid and bake for an additional 4 to 5 minutes.
9. When cooking is complete, carefully remove pan from pot and place it on a cooling rack. Let cool. Using a fine mesh sieve, garnish the coffee cake with confectioners' sugar.

Nutrition:
- InfoCalories: 1152, Total Fat: 65g, Sodium: 464mg, Carbohydrates: 132g, Protein: 13g.

Molten Lava Cake

Servings: 4
Cooking Time: 20 Min
Ingredients:
- 3 ½ oz. butter, melted /105ml
- 3 ½ oz. dark chocolate, melted /105ml
- 2 eggs
- 3 ½ tbsp sugar /52.5g
- 1 ½ tbsp self-rising flour /22.5g

Directions:
1. Grease 4 ramekins with butter. Beat the eggs and sugar until frothy. Stir in the butter and chocolate.
2. Gently fold in the flour. Divide the mixture between the ramekins and bake in the Foodi for 10 minutes on Air Crisp mode at 370 °F or 185°C. Let cool for 2 minutes before turning the lava cakes upside down onto serving plates.

Carrot Cake

Servings: 8
Cooking Time: 40 Minutes
Ingredients:
- Butter flavored cooking spray
- 3 eggs
- 1 cup almond flour, sifted
- 1/3 cup Stevia
- 1 tsp baking powder
- 1 tsp apple pie spice
- ¼ cup coconut oil, melted
- ½ cup + 1 tbsp. heavy cream
- 1 cup carrots, grated
- ½ cup walnuts, chopped
- 4 oz. cream cheese, soft
- ¼ cup butter, soft
- ½ tsp vanilla
- ½ - 1 cup powdered Stevia

Directions:
1. Lightly spray a 6x3-inch cake pan with cooking spray.
2. In a large bowl, beat eggs, flour, Stevia, baking powder, apple pie spice, oil, and ½ cup cream until fluffy.
3. Fold in carrots and nuts and pour into prepared pan.
4. Place in cooking pot and add tender-crisp lid. Set to bake on 350 °F (175°C). Bake 30-35 minutes or until cake passes the toothpick test. Transfer to wire rack and let cool 10 minutes in pan, then invert onto serving plate.
5. In a large bowl, beat cream cheese, butter, and remaining cream until smooth and creamy.
6. Stir in vanilla and enough powdered Stevia until frosting is thick enough to spread. Cut cake in half horizontally and spread with 1/3 of the frosting in the middle, then frost outside. Serve.

Nutrition:
- InfoCalories 345,Total Fat 34g,Total Carbs 25g,Protein 8g,Sodium 137mg.

Mexican Chocolate Walnut Cake

Servings: 8
Cooking Time: 2 ½ Hours
Ingredients:
- Butter flavored cooking spray
- 1½ cups flour
- ½ cup cocoa powder, unsweetened
- 2 tsp baking powder
- 2 tsp ground cinnamon
- ¼ tsp cayenne pepper
- 1/8 tsp salt
- 1 cup sugar
- 3 eggs, beaten
- ¾ cup coconut oil melted
- 2 tsp vanilla
- 2 cups zucchini, grated
- ¾ cup walnuts, chopped, divided

Directions:
1. Spray the cooking pot with cooking spray and line the bottom with parchment paper.
2. In a medium bowl, combine dry ingredients and mix well.
3. In a large bowl, beat sugar and eggs until creamy.
4. Stir in oil, vanilla, zucchini, and ½ cup walnuts until combined. Fold in dry ingredients just until combined.
5. Pour batter into cooking pot and sprinkle remaining nuts over the top. Add the lid and set to slow cooking on high. Cook 2 ½ hours or until cake passes the toothpick test. Transfer cake to a wire rack to cool before serving.

Nutrition:
- InfoCalories 452,Total Fat 28g,Total Carbs 48g,Protein 7g,Sodium 189mg.

Almond Milk

Servings: 4
Cooking Time: 20 Min
Ingredients:
- 1 cup raw almonds; soaked overnight, rinsed and peeled /130g
- 2 dried apricots; chopped
- 1 cup cold water /250ml
- 4 cups water /1000ml
- 1 vanilla bean
- 2 tbsp honey /30ml

Directions:
1. In the pot, mix a cup of cold water with almonds and apricots. Seal the pressure lid, choose Pressure, set to High, and set the timer to 1 minute.
2. When ready, release the pressure quickly. Open the lid. The almonds should be soft and plump, and the water should be brown and murky. Use a strainer to drain almonds; rinse with cold water for 1 minute.
3. To a high-speed blender, add the rinsed almonds, vanilla bean, honey, and 4 cups or 1000ml water. Blend for 2 minutes until well combined and frothy. Line a cheesecloth to the strainer.
4. Place the strainer over a bowl and strain the milk. Use a wooden spoon to press milk through the cheesecloth and get rid of solids. Place almond milk in an airtight container and refrigerate.

Mocha Cake

Servings: 6
Cooking Time: 3 Hours 37 Minutes
Ingredients:
- 2 ounces 70% dark chocolate, chopped
- ¾ cup butter, chopped
- ½ cup heavy cream
- 2 tablespoons instant coffee crystals
- 1 teaspoon vanilla extract
- 1/3 cup almond flour
- ¼ cup unsweetened cacao powder
- 1/8 teaspoon salt
- 5 large eggs
- 2/3 cup Erythritol

Directions:
1. Grease the Ninja Foodi's insert.
2. In a microwave-safe bowl, stir in the chocolate and butter and microwave on High for about 2 minutes or until melted completely, stirring after every 30 seconds.
3. Remove from the microwave and stir well.

4. Set aside to cool.
5. In a small bowl, stir in the heavy cream, coffee crystals, and vanilla extract and beat until well combined.
6. In a suitable bowl, mix the flour, cacao powder and salt.
7. In a large bowl, stir in the eggs and with an electric mixer, beat on high speed until slightly thickened.
8. Slowly, stir in the Erythritol and beat on high speed until thick and pale yellow.
9. Stir in the chocolate mixture and beat on low speed until well combined.
10. Stir in the dry flour mixture and mix until just combined.
11. Slowly stir in the cream mixture and beat on medium speed until well combined.
12. In the prepared Ninja Foodi's insert, add the mixture.
13. Close the Ninja Foodi's lid with a crisping lid and select "Slow Cooker".
14. Set on "Low" for 2½-3½ hours.
15. Press the "Start/Stop" button to initiate cooking.
16. Transfer the pan onto a wire rack for about 10 minutes.
17. Flip the baked and cooled cake onto the wire rack to cool completely.
18. Cut into desired-sized slices and serve.

Nutrition:
- InfoCalories: 407; Fats: 39.7g; Carbohydrates: 6.2g; Proteins: 9g

Blueberry Lemon Pound Cake

Servings: 12
Cooking Time: 1 Hour 5 Minutes
Ingredients:
- Butter flavored cooking spray
- 1 ¾ cups + 2 tsp flour, divided
- 2 tsp baking powder
- ½ tsp salt
- 1 ½ cups blueberries
- ¾ cup butter, unsalted, soft
- 1 cup ricotta cheese, room temperature
- 1 ½ cups sugar
- 3 eggs, room temperature
- 1 tsp vanilla
- 1 tbsp. lemon zest

Directions:
1. Spray a loaf pan with cooking spray
2. In a medium bowl, combine flour, baking powder, and salt, mix well.
3. Add the blueberries to a bowl and sprinkle 2 tsp flour over them, toss to coat.
4. In a large bowl, beat together butter, ricotta, and sugar on high speed, until pale and fluffy.
5. Reduce speed to medium and beat in eggs, one at a time. Beat in zest and vanilla.
6. Stir in dry ingredients, a fourth at a time, until combined. Fold in blueberries and pour into prepared pan.
7. Add the rack to the cooking pot and place the pan on it. Add the tender-crisp lid and set to bake on 325°F (160°C). Bake 1 hour 10 minutes or until cake passes the toothpick test. After 40 minutes, cover the cake with foil.
8. Transfer to wire rack and let cool in pan 15 minutes. Then invert and let cool completely before serving.

Nutrition:
- InfoCalories 303,Total Fat 17g,Total Carbs 32g,Protein 6g,Sodium 147mg.

Chocolaty Fudge

Servings: 8
Cooking Time: 55 Min
Ingredients:
- 1 oz. cocoa powder /30g
- 4 oz. butter /120g
- 7 oz. flour, sifted /210g
- 1 cup sugar /130g
- ¼ cup milk /62.5ml
- 2 eggs
- 1 tbsp honey /15ml
- 1 tsp vanilla extract /5ml
- 1 orange, juice and zest
- Icing:
- 4 oz. powdered sugar /120g
- 1 oz. butter, melted /30ml
- 1 tbsp milk /15ml
- 1 tbsp brown sugar/15g
- 2 tsp honey /10ml

Directions:
1. In a bowl, mix the dry ingredients for the fudge. Mix the wet ingredients separately. Combine the two mixtures gently. Transfer the batter to a prepared Foodi basket. Close the crisping lid and cook for about 35 minutes on Roast mode at 350 °F or 175°C.
2. Once the timer beeps, check to ensure the cake is cooked. For the Topping: whisk together all of the icing ingredients. When the cake is cooled, coat it with the icing. Let set before slicing the fudge.

Chocolate Brownie Cake

Servings: 6
Cooking Time: 35 Minutes.
Ingredients:
- ½ cup 70% dark chocolate chips
- ½ cup butter
- 3 eggs
- ¼ cup Erythritol
- 1 teaspoon vanilla extract

Directions:
1. In a microwave-safe bowl, stir in the chocolate chips and butter and microwave for about 1 minute, stirring after every 20 seconds.
2. Remove from the microwave and stir well.
3. Set a "Reversible Rack" in the pot of the Ninja Foodi.
4. Close the Ninja Foodi's lid with a crisping lid and select "Air Crisp".
5. Set its cooking temperature to 350 °F (175°C) for 5 minutes.
6. Press the "Start/Stop" button to initiate preheating.
7. In a suitable, add the eggs, Erythritol and vanilla extract and blend until light and frothy.
8. Slowly add in the chocolate mixture and beat again until well combined.
9. Add the mixture into a lightly greased springform pan.
10. After preheating, Open the Ninja Foodi's lid.
11. Place the springform pan into the "Air Crisp Basket".

12. Close the Ninja Foodi's lid with a crisping lid and select "Air Crisp".
13. Set its cooking temperature to 350 °F (175°C) for 35 minutes.
14. Press the "Start/Stop" button to initiate cooking.
15. Place the hot pan onto a wire rack to cool for about 10 minutes.
16. Flip the baked and cooled cake onto the wire rack to cool completely.
17. Cut into desired-sized slices and serve.

Nutrition:
- InfoCalories: 302; Fats: 28.2g; Carbohydrates: 5.6g; Proteins: 5.6g

Fried Snickerdoodle Poppers

Servings: 6
Cooking Time: 30 Min
Ingredients:
- 1 box instant vanilla Jell-O
- 1 ½ cups cinnamon sugar /195g
- 1 can of Pillsbury Grands Flaky Layers Biscuits
- Melted butter, for brushing

Directions:
1. Unroll the flaky biscuits and cut them into fourths. Roll each ¼ into a ball. Arrange the balls on a lined baking sheet, and cook in the Foodi for 7 minutes, or until golden, on Air Crisp mode at 350 °F or 175°C.
2. Prepare the Jell-O following the package's instructions. Using an injector, inject some of the vanilla pudding into each ball. Brush the balls with melted butter and then coat them with cinnamon sugar.

Raspberry Lemon Cheesecake

Servings: 8
Cooking Time: 30 Minutes
Ingredients:
- Butter flavored cooking spray
- 8 oz. cream cheese, fat free, soft
- 1/3 cup sugar
- ½ tsp lemon juice
- 1 tsp lemon zest
- ½ tsp vanilla
- ½ cup plain Greek yogurt
- 2 eggs, room temperature
- 2 tbsp. white whole wheat flour
- Fresh raspberries for garnish

Directions:
1. Spray an 8-inch baking dish with cooking spray.
2. In a large bowl, beat cream cheese, sugar, lemon juice, zest, and vanilla until smooth.
3. Add yogurt, eggs, and flour and mix well. Spoon into prepared pan.
4. Place pan in the cooking pot and add the tender-crisp lid. Set to bake on 350°F (175°C). Bake 25-30 minutes or until cheesecake passes the toothpick test.
5. Transfer to a wire rack to cool. Cover with plastic wrap and refrigerate 2-3 hours. Serve garnished with fresh raspberries.

Nutrition:
- InfoCalories 93,Total Fat 6g,Total Carbs 14g,Protein 5g,Sodium 127mg.

Irish Cream Flan

Servings: 3
Cooking Time: 10 Minutes
Ingredients:
- ¼ cup + 2 tbsp. sugar, divided
- 1 tbsp. water
- 1 cup half and half
- ¼ cup Irish cream flavored coffee creamer
- ¼ cup Irish cream liqueur
- 2 eggs

Directions:
1. In a small saucepan over medium heat, heat ¼ cup sugar until melted and a deep amber color. Swirl the pan occasionally to distribute the heat.
2. When the sugar reaches the right color remove from heat and carefully stir in the water until combined. Drizzle over the bottoms of 3 ramekins.
3. In a small oven-safe bowl, whisk the eggs.
4. In a small saucepan over medium heat, stir together half and half, creamer, Irish cream, and remaining sugar. Heat to simmering.
5. Gradually whisk the warm liquids into the eggs 2 tablespoons at a time, whisking constantly. After a 1/3 of the cream mixture has been added, slowly pour the remaining mixture into the eggs, whisking constantly until combined.
6. Pour 1 cup water into the cooking pot and add the trivet.
7. Pour the egg mixture into the ramekins and cover tightly with foil. Place them on the trivet.
8. Secure the lid and set to pressure cooking on high. Set the timer for 5 minutes. When the timer goes off, use natural release to remove the lid. Transfer custards to a wire rack and uncover to cool.
9. Cover with plastic wrap and refrigerate at least 4 hours before serving. To serve, use a small knife to loosen the custards from the sides of the ramekin and invert onto serving plate.

Nutrition:
- InfoCalories 215,Total Fat 9g,Total Carbs 25g,Protein 7g,Sodium 134mg.

Bacon Blondies

Servings:6
Cooking Time: 35 Minutes
Ingredients:
- 6 slices uncooked bacon, cut into ¼ slices
- 1½ cups unsalted butter, at room temperature, plus additional for greasing
- 1 cup dark brown sugar
- 2 cups all-purpose flour
- Ice cream, for serving

Directions:
1. Grease the Ninja Multi-Purpose Pan with butter.
2. Select SEAR/SAUTÉ and set to HI. Select START/STOP to begin. Let preheat for 5 minutes.
3. Place the bacon in the pot. Cook, stirring frequently, for about 5 minutes, or until the fat is rendered and bacon starts to brown. Transfer the bacon to a paper towel-lined plate to

drain. Wipe the pot clean of any remaining fat and return to unit.

4. In a medium bowl, beat the butter and brown sugar with a hand mixer until well incorporated. Slowly add in the flour and continue to beat until the flour is fully combined and a soft dough forms. Next, fold the cooked bacon into the dough.

5. Press the dough into the prepared pan. Place pan on Reversible Rack, ensuring it is in the lower position. Lower rack into pot. Close crisping lid.

6. Select BAKE/ROAST, set temperature to 350°F (175°C), and set time to 25 minutes. Select START/STOP to begin.

7. After 20 minutes, open lid and check for doneness by sticking a toothpick through the center of the dough. If it comes out clean, remove rack and pan from unit. If not, close lid and continue cooking.

8. When cooking is complete, remove rack and pan from unit. Let the blondies cool for about 30 minutes before serving with ice cream, if desired.

Nutrition:
- InfoCalories: 771,Total Fat: 54g,Sodium: 453mg,Carbohydrates: 60g,Protein: 12g.

Peach Cobbler

Servings: 6
Cooking Time: 35 Minutes
Ingredients:
- Nonstick cooking spray
- 5 fresh peaches, peeled, pitted & sliced
- 3 tbsp. Stevia
- 1 tsp coconut flour
- ¼ tsp cinnamon
- 1/8 tsp nutmeg
- ½ cup almond flour, sifted
- 1 cup oats, ground fine
- 1 ½ tsp baking powder
- ¼ cup almond milk, unsweetened
- 1 tsp almond extract
- 2 tbsp. honey

Directions:
1. Place the rack in the cooking pot. Spray an 8-inch baking dish with cooking spray.
2. In a large bowl, toss peaches with Stevia, coconut flour, cinnamon, and nutmeg. Place in prepared baking dish.
3. In a medium bowl, combine almond flour, oats, baking powder, milk, almond extract, and honey, mix well. Drop by large spoonful over the top of the peaches. Place in the cooking pot.
4. Add the tender-crisp lid and set to air fry on 350 °F (175°C). Bake 35-40 minutes until top is lightly browned. Serve warm.

Nutrition:
- InfoCalories 204,Total Fat 7g,Total Carbs 39g,Protein 7g,Sodium 11mg.

Créme Brulee

Servings: 4
Cooking Time: 30 Min + 6 Hours Of Cooling
Ingredients:
- 3 cups heavy whipping cream /750ml
- 7 large egg yolks
- 2 cups water /500mll
- 6 tbsp sugar /90g
- 2 tbsp vanilla extract /30ml

Directions:
1. In a mixing bowl, add the yolks, vanilla, whipping cream, and half of the swerve sugar. Use a whisk to mix them until they are well combined. Pour the mixture into the ramekins and cover them with aluminium foil.
2. Open the Foodi, fit the reversible rack into the pot, and pour in the water.
3. Place 3 ramekins on the rack and place the remaining ramekins to sit on the edges of the ramekins below.
4. Close the lid, secure the pressure valve, and select Pressure mode on High for 8 minutes. Press Start/Stop.
5. Once the timer has stopped, do a natural pressure release for 10 minutes, then a quick pressure release to let out the remaining pressure.
6. With a napkin in hand, remove the ramekins onto a flat surface and then into a refrigerator to chill for at least 6 hours. After refrigeration, remove the ramekins and remove the aluminium foil.
7. Equally, sprinkle the remaining sugar on it and return to the pot. Close the crisping lid, select Bake/Roast mode, set the timer to 4 minutes on 380 °F or 195°C. Serve the crème brulee chilled with whipped cream.

Apricots With Honey Sauce

Servings: 4
Cooking Time: 15 Min
Ingredients:
- 8 Apricots, pitted and halved
- ¼ cup Honey /62.5ml
- 2 cups Blueberries /260g
- ½ Cinnamon stick
- 1 ¼ cups Water /312.5ml
- ½ Vanilla Bean; sliced lengthwise
- 1 ½ tbsp Cornstarch /22.5g
- ¼ tsp ground Cardamom /1.25g

Directions:
1. Add all ingredients, except for the honey and the cornstarch, to your Foodi. Seal the pressure lid, choose Pressure, set to High, and set the time to s 8 minutes. Press Start. Do a quick pressure release and open the pressure lid.
2. Remove the apricots with a slotted spoon. Choose Sear/Sauté, add the honey and cornstarch, then let simmer until the sauce thickens, for about 5 minutes. Split up the apricots among serving plates and top with the blueberry sauce, to serve.

Chocolate Cake

Servings: 16
Cooking Time: 30 Minutes
Ingredients:
- Butter flavored cooking spray
- 8 Eggs
- 1 lb. semi-sweet chocolate chips
- 1 cup butter

Directions:

1. Place the rack in the cooking pot. Line the bottom of an 8-inch springform pan with parchment paper. Spray with cooking spray and wrap foil around the outside of the pan.
2. In a large bowl, beat eggs until double in size, about 6-8 minutes.
3. Place the chocolate chips and butter in a microwave safe bowl. Microwave at 30 second intervals until melted and smooth.
4. Fold 1/3 of the eggs into chocolate, folding gently just until eggs are incorporated. Repeat two more times.
5. Pour the batter into the prepared pan. Pour 1 ½ cups water into the cooking pot. Place the cake on the rack.
6. Add the tender-crisp lid and set to air fry on 325°F (160°C). Bake 25-30 minutes or until center is set.
7. Transfer to wire rack to cool. When cool, invert onto serving plate, top with fresh berries if desired. Slice and serve.

Nutrition:
- InfoCalories 302, Total Fat 25g, Total Carbs 15g, Protein 5g, Sodium 130mg.

Cherry Almond Bar Cookies

Servings: 9
Cooking Time: 15 Minutes
Ingredients:
- Butter flavored cooking spray
- ¼ cup dates
- 2 bananas
- 1 cup oats
- ½ cup cherries, dried, chopped
- ½ cup almond flour
- ½ cup almonds, chopped

Directions:
1. Place the rack in the cooking pot. Spray an 8x8-inch baking pan with cooking spray.
2. Place the dates in a food processor and pulse until they form a paste.
3. In a large bowl, mash the bananas with a fork.
4. Mix in remaining ingredients. Spread evenly in prepared pan.
5. Place the pan on the rack and add the tender-crisp lid. Set to bake on 325°F (160°C). Bake 15 minutes or until top is golden brown. Remove to wire rack to cool before cutting.

Nutrition:
- InfoCalories 177, Total Fat 5g, Total Carbs 30g, Protein 5g, Sodium 2mg.

Hearty Apricot Cobbler

Servings: 4
Cooking Time: 25 Minutes
Ingredients:
- 4 cups (1 L) sliced apricots
- 2 tablespoons plus ¾ cup (188 mL) all-purpose flour, divided
- ½ teaspoon cinnamon powder
- ¼ teaspoon nutmeg powder
- 1 teaspoon vanilla extract
- ½ cup (125 mL) plus ¼ cup (63 mL) brown sugar, divided
- 1½ teaspoons salt, divided
- 1¼ cup (63 mL) water, divided
- ½ teaspoon baking powder
- ½ teaspoon baking soda
- 3 tablespoons butter, melted

Directions:
1. In a baking pan, mix the apricots, 2 tablespoons of flour, cinnamon, nutmeg, vanilla, ½ cup of brown sugar, ½ teaspoon of salt, and ¼ cup of water; set aside.
2. In another bowl, mix the remaining flour, salt and brown sugar, baking powder and soda, and butter. Spoon mixture over apricot mixture and spread to cover.
3. Pour 1 cup of water in the pot, then place the reversible rack in pot and place the pan on top.
4. Assemble pressure lid, making sure the pressure release valve is in the Seal position. Select Pressure and set to high. Set time to 25 minutes. Press Start to begin.
5. When cooking is complete, perform a natural pressure release for 10 minutes, then release any remaining pressure.
6. Carefully open the lid. Remove the pan and serve.

RECIPE INDEX

A

All-tim Favorite Beef Chili 84
Almond Milk 105
Aloo Gobi With Cilantro 37
Apple And Cranberry Oatmeal With Vanilla 21
Applesauce Pumpkin Muffins 30
Apricot Bbq Duck Legs 90
Apricot Oatmeal 26
Apricot Salmon With Potatoes 55
Apricots With Honey Sauce 108
Artichoke With Mayo 34
Artichokes With Melted Butter 10
Asian Chicken Nuggets 10
Asian-glazed Pork Shoulder 81
Authentic Belizean Stewed Chicken 95
Awesome Ligurian Chicken 86

B

Baby Back Ribs With Barbeque Sauce 80
Bacon & Cranberry Stuffed Turkey Breast 99
Bacon And Cheese Custards 20
Bacon And Gruyère Cheese Quiche 28
Bacon Blondies 107
Bacon Strips 70
Baked Cod Casserole 62
Baked Ziti With Rich Meat Sauce 83
Balsamic Pot Roast Of Beef 80
Banana Rum Pudding 103
Barbeque Chicken Drumettes 86
Basil Lemon Shrimp & Asparagus 57
Bbq Chicken Sandwiches 30
Beef And Pork Chili 47
Beef And Turnip Chili 80
Beef Chicken Meatloaf 19
Beef Congee 84
Beef Lasagna 72
Beef Prime Roast 74
Beef Short Rib & Ale Stew 77
Beef Stew With Beer 71
Beer Braised Bacon & Cabbage 82
Blackberry Crisp 100
Blueberry Lemon Pound Cake 106
Breakfast Egg Pizza 24
Broccoli & Pesto Penne 34
Butter Cookies 28
Butternut Breakfast Squash 22
Butternut Squash And Orzo Soup 47
Butternut Squash Apple Soup With Cinnamon . 25
Butterscotch Almond Brownies 101
Buttery Lemon Cod Over Couscous 66
Buttery Salmon With Green Beans And Rice ... 68
Buttery Scallops 62

C

Cabbage And Chicken Meatballs 87
Cajun Red Beans And Rice 76
Calzones With Sausage And Mozzarella 74
Caramelized Sweet Potatoes 36
Carrot Cake 105
Cauliflower And Chickpea Green Salad 73
Cauliflower And Egg Dish 17
Cauliflower Cakes 42
Cauliflower Chunks With Lemon Sauce 35
Cheddar Shrimp And Grits 30
Cheeseburger Boats 17
Cheesy Chicken & Zucchini Rolls 88
Cheesy Chicken And Broccoli Casserole 91
Cheesy Chicken Dip 11
Cheesy Chilies 38
Cheesy Egg Bake With Ham 21
Cheesy Green Beans With Nuts 36
Cheesy Smashed Sweet Potatoes 15
Cheesy Spicy Pasta 36
Cheesy Stuffed Onions 13
Cheesy Tex-mex Breakfast Egg Bake Casserole ... 27
Cherry Almond Bar Cookies 109
Chicken & Black Bean Chowder 90
Chicken And Black Bean Enchilada Soup 48
Chicken And Broccoli Stir-fry 93
Chicken And Crispy Dumplings 81
Chicken Burgers With Avocado 98
Chicken Enchilada Soup 52
Chicken Gumbo 90
Chicken Pasta With Pesto Sauce 97
Chicken Pork Nuggets 18
Chicken Posole 96
Chicken Potpie Soup 48
Chicken Wings 16
Chicken With Bacon And Beans 88
Chicken With Bbq Sauce 93
Chicken With Black Beans 88
Chicken With Cilantro Rice 97
Chicken With Rice And Peas 89
Chili Cheese Quiche 29
Chili Chicken Dip 16
Chinese Bbq Ribs 83
Chipotle Burgers 79
Chives And Radishes Platter 41
Chocolate Brownie Cake 106
Chocolate Cake 108
Chocolate Chip And Banana Bread Bundt Cake ... 32
Chocolate Mousse 101
Chocolaty Fudge 106
Chorizo Omelet 21
Cinnamon Bun Oatmeal 28
Cinnamon Oatmeal With Cream Cheese 31
Cinnamon Sugar Donuts 25
Citrus Mahi Mahi 60
Classic Cheesecake 100
Classic Crab Imperial 60
Coconut And Shrimp Bisque 50
Coconut Cilantro Shrimp 64
Coconut Lime Snack Cake 101
Coconut Shrimp And Pea Bisque 46

Cod Cornflakes Nuggets	61
Cod Over Couscous	59
Coffee Cake	104
Complete Cauliflower Zoodles	41
Coq Au Vin	96
Crab Alfredo	58
Cranberry And Toasted Almond Grits	23
Cranberry Lemon Quinoa	24
Cranberry Pork Bbq Dish	81
Creamy Crab Soup	60
Creamy Italian Sausage, Potato, And Kale Soup	44
Creamy Polenta & Mushrooms	40
Creamy Pumpkin And Squash Bisque With Apple	44
Créme Brulee	108
Crispy Brussels Sprouts With Aioli Sauce	12
Crispy Cheesy Zucchini Bites	10
Crispy Chicken With Carrots And Potatoes	94
Crispy Fries	13
Crispy Korean-style Ribs	76
Crispy Pork Chops	70
Crispy Spiced Cauliflower Bites	19
Crunchy Chicken Schnitzels	89
Cuban Flank Steak	72
Curried Chickpea And Roasted Tomato Shakshuka	23
Curried Salmon & Sweet Potatoes	54
Curry Acorn Squash Soup	49
Curry-flavored Shrimp	61

D

Dark Chocolate Brownies	103
Delicious Bacon- Wrapped Drumsticks	15
Delicious Hungarian Goulash Soup	44
Delightful Salmon Fillets	67
Deviled Eggs(1)	23
Dijon Flavored Lemon Whitefish	54
Dill Butter	14
Dried Beet Chips	10

E

Easy Cheesy Egg Bake	20
Easy Homemade Yogurt	25
Egg And Ham Pockets	100
Eggplant Casserole	34
English Pub Split Pea Soup	46

F

Farro, Fennel And Arugula Salad	74
Faux Daikon Noodles	10
Favorite Salmon Stew	66
Fish Finger Sandwich	67
Fluffy Whole Chicken Dish	87
Fried Oreos	104
Fried Snickerdoodle Poppers	107

G

Garlic And Butter Chicken Dish	90
Garlic And Mushroom Crunchies	11
Garlic Sauce And Mussels	67
Garlic-herb Roasted Chicken	92
Garlicky Shrimp With Broccoli	58
Garlicy Roasted Cauliflower And Potato Soup	45
Generous Shepherd's Pie	75
Ginger Orange Chicken Tenders	89

Goulash (hungarian Beef Soup)	53
Great Seafood Stew	59
Greek Lamb Gyros	71
Greek Style Turkey Meatballs	86
Green Cream Soup	39
Green Lasagna Soup	43
Green Squash Gruyere	33

H

Haddock And Biscuit Chowder	47
Haddock With Sanfaina	55
Ham & Broccoli Frittata	22
Ham, Bean & Butternut Soup	77
Hanging Bacon	25
Hawaiian Pinna Colada Chicken Meal	94
Hawaiian Tofu	41
Heartfelt Sesame Fish	66
Hearty Apricot Cobbler	109
Hearty Crème Brulee	103
Hearty Veggie Soup	41
Homemade Vanilla Yogurt	31
Honey Garlic Chicken	91
Horseradish Roasted Carrots	12
Hungarian Cornmeal Squares	17

I

Irish Cream Flan	107
Italian Chicken Muffins	88
Italian Pot Roast	80
Italian Rigatoni, Sausage, And Meatball Potpie	69
Italian Sausage Soup	46
Italian Sausage With Garlic Mash	43
Italian Sausage, Potato, And Kale Soup	49
Italian Spinach & Tomato Soup	40

J

Japanese Pancake	31

K

Kale-egg Frittata	20
Korean Barbecued Satay	90

L

Lamb Chops And Potato Mash	73
Lasagna Soup	48
Lemon Chicken	95
Lemon Cod Goujons And Rosemary Chips	58
Lemon Turkey Risotto	97
Lemony Shrimp	55
Lentil Spinach Soup With Lemon	53
Lime And Cilantro Chicken Meal	95
Lime And Ginger Low Carb Pork	72
Loaded Potato Soup	52
Loaded Smashed Potatoes With Bacon	13
Lone Star Chili	85

M

Mackerel En Papillote With Vegetables	54
Maple Apples & Pork Chops	75
Maple Giant Pancake	26
Maple Glazed Pork Chops	78
Mediterranean Quiche	29
Mesmerizing Spinach Quiche	40

Mexican Chocolate Walnut Cake 105
Mexican Style Green Chili Chicken 92
Minestrone With Pancetta 43
Mississippi Pot Roast With Potatoes 69
Mocha Cake 105
Molten Lava Cake 104
Moon Milk 103
Mushroom And Cheddar Poutine 84
Mushroom And Swiss Cheese Tarts 39
Mushroom Brown Rice Pilaf 34
Mushroom Goulash 33

N

Nawesome Cherry Tomato Mackerel 57
Ninja Foodi Hard-boiled Eggs 32

O

Okra Bhindi Masala 39
One Pot Ham & Rice 70
Orange Chicken And Broccoli 82

P

Pancetta Hash With Baked Eggs 25
Panko Crusted Cod 65
Paprika Hard-boiled Eggs 32
Paprika Pork And Brussels Sprouts 71
Parmesan Broccoli Florets 84
Parmesan Tilapia 61
Peach Cobbler 108
Pecan And Cherry Stuffed Apples 102
Pecan Steel-cut Oats 28
Pepper Smothered Cod 63
Pesto Pork Chops & Asparagus 82
Philippine Pork Chops 77
Pho Tom 45
Pineapple Appetizer Ribs 43
Pineapple Cake 102
Pineapple Rack Ribs 71
Pineapple Rice With Coconut-crusted Shrimp 62
Poached Breakfast Eggs 21
Poached Chicken With Coconut Lime Cream Sauce 91
Pork And Peanut Lettuce Wraps 72
Pork, Green Beans, And Corn 70
Potato Filled Bread Rolls 37
Premium Mexican Beef Dish 79
Prosciutto Egg Bake 27
Pumpkin Breakfast Bread 24

Q

Quick Turkey Cutlets 15
Quinoa Stuffed Peppers With Pesto 33
Quinoa, Nut, And Chickpea Stuffed Butternut Squash 83

R

Ranch Warm Fillets 64
Raspberry Lemon Cheesecake 107
Rhubarb, Raspberry, And Peach Cobbler 102
Rich Beef Rendang 69
Rise And Shine Breakfast Casserole 11
Risotto And Roasted Bell Peppers 41
Ritzy Vegetable Mix 37
Roasted Red Pepper And Caramelized Onion Soup With Grilled Cheese 49
Roasted Tomato And Seafood Stew 51
Roasted Vegetable Salad 37
Rosemary Pork Roast 69
Rustic Veggie Tart 35

S

Salmon Chowder 64
Salmon Florentine 66
Salmon Paprika 64
Salmon With Dill Sauce 56
Salsa Verde Chicken With Salsa Verde 95
Saucy Chicken Breasts 93
Sausage & Roasted Red Pepper Linguine 78
Savory Custards With Ham And Cheese 22
Seafood Minestrone 67
Seafood Paella 56
Sesame Beef Ribs 81
Sesame Chicken Wings(2) 98
Sesame Radish 33
Short Ribs With Mushroom And Asparagus Sauce 78
Shredded Chicken & Black Beans 87
Shrimp And Sausage Paella 62
Shrimp Fried Rice 59
Shrimp Scampi With Tomatoes 64
Shrimp Spaghetti With Parmesan 65
Simple Beef & Shallot Curry 75
Slowly Cooked Lemon Artichokes 38
Southern Grits Casserole 30
Southern Pineapple Casserole 35
Spaghetti Squash And Chicken Parmesan 15
Spanish Chorizo And Lentil Soup 46
Spanish Rice 39
Spanish Steamed Clams 63
Spanish White Quinoa 75
Speedy Clams Pomodoro 65
Spiced Red Snapper 63
Spicy "faux" Pork Belly 79
Spicy Chicken Tortilla Soup 87
Spicy Pork Stew With Black Benas And Tomatoes 51
Spicy Shrimp Pasta With Vodka Sauce 65
Spinach And Chicken Curry 98
Spinach Casserole 27
Spinach Hummus 18
Spiralized Carrot 12
Steamed Lemon Pudding 102
Steamed Shrimp With Asparagus 56
Sticky Drumsticks 97
Stir-fried Chicken And Broccoli Rice Bowl 94
Strawberry Muffins 23
Strawberry Oat Breakfast Bars 32
Strawberry Snack Bars 17
Stuffed Baked Potatoes 29
Stuffed Chicken Mushrooms 16
Stuffed Manicotti 38
Super Cheesy Pepperoni Calzones 85
Sweet & Spicy Shrimp 57
Sweet And Salty Bars 100
Sweet Potato Fries 13
Sweet Potato Hash And Eggs 26
Sweet Potato Skins 11
Swiss Bacon Frittata 22

T

Taiwanese Chicken Delight 87

Teriyaki Chicken Wings 14
Tex-mex Chicken Tortilla Soup 51
The Borderline Crack Chicken 93
The Calabacita Squash Meal 78
The Chipotle Copycat Dish 73
The Ginger Flavored Tilapia 58
The Great Poached Salmon 54
The Kool Poblano Cheese Frittata 16
The Original Braised Kale And Carrot Salad 14
The Original Zucchini Gratin 12
The Veggie Lover's Onion And Tofu Platter 38
Tomatillo Chicken Thigh Stew 50
Tomato And Poblano Stuffed Squash 39
Tomato-basil Bread Pizza 73
Tropical Fruit Steel Cut Oats 20
Turkey & Pasta With Lemon Pesto 94
Turkey And Wild Rice Salad With Walnuts 18
Turkey Cutlets 96
Turkey Rellenos 91
Turkey Scotch Eggs 15
Tuscan Cod With Red Potatoes 61
Tuscan Cod 56

V

Vegetable And Lamb Stew 45
Vegetable Wild Rice Soup 53
Veggie And Quinoa Stuffed Peppers 42
Veggie Loaded Pasta 36
Very Berry Puffs 24
Very Low Carb Clam Chowder 60

W

Walnut Orange Coffee Cake 27
White Bean Hummus 14
White Wine Mussels With Saffron Threads 66
Whole Farro And Leek Soup 50
Worthy Caramelized Onion 35

Y

Your's Truly Lime Chicken Chili 92

Z

Zesty Brussels Sprouts With Raisins 11
Zinfandel Braised Beef 76
Zucchini And Artichoke Platter 42
Zucchini Cream Soup 42

Printed in Great Britain
by Amazon